Biology and Theology Today

Biology and Theology Today

Exploring the Boundaries

Celia Deane-Drummond

scm press

0 334 02823 X

This edition first published 2001 by
SCM Press,
9–17 St Albans Place, London N1 0NX

SCM Press is a division of
SCM-Canterbury Press Ltd

Typeset by Regent Typesetting, London
and printed in Great Britain by
Biddles Ltd, Guildford and King's Lynn

For Henry

Contents

Preface

This book is designed to be accessible to undergraduates and those interested in current issues of public concern, including the new genetics and environmental issues. Throughout this book I have tried to show not just where the issues in biological science raise important questions for Christian theology, but also how exploring the boundaries between the two disciplines serves to point to particular ways forward for the further development of both biology and theology. For the engagement of Christian theology with serious questions about how the natural world comes to be perceived from a scientific perspective affects the theological task as much as it challenges the framework for further scientific developments.

I am also conscious that the whole field of biology is so vast in scope that an adequate and comprehensive engagement with Christian theology would take many more volumes to complete. The focus is deliberately illustrative, rather than exhaustive, drawing on biological science from two very contrasting perspectives of genetics and ecology. While recognizing the influence of Charles Darwin, I have not tackled in detail particular scientific issues that arise in evolutionary biology. It seems to me that other excellent texts are available that deal with this question in a more theoretical and comprehensive way from a theological and scientific perspective.[1] I have also not dealt with questions relating to the psychology of mind and the particular issues this raises for theology and philosophy. Again, there are other textbooks that cover this area of debate.[2]

The purpose of this book is to show the relevance of theology to scientific applications of biology in current situations of popular debate. It is also intended to be accessible to as wide an audience as possible. It therefore includes ethical as well as theological discussion, using particular case studies. The tendency for many current texts in science and religion is to ignore ethical questions altogether, or separate them from theological issues. One of the intentions of this book is to demonstrate that the ethics of nature can have a theological basis from a Christian perspective.

Easter, 2000   *Celia Deane-Drummond*

Acknowledgments

Some of the material for sections of this book first appeared in a draft form as a course of lectures entitled *New Frontiers in Biology and Theology* for final-year undergraduates taking combined honours degrees, as well as masters' students in applied theology at Chester College of Higher Education. This course won a John Templeton Course Award in Science and Religion in 1998 and a Development Grant in 1999. I am therefore grateful to the John Templeton Foundation for supporting this course and also for providing helpful feedback on matters of content and pedagogical methods. I am also grateful to many of my students who have taken the course in the academic years 1998/9 and 1999/2000 for helpful comments, all of which have contributed to making this text more accessible from their perspective. I am grateful to the department of theology and religious studies at Chester College for allowing me to take a term's sabbatical leave in the autumn of 1999, which provided a welcome opportunity to work on material for this book.

There are some sections of this book that have appeared in slightly different forms elsewhere. Nonetheless, I have substantially rewritten and revised and enlarged the texts to make them suitable for publication in this book. In particular, I have drawn on an article published recently in *New Blackfriars* for part of Chapter 2.[1] I have also made use of two articles recently published in *Ecotheology* for parts of Chapter 2 and Chapter 5.[2] I also draw on some material from *Genetic Engineering for a New Earth? Theology and Ethics of the New Biology* and *Creation Through Wisdom: Theology and the New Biology*.[3] Nonetheless, the core material for this book has not been published previously, and where I have drawn on other published sources, it has undergone considerable revision so as to be appropriate to the particular context of the questions addressed in this book.

I am particularly indebted to Christopher Southgate, who graciously agreed to read an early draft of the complete manuscript. I am very grateful for his astute and constructive criticism, and I am aware that the book would be far poorer without his helpful comments. I would like to thank my husband, Henry, for his patience and support while I wrote this book. Finally, thanks to the publisher, SCM Press and particularly to Margaret Lydamore, formerly associate editor, and to Anna Hardman, current editorial manager, for their encouragement and positive feedback.

Introduction

Is the conversation between biology and Christian theology still possible if we can explain both the origin and the apparent purpose of the natural world simply by reference to processes in nature itself? For some theologians we can only answer this question with a resounding 'No'. Furthermore, others would suggest that any attempt to do so amounts to a watering down of the real point of theology, which is to bring the message of salvation to humanity. All forms of natural theology are rejected as they lead to a false understanding of God, who can only be understood in terms of the coming of the Word in Christ. Even more subtle is the idea that theology is somehow weakened by its engagement with science, since it loses sight of its own aims and purposes, hence any particular contribution to *theology* of those engaged in science and religion is dismissed. We should leave the question of nature to the biologists, and we should get on with where theology is more at home, namely, the salvation of souls.

However, such a truncated view of theology reinforces the stereotype of its activity common in the popular mind, that it is so heavenly minded that it is of no earthly use. A slightly weaker version of the same sort of idea comes with an equally popular notion that suggests that theology answers the 'why' questions, while science answers the 'how' questions. In this case the two are still speaking completely different languages; they may speak of the same things, including creation, but the overall effect is the same, namely, that genuine conversation is no longer possible.

I will argue in this book that such a retreat of theology into either the realms of salvation history, or simply the heavenly purpose of the universe, needs to be vigorously resisted, as it ignores at least five issues:

- The first is that science as practised does show a religious dimension, so that the language between religion and science is not as disparate as we might presuppose. Nonetheless, this religious dimension needs to be the subject of careful theological critique.

- The second issue is that we cannot escape from the fact that science has shaped and continues to shape the culture in which we live. In some cases science even invades all other forms of knowledge, becoming what is known as scientism. Theology is no exception, and many of the methods of modern theology draw on the insights of the sciences.

- The third issue is that science does have values that both feed off the culture in which it is based and in turn influence that culture. Science is not detached from culture any more than religion is. Hence to ignore areas of interconnection amounts to a failure of perception, a failure to see how different areas of knowledge do interact and inform each other.

- Fourthly, religious beliefs can themselves be the object of scientific inquiry, just as science can be subject to scrutiny from the perspective of theologians. Scientists themselves may have an interest in religion from a particular perspective, for example, psychology or medicine. Nonetheless, most of the scientific analysis of religion is dominated by social-scientific research. In the past social science has drawn on classic scientific method in an effort to be as objective as possible. More recently, a simple reliance on traditional scientific method in the social sciences has become less fashionable, with a shift towards more inter-active participatory research known collectively as new paradigm research. Social-scientific analysis of religion has come to dominate the way religious studies has developed.

- Fifthly, given the way such an interaction between science and religion may be presumed in our culture, the influences of science on theology and theology on science are often largely unnoticed. Once we have identified the ways these influences take place we may wish to move the dialogue in a more self-conscious way in another direction altogether. This is the area of creative conversation, of careful listening and dialogue in a way that leads to mutual understanding and enlargement of vision, rather than rejection and hostility.

I begin this book with an exploration of historical issues in our relationship with the natural world. In particular, human perception of nature has changed significantly over the centuries, from an early understanding of nature as symbol, through to modern perceptions of nature as self-sufficient and autonomous. Theologians have frequently drawn attention to the contrast between a metaphor of the world as organic, as opposed to a metaphor of the world as mechanistic. While these are important frameworks in which to understand modern science, I argue that to view the emergence of modern science in the seventeenth century simply in terms of a replacement of the idea of organism with mechanism is too simplistic. In particular, other images of nature are worth consideration, such as the fading image of nature as symbol and the increasing popularity of ideas such as nature as mirror to the divine mind and nature as autonomous. How might we respond to such a shift towards the idea of the autonomy of nature, seemingly detaching the natural world from any religious understanding? One approach, followed by Charles Raven, is to go back to the early work of the seventeenth-century scientists, such as John Ray, and see ways in which they were able to arrive at a synthesis between their Christian faith and their science. Another approach is to explore the pioneering work of Pierre Teilhard de Chardin, a modern-day Jesuit priest who was also a committed scientist.

How far are such syntheses between Christianity and science compatible with the contemporary practice of science? The second chapter explores scientific method, but in a way that seeks to move beyond classic models of scientific method that have influenced debates in science and religion. Instead, I shall be asking questions about the values in science and why in particular it was important and still is important for many scientists to hold on to the notion of science as a value-free, neutral activity. Yet a particular value in science to search for truth does have some resonance with theology. There may be exaggerated claims for such scientific truth, and I suggest that much of the writing of Richard Dawkins amounts to a form of scientism. On the other hand, buried in the story of another geneticist, namely Barbara McClintock, lies a rather different approach to scientific method. Her work shows openness to spiritual insights in a way that suggests that scientific research at its best, even in a field such as genetics, may be more inclusive of other forms of knowledge. I also argue that an exploration of a particular narrative within a scientific field can give us insights into how science moves forward. The story of the unfolding science of ecology and its need to develop its own particular philosophy of ecology is such a case study.

The second chapter also introduces the twin focus of this book, namely, the biological science of genetics in contrast with that of ecology. I use additional examples from genetic science in Chapter 3, and environmental science, in particular Lovelock's Gaia hypothesis, in Chapter 7. What is the basic philosophy behind genetic engineering? Many medical experiments suggest an altruistic motive, but what about the techniques themselves? Biotechnology, that is, the commercial application of biological science, relies on a view of the world which treats 'nature' as other than human and in which all living things, including I suggest humans, are viewed as a mechanism. Those who reacted against this philosophy in the eighteenth century developed a school of thought known as 'nature philosophy', more akin to Lovelock's Gaia hypothesis. In physics there was a similar reaction against the static Newtonian ideas, though in this case the new physics was indebted to Einstein. The greater degree of uncertainty that is part of Einstein's thesis allowed a more mystical view of physics to emerge, such Capra's well-known *The Tao of Physics*. While some historians argue, I believe quite correctly, that the new physics is still indebted to Newtonian ideas, the shift to a more open approach in physics seems undeniable. The difference between the new physics and the new biology is that while the former seemed to challenge the idea of mechanism, the latter has rarely moved beyond it.

In Chapter 3, I explore the scientific approach to genetic engineering and its applications along with other areas in the new
biology, such as cloning, in order to ground later theological and
ethical discussion. In particular, I explore the practice of genetic
engineering from a scientific perspective. Those readers who have
no background in biological science may find parts of this chapter
rather technical. I have, nonetheless, attempted to make the
biology as accessible as possible while not shrinking from giving
illustrative examples. I suggest that it is through coming to terms
with these details that the reality of the practice of genetics comes
alive. I also look at applications of the new genetics, in humans,
animals and plants. A broad approach to this topic serves to show
how knowledge from one area can feed into other areas and so
stimulate future research. I also examine the possible risks of
genetic engineering, both for human health and the environment,
and I touch on a subject often avoided in discussions, namely, the
potential use of genetic engineering in biological warfare.

Given the richness of possible interpretations of the way to do
theology in different Christian traditions, how is the issue of
science and religion approached from an ecumenical perspective? How have different churches responded to the complex
questions that revolve around genetic engineering? The exploration of these issues will be the subject of the fourth chapter. I
examine the responses of the World Council of Churches, and
also those of the Anglican Church, Roman Catholic Church,
Church of Scotland and Methodist Church. I argue that one way
of taking the ecumenical response further is to explore the
Wisdom traditions of the church. The theological basis for
Wisdom is rooted not just in the biblical accounts, but also in
the writings of Thomas Aquinas and Sergii Bulgakov. I explore
the idea that Wisdom may be of special relevance in dealing with
the complex issues surfacing in the new genetics.

I then move on to discuss the theological implications of genetic
science. A complete survey of all the possible applications of
genetic science and their implications for theology would be outside the scope of this book. I have, therefore, deliberately focused
on two areas that are of interest in public debates. The first area I

discuss in detail is the genetic modification of food, and the second is the cloning of animals and possibly humans. There are theologians who are supportive of both developments in science from a theological perspective. I examine their arguments, alongside counter theological arguments that are more resistant to genetic change. I argue, instead, that a more subtle approach to the issue comes through drawing on the Wisdom motif, especially as it takes into account issues of social justice that are easily lost once topics are viewed in narrowly scientific terms.

The subject of genetic engineering cannot avoid ethical concerns, even though many texts in science and religion have tended to give short shrift to the ethical implications of science. Genetic science is, perhaps, an exception, in that – if anything – theological discussion has become eclipsed by a focus on ethical dilemmas. In Chapter 6 I explore the dominant approach to the ethics of genetic engineering, namely, consequentialism. I will ask how far a consequentialist approach really assists in resolving the difficult issues to hand. I illustrate the partial adequacy of this approach in dealing with specific examples, such as the cloning of animals and the genetic engineering of humans. I suggest that arguments for or against genetic engineering from first principles are more often hidden from view. I also offer an alternative approach to the ethics of genetic engineering that ties in with the theological arguments introduced in the previous two chapters, namely, an ethic based on Wisdom.

Chapter 7 marks the transition to a new way of approaching science and biology, in examining the Gaia hypothesis of James Lovelock. I explore different possible scientific models for Gaia, along with scientific arguments for these models. The extent to which Gaia becomes ideological reflects the philosophical presuppositions of the scientists involved. Chapter 8 moves the scientific debate into theological, philosophical and ethical analysis. I ask in what ways theologians and philosophers have used Gaia for their own purposes, and whether this is justified. I argue that Gaia is especially significant in the work of some feminist theologians. Gaia represents an alternative approach to science that seems to set it in sharp contrast to genetics. I explore the possibility suggested by some scientists that Gaia does have its own particular molecular biology.

Given that Gaia is popular among feminist theologians, how have feminists attempted to critique the practice of science? Chapter 9 explores a boundary that has far less coverage than it deserves in texts in science and religion, namely, the place of women in science. In particular, I ask how far feminists have critiqued both the exclusion of women from science and the portrayal of women as insignificant in science. One approach, that is also characteristic of feminist theology, is to 'set the record straight' and examine historical examples of women who have made a significant contribution to the field. Another approach is to critique the practice of science by pointing to the lack of access of women to science, the cause of liberal feminism, or the cultural exclusion of women from scientific pursuits, the cause of cultural feminism. More radical is the attempt by more romantic eco-feminists to challenge the way science is done as being inappropriate for half of the human race. In other words, since science operates according to a particular gender bias the only option is a rejection of scientific method. Such radical feminists argue that women instead need to recover their affinity with the earth and celebrate this as an alternative to the detached mode of thinking that has dominated Western male-orientated science. It is of interest that in this group we find alignment with religious interpretations of reality. Not all feminists argue for a rejection of science per se. I suggest that those who seek alternative models for science are those worth taking the most seriously from the point of view of exploring the boundaries between theology and biological science. For the romantic eco-feminist rejection of science, even though it seems to carry a religious gloss, fails to engage with scientific practice. Moreover, it also rejects all traditional forms of religion, tainted as they seem with patriarchy.

Then, in the final chapter, I ask what kind of future we can expect for biological science, given the current trends in science and associated ethical, philosophical and theological discussion. Chapter 10 draws together the themes of the book and argues the case for a holistic approach to science, one that is informed by the current debates in the humanities rather than is dismissive of them. I suggest that the ultimate future of both biological science and theology depend on such mutual collaboration. I argue that the Wisdom motif is fruitful in allowing for both creativity in science and a critique of associated social justice issues.

1

Historical issues

Be praised thee, my Lord God,
In and through all your creatures.
Especially among them,
Through your Noble Brother Sun,
By whom you light our day;
In his radiant splendid beauty
He reminds us, Lord, of you.

Be praised, my Lord, through Sister Moon and all the stars;
You have made the sky shine in their lovely light.

In Brother Wind be praised, my Lord,
And in the air,
In clouds, in calm,
In all weather moods that cherish life.

Be praised my Lord through Sister Water,
She is most useful, humble, precious, pure.

And Brother Fire, by whom you lighten night,
How fine is he, happy, powerful, strong.

Through our dear Mother Earth be praised, my Lord.
She feeds us, guides us, gives us plants, bright flowers,
And all her fruits.

An extract from *The Canticle of the Creatures* [1]

This well-known eulogy of the natural world attributed to St Francis of Assisi epitomizes the poetic, romantic and nature mysticism that has inspired many theologians searching for ways of expressing the fundamental unity of all creatures in praise of God. Francis of Assisi is also commonly adopted by contemporary conservationists as their patron saint.

If we consider the modern techniques of genetic manipulation, a very different image of human relatedness to nature seems to be presented. The possibility that is before us now, for the first time in the history of the world, is one where the very fabric of life, even the human genetic make-up itself, lies open to human manipulation. The natural world becomes a resource to be managed for human convenience and advantage. We seem to have searched into the heart of the natural world and found the keys for its reconstruction for our own particular purposes and uses.

Is such a view compatible with the Franciscan idea of wonder? Has the trend in biology been to reduce nature to mere mechanism, most notably in the science of genetic engineering? In this chapter I will highlight key shifts in our perception of nature from a historical perspective. This may give us some clues on how we have arrived at our present ambiguous relationship with the natural world. Nature is, in a sense, idealized in very different forms, and it is from this idealization that particular human interaction becomes both permissible and fostered. I suggest that key examples of the images of nature are nature as *organic*, *mechanistic*, *symbolic*, *mirror* or *autonomous*.

The historical development of the concept of nature as organic or as mechanism is well rehearsed in other sources, and I do not intend to develop these concepts in detail here.[2] I will be showing their significance in later chapters, especially the idea of nature as mechanism influencing genetic engineering in Chapter 3 and the idea of nature as organic influencing the science of Gaia in Chapter 7. It is clear, however, that the organic and mechanistic views of the natural world have existed side by side right from the early beginnings in classical Greek science. To portray the mechanistic view as in any sense causative of the ecological crisis or environmental collapse gives philosophy far too high a status in the multiplicity of factors involved. Furthermore, a view of nature as mechanism as an alternative to organicism misses out three other particularly striking and historically important images of nature. These are images of nature as symbolic, as mirror and as autonomous. I suggest that the focus of our attention needs to be on these images of nature, as much as the above.

In this chapter I will also show how the idea of nature as autonomous is particularly significant in that it encourages a detachment of science from religion. There are two possible responses to this trend that I will discuss here as found in the work of early twentieth-century writers and beyond. The first response is to return to a careful historical examination of the early practice of science in the seventeenth century before the fragmentation from religion had flowered. The second response is to arrive at a new synthesis, as found in the work of Teilhard de Chardin.

Historical images of nature

An overview of the key different images of nature is as follows:

Nature as organic

The idea that the earth is like an organism, working together as a whole, goes as far back as the philosophy of the Stoics in the classical Greek era. We find associated with this concept that of the world soul, where not only is the earth an organic system, but it contains within it a principle of order that has a purpose, direction or *telos*. Historically an organic understanding of the earth is more often than not attributed to the wider cultural movement of romanticism. However, contrary to what one might expect, an organic view of nature is compatible with some forms of science. An organic view of nature is also associated with the idea of *vitalism*. This is the belief that life contains something special in and of itself that cannot be explained in terms of its constituent parts. While vitalism was eventually discarded from institutional science, more organic approaches to nature survived on its fringes.

Nature as machine

The idea that nature is a mechanism that could be explained by reference to its constituent parts is often attributed to the philosophy of René Descartes (1596–1650). He imagined nature was like a giant clock, using the great clock of Strasbourg as a model for his deliberations. However, the idea that we could explain the world by its constituent parts goes much further back in history. It is also associated with the classical Greek view that the earth could be broken up into its constituent parts, known as *atomism*. In ancient Greek and Egyptian cultures the concept that a perceiving subject could be separated from an object began to shatter the belief that everything is connected to everything else in an organic way. It is likely that the shift to seeing a separation between subject and object allowed atomism to emerge in these early cultures. Isaac Newton was influenced by Descartes, though it is noteworthy that in places he criticises his science as being too influenced by mechanistic philosophy. Such a view still pervades the methods of modern science.

Nature as symbolic

The concept that nature might be symbolic of a higher, spiritual order goes back to the early history of the church. The basic idea is that just as scripture presents us with a story about the world that has spiritual meaning, so too the natural world points to a symbolic meaning into the spiritual realm. This interpretation of nature was popular right up to the Middle Ages, and was the dominant view for many centuries before the advent of modern science. It is possible that the idea of the symbolic significance of nature actually held back a more empirical approach to the natural world in that those who tried to discover the inner workings of nature were considered to miss nature's 'true' significance, namely, its link to spiritual insights. This concept of nature will be discussed in more detail below.

Nature as mirror

The view of nature as mirror moves on from the concept of symbol in that now nature can be investigated by human beings since it is a mirror of the divine mind. The idea of nature as mirror began to appear in the Middle Ages, but flowered in the seventeenth century. This concept, unlike the idea of nature as symbol, actually seemed to encourage the active pursuit of biological science, for those who searched into the deep workings of nature were 'thinking God's thoughts after him'. This was not 'natural theology' in the sense of proving the existence of God from nature; rather, it reinforced faith in a divine Creator and designer, and encouraged those who believed to find God in their scientific discoveries.

Nature as autonomous

One of the core quests of the early scientists, such as Francis Bacon, was to demystify the idea of nature so that it was no longer a realm of mysterious magic. Rather, the practice of science would show humanity how to manage and control nature for the purposes of human advancement. Humanity thus becomes autonomous, free from the clutches of a mysterious nature pervaded by magical forces. There were some scientists who were Christians who still held on to the concept that nature could provide evidence for God's design, as in the idea of nature as mirror. Others believed that even this link between Christian spirituality and nature was spurious. Charles Darwin's approach to nature gave ammunition to those who wished to evacuate any sense of the divine in nature. His theory of evolution shook to the core the idea of nature as mirror of the divine mind and natural theology in general. Now, for the first time, the idea that nature evolved independently of a divine designer took hold, and thus seemed to dispense with the idea of God altogether. Nature itself now becomes autonomous, subject to internal natural laws. It is these laws that natural science seeks to elucidate.

Nature as symbolic

The idea that nature is symbolic[3] of another realm goes back to an understanding of creation in the early history of the church. It is linked with a particular understanding of how to interpret scriptural texts, or hermeneutics. Origen and other Alexandrian Fathers constructed a hermeneutic that allowed the objects of the physical world to take on particular spiritual meanings. The world was like a moral training ground for the human race. St Ambrose, for example, believed that the stones, plants and animal behaviour all showed forth in some way an aspect of human nature, a vice to be avoided or a virtue to be emulated. Hence scripture and the natural world were read as parallel texts in a symbolic way.

Speculative books about nature, such as *Physiologus*, written by an anonymous contemporary of Origen, were fantastic speculations that are somewhat entertaining to read. According to some scholars, no other book other than the Bible has had such an influence on such a wide range of people. It was used as a source book for centuries, and translated into Latin, Ethiopic, Arabic, Armenian, Syriac, Anglo-Saxon, Icelandic, Spanish, Italian, Provençal and all the major German dialects. This book is a collection of reflections about the natural world, but it includes not just the plants and animals that are familiar to us today, such as the pelican and the lion, but stories and legends about serpents, the phoenix and the unicorn. The stories were wrapped in folklore with the deliberate intention of addressing a particular moral concern or need. Authors like the writer of *Physiologus* believed that Christ himself gave the justification for this kind of treatment of the natural world. He had spoken of himself as the vine, while pointing to its moral significance; he had called the disciples to be fishers of men, hence drawing moral lessons from the use of natural objects, such as fish.

According to *Physiologus*, the serpent has four natures, all of which give us a lesson in spiritual practice. The first nature is how a serpent, on growing old, will fast for forty days until the skin is loose and then rub it free from his body using a crevice in a rock. The new skin then reappears, fresh and free from blemish. This mirrors the practice of fasting whereby we throw off our old natures and put on the nature of Christ. Or again, the pelican delivers young that attack the parents. However, they kill their offspring, weeping over them for three days; eventually the mother strikes her side and spills blood over their dead bodies. The blood awakens the dead chicks to life again.

Such embellished stories mixing fact, fiction and animal lore held sway in the ancient world for centuries. The pelican, for example, became a central image in the iconography and sculpture of the Middle Ages and beyond. However, for these writers, such images of nature were quite appropriate. It is hard for us to imagine being without empirical knowledge about the natural world that we are so familiar with today. Fantastic speculations about the natural world characterized the early history of the church.

For St Augustine of Hippo one of the most appropriate methods for the interpretation of scriptural texts is the use of allegory. In this case scriptural text points to the material basis of the natural world, which itself acts as a sign for something else. When we find a reference to Jerusalem in a biblical account, it more often than not just points to the historic city itself. However, Jerusalem has a number of different meanings for believers, acting as a sign or pointing to other images, such as the Jews, the church, the heavenly city or the soul, and so on. It is difficult to appreciate this mindset, but allegory is not simply a multiple meaning of a text; rather, the text points to an object that itself bears a number of different meanings. The fact that the object itself had these deeper spiritual meanings leads to an attitude of non-interference. Moreover, the real significance of the objects in the natural world was their spiritual significance. To focus on material nature alone seemed like idolatry and hence inhibited scientific investigation.

St Augustine assumed a thoroughly Platonic understanding of the world, so that reality was to be found not in the visible and bodily material of the world, but in the eternal realm of ideas. The physical world represented patterns of the truth, but was not the actual truth. Hence to search for the truth in the material world amounted to delusion. According to St Augustine, pagan philosophers possessed knowledge of things, but failed to see their transcendental significance. They had *scientia*, but lacked *sapientia*, the Wisdom that comes from knowledge of the eternal. The confusion of the signs with the thing signified could eventually lead to worship of the material world, hence idolatry. To be concerned with just the natural objects alone was to be a slave to sign. Experimental scientific investigation is clearly problematic once we see the world in such symbolic terms. It can also lead to a negative attitude to the natural world as the harbinger of all kinds of dark forces and temptations of the flesh away from the spiritual graces.

In the Middle Ages we find much more positive interpretations of the natural world beginning to emerge again. Instead of the image of the earth as a loose collection of religious symbols, gradually we discover the earth described as ordered according to a metaphor of a machine, a body, a chain or even a musical instrument. Nature was like a book that we could read and in which we could detect signs of the finger of God. While some sense of symbolism remained, it was now possible and permissible to look for signs of such ordering in the world of nature. In this sense the idea of the earth as organic or machine is not so important; the importance is that it is ordered and that we can see signs of this ordering.

Thomas Aquinas added to the theological respectability of looking for order in the natural world by retrieving the philosophy of Aristotle. His philosophy affirmed the worth of scientific investigations and detailed observations of the natural world. For Aquinas the world was characterized by natural law, which reflected the eternal law of God. The law that operated in human society, the moral law, mirrored the natural law of nature. Seeking out this law in the natural world was one way to discover the Wisdom and purposes of God.

Humanity's quest also became a search for a paradise lost. It is interesting that this search, commonly associated with Francis Bacon, appears much earlier, in writings of the twelfth and thirteenth centuries. The scholastics often used the texts of the ancients, rather than direct experience, for their reflections on the natural world. This hampered any real progress in understanding nature, as it was assumed that these texts were accurate descriptions. However, such trust in the authority of these texts suffered when inconsistencies were discovered between different accounts.

As the sixteenth century progressed, scholars found even more difficulties in reconciling what they observed with the account of the classic writers. The unfolding New World opened up a rich variety of creatures of all kinds. However, such creatures were nowhere to be found in the classic texts. The Protestant interpretation of scriptural texts fostered even further the breakdown of the symbolic approach to nature. In this case the authority of the church and all ancient scholarship was tested in the light of more literal interpretations of scripture, and in many cases found wanting. This reformation in interpretation of scripture made it impossible to view nature as a symbolic realm.

Once the allegorical interpretation of scripture was abandoned, following the rise of Protestantism, the natural world was perceived rather differently. It was no longer thought of as primarily a symbolic realm into the transcendent. The medieval images of nature as chain, mirror, machine or musical instrument all speak of a new-found intelligibility in the natural world. However, this was superimposed on the symbolism inherited from the early church Fathers. I suggest that it was the fading image of nature as symbol that allowed experimental science to flourish in the seventeenth century. In other words, a move away from a perception of nature as symbolic was a necessary prerequisite for experimental science's full development.

Nature as mirror

Many of the seventeenth-century writers deliberately tried to integrate their discoveries of science with a particular way of interpreting their religious understanding. John Ray's *The Wisdom of God Manifested in the Glory of Creation*, published in 1695, went through numerous editions – ten by 1835.[4] It is interesting that in 1678 he had published a tribute to his naturalist friend Francis Willughby, *The Ornithology of F. Willughby*. In the preface Ray robustly denied any hint that the natural world could be discovered in any other way other than through careful observations. In one sense he was a clear pioneer of modern experimental science. He intended his work to be firmly rooted in the natural sciences, rather than the human sciences. It is curious, perhaps, that while on the one hand he castigated his colleagues for including 'Hierglyphics, Morals, Divinity and Ethics' in their natural history, he still allowed himself in *The Wisdom of God* to speculate on the purposes of God as discoverable in the realms of nature.

The difference relates to the way Ray interpreted the natural world. Previous accounts had subsumed their scientific research under particular religious judgments, and lacked reference to any detailed observation of the natural world. By contrast, he sought to elucidate natural history through careful study and research of an empirical nature. He suggested that it was in the world of science alone that we could see the work of God as the designer. In other words, the Wisdom of God is manifested in the exploration of the work of science according to scientific methods.

If we look carefully at Ray's work, we see him giving glory to God for the intricacy of creation as discovered by science. He cites the work of the Wisdom writers as support for his interpretation. For example, he uses verses from the Psalms, such as 8.3, to give a scriptural basis for his research: 'When I Consider the Heavens, the Works of Thy Fingers, the Moon and the Stars which Thou hast ordained . . .' It is unlikely from a purely exegetical point of view that the Wisdom writers would have intended the text to be understood as a basis for natural theology. Their understanding of natural science as such was, at best, rudimentary. Nonetheless, they did affirm the created order, and used it to celebrate the glory of God's creative activity. By contrast, natural theologians like John Ray and others who followed in his wake, such as Paley, pointed to the intricate work of creation as *evidence* for divine design. The world in this view becomes a mirror of the mind of God. Ray's work has recently enjoyed something of a revival among more conservative Christians, with the establishment of the John Ray Institute, set up to promote Christian environmental values.

For writers like John Ray the medieval interpretation of the natural world as symbolic order had failed to take adequate account of sin. They rejected the medieval idea that the book of nature was a source of equal weight with scripture; for them it could neither lead to salvation nor point the way to spiritual practice. Instead, the book of nature needed to be investigated by arduous empirical investigation. Even then, the knowledge of the Deity was always indirect; nature was a somewhat cloudy mirror of the divine, rather than a translucent window into the divine mind. We might be able to deduce something of God's attributes from the natural world, but not the divine image itself. Attributes of God, such as God's Wisdom and power and goodness, were like indirect pointers to the Author of creation.

Nonetheless, some features characteristic of the medieval approach to interpretation of scripture, such as typological interpretation of texts, remained popular even in the seventeenth century. Typology was a way of interpreting historical events rather than a way of interpreting the natural world. Typology viewed a historical event as a type of what was to come – for example, the Israelites' entry into Canaan in the Exodus story prefigured Christ's entry into Jerusalem. In other words, typology was a certain way of understanding history that was still largely accepted.

Writers of the seventeenth century, like John Ray, believed that God had designed the world for particular purposes, and more often than not for human utility. Those who studied the natural world assisted God by pointing to possible fulfilment of the original design, namely for practical usefulness. Furthermore, it became a *religious duty* to discover the usefulness of creatures for humanity, as this was the key to God's design of the world, the purpose of creation. Scientists became the new priests of creation, showing the true purpose of creation by uncovering its particular significance in practical, utilitarian terms.

In the case of some writers of the seventeenth century, their forced interpretation of all natural activity according to specific purposes, most particularly the benefit of humanity, strikes the modern reader as somewhat bizarre. All parts of the anatomy of all beasts and birds alike had a particular explanation. Henry More, for example, in the *Antidote to Atheism* (1653) suggested the following: God designed the silkworm for the sole purpose of giving humanity a means to make costly clothing. The two humps of a camel are designed to hold a packsaddle. In human anatomy, also, we find specific design: the eyebrows are to prevent sweat running down the forehead, while the eyelids are to ward off flies and insects.

Some historians argue that the search for purpose, or teleology, hindered scientific progress, but it is equally plausible that the search for usefulness for humanity may actually have spurred on scientific investigations. Once the purposes of nature could be identified with God's purposes, this would lead to worship and praise of the Creator. Extremes of these so-called physico-theologies abounded.

More interesting, perhaps, was the belief, shared by Isaac Newton, that science actually had the capacity to elucidate hidden meanings in scripture, representing a reversal of previous conceptions where scripture was used to find the meaning of nature. Some alchemists of the seventeenth century suggested that their methods mirrored those of God in the creation of the world. The symbolic understanding of nature had presumed that the natural and the supernatural were distinct; matter and spirit were in a dualistic relationship to each other. Such a dualistic understanding was eroded in this period, so that in more extreme accounts the resurrection becomes just another natural process.

Such a collapse of the concept of the supernatural heightens the theodicy question – that is, the spectre of the problem of suffering in the natural world if God is considered to be good. However, the writers of the seventeenth century were particularly adept at explaining reasons for violence in the natural world according to the good purposes of God. Poisonous plants, toadstools and snakes, for example, were God's way of extracting poisons from the earth. We should be grateful that snakes, such as the rattlesnake and other poisonous or dangerous creatures, were so designed that they warned their potential victims in various ways, even carrying an antidote in their own bodies! Those creatures that seemed useless or dangerous to us merely reflected our own human idleness, rather than the careful design of the Creator. It was only through active human intervention that such usefulness might be discovered, for the greater glory of God and the utility of humanity.

Nature as autonomous

The seventeenth century saw another shift in the perception of nature that was also highly significant. Whereas previously the natural world had seemed a threatening place, one that was full of magic, unknown forces and the like, now humans sought to control and contain the natural world. It is hardly surprising that pioneers like Francis Bacon spoke in the following way:

> That the state of knowledge is not prosperous nor greatly advancing, and that a way must be opened up for the human understanding entirely different from any hitherto known, and other helps provided, in order that the mind may exercise over the nature of things the authority which properly belongs to it.[5]

Bacon's strong confidence in the power of the mind over the natural world might seem rather strange to our modern ears. However, it shows the extent to which scientists were determined to challenge the myth that nature held us in her mysterious grip.

The shift in interpretation of the Genesis texts on creation in Protestant theology was also particularly significant. If Adam was a mythological figure, then the fact that he had dominion over the earth had no real practical consequence for human behaviour. In this case Adam's only significance was the way he points to the figure of Christ as a model for all humanity. Once Adam was thought to be a literal historical figure, ideas such as that of humanity having dominion over the earth became a reality that could be applied to present circumstances. The idea of humanity as having dominion over the earth seemed to encourage scientific pursuits of all kinds.

A controversial thesis is whether this command for humans to have dominion over the earth could become distorted to mean human domination of the earth. Fostering notions of domination would have clear negative consequences for the environment. Authors such as Lynn White have even gone as far as blaming Christianity for the ecological crisis. Some have argued that the Protestant Calvinistic tradition was particularly responsible for encouraging this view. This seems to me to be an oversimplification, both of Calvinism and of the influence of the interpretation of this text in terms of domination. I suggest, instead, that the idea of human domination was rooted primarily in the ideal of autonomy, both for humanity and nature.

It is more likely that the desire to have dominion over the natural world was related to the search for an ideal state, rather than a search for domination. This links up with the Genesis narrative as a whole, where Adam and Eve were initially in paradise. Some authors of the early modern period continued to believe that this paradise was a physical reality on earth that we could discover for ourselves through searches in the New World. Others believed that this represented the goal for human efforts in the sciences. Now flaws could be rectified and paradise could once more become a reality. This optimistic view of science clearly led to some problems, since it presumed that humanity has the capacity to reconstruct nature according to its own perceived view of Eden. Francis Bacon, in particular, believed that it was necessary for humans to work towards the restoration of the earth to Eden before the second coming of Christ. Such optimistic views, like Bacon's concept of the New Atlantis, fail to take into account the real possibility of human error and sinfulness.

In other words, in the seventeenth century a sense of detachment from the world led scientists to observe the world in a very different way from the contemplative stance of the medieval mystics. Such a detached attitude bore fruit in the experimental sciences of the next two centuries. However, science was still very slow to bring in the new age promised by Bacon in the seventeenth century. Furthermore, Bacon's assumptions about the method of science as simply cataloguing observations miss out the important role of theory and the imagination in the emergence of science.

The concept of science born in the seventeenth century also

relied on a new philosophy of knowledge. For the first time there was awareness that knowledge could be gained through doing, through construction. Human beings were autonomous in a self-conscious way and could create their own futures. This attitude applied initially to social construction of reality, as in, for example, the writing of Hobbes. The possibility of self-conscious human construction could not be applied to the natural world. This was the realm where God alone acted as Creator. However, they considered that even God's knowledge of nature came through the constructive acts of creation. This fostered an attitude to the natural world that encouraged active human intervention rather than just passive observation. We know by intervening through experiment and then observation. Eventually a more secularized approach to the natural world ensued, and the idea of the Creator was discarded. In this case the belief that humans could actively and autonomously construct the world of nature became a real possibility.

While the early-seventeenth-century scientists were highly confident of their potential for success, it took much longer for science to be accepted in the public domain. Gradually, over the eighteenth and into the nineteenth centuries the successes of science accumulated. However, it was not until the nineteenth century that real improvements to medicine were made. Scientific discoveries of the nineteenth century included basic properties such as atomic structure and the relationship of magnetism to electricity.

Darwin's theory of evolution, conceived in the nineteenth century, was born in a climate of optimism about the success of science and the progress of humanity. Ideals connected with social progress, common at the time, in all probability encouraged him to formulate his theory. He rejected the idea of a preconceived divine plan for each species. Rather, Darwin argued instead that there is variety in the population, and only those best suited for survival produce the offspring for the next generation. In other words, the variety we see around us can be explained by the operation of natural laws, without any need for supernatural intervention.

The idea that every creature in the world and every organ in every creature were the result of divine design seemed to be unnecessary and counter-intuitive. A religious explanation of creation would not explain a number of facts, for example, why useless organs exist. Darwin's theory could account for these by suggesting that their purpose relates to some earlier stage of evolution. Nature emerges through principles that are inherent in nature itself rather than through any divine intervention. Not only is human activity autonomous. Now the world of nature is self-contained, autonomous as well.

The religious controversy and the debates surrounding Darwin's theory revolved round the idea of divine agency. For some Christians of the nineteenth century Darwin's ideas seemed to point to atheism. This led to a rejection of Darwin's theory as incompatible with Christianity. For others Darwin could be accommodated. Such an accommodation could come from modifying their view of God, as in the liberal tradition exemplified by the work of the Scottish theologian Henry Drummond. In his view God is immanent in creation, and human evolution is a positive fulfilment of the spiritual presence of God in creation. An alternative method of accommodation came through modifying the understanding of the way God creates the world. In this case God is the Creator of the process itself. The more conservative Harvard biologist Asa Gray, for example, held this view.

In both methods of accommodation the problem of suffering in the natural world seemed to conflict with images of God as good. Where God was intricately part of the process, as in Henry Drummond, how could the cruel and insensitive aspects of evolution possibly be attributed to God? On the other hand, if God just started the process and then left it to its own devices, how could God in any real sense be the Creator of the world? Is God no longer all-powerful if such suffering takes place? Such problems of how to explain the apparent immorality in the natural world are a permanent aggravation for those seeking to reinstate any kind of natural theology today in a post-Darwinian world.

The synthesis of science and religion

Hints at synthesis in seventeenth-century science

Once the idea of nature as autonomous became popular, the perceived unity between science and religion characteristic of the seventeenth century began to fragment. A closer examination of the way these early scientists combined religious belief with their scientific practice may give us some more clues on how science and religion can become re-engaged. Charles Raven (1885–1964), one of the foremost thinkers in science and religion in the early twentieth century, stressed the importance of the recovery of seventeenth-century science as a way of healing the breach between science and religion.[6] Raven was particularly fascinated with the work of the biologist John Ray, and he became well known for his extensive biography of Ray's life, research and significance.[7] Raven wrote primarily as a historian rather than an experimental scientist, and sought to explain how the breach between science and theology had happened by his study of the history of seventeenth-century science.[8] His work demonstrates one possible response to the idea of nature as autonomous, namely, to examine more closely how scientists of the early seventeenth century were able to arrive at a synthesis between their faith and science.

Raven's work is far less well known than that of Teilhard de Chardin, even though he lived in the same period. There are also some remarkable parallels in their work in that both sought to find a holistic synthesis of evolutionary ideas with theology, even though Raven's main influence came from his work as a historian. Like Teilhard, he believed that the creative process needed to be seen as a whole, culminating in Christ and infused by the action of the indwelling Spirit of God. He was also perhaps more aware than Teilhard of the cost of the evolutionary process in terms of suffering and pain, with the true symbol of reality being for him Christ crucified.[9] Yet for Raven it was the seventeenth-century scientists who provided the main inspiration for his work, before the 'moral, intellectual and religious rot' had set in.[10] Raven believed that:

No one can study the pioneers of the scientific movement without realising that they were men who found in their 'new philosophy' and in the observation and interpretation of the natural order a religious experience. There is in all their work a sense of curiosity, of wonder as of children exploring a new country.[11]

Yet it was also the humility of these early scientists that struck Raven as significant. He suggests that even today scientists need to be aware of the fragmentary nature of their accounts of the natural world, so that any dogmatism in science is positively 'indecent'.[12] He also believed that while it is difficult for modern scientists of the twentieth century to return to a more holistic understanding of the natural world, a failure to do so would prove disastrous both for individuals and civilization. If biologists or theologians were to focus on either romantic images of nature such as lilies, or more insidious examples such as parasites, then they lose sight of the whole picture. For Raven, the evil we find in nature is analogous to, but not homologous with, evil in the human world. Above all, he wishes us to seek to understand nature, like the early scientists, by close observation, so that we begin to learn of the quality of the world from the perspective of other living creatures. While he still supported modern scientific methods, Raven believed that it needed to be disciplined by an organic rather than a mechanistic framework.

As I suggested above, many scientists of the seventeenth century believed that their science constituted a serious religious duty, as it paved the way for discovering the real purpose of creation in terms of practical usefulness. Yet John Ray and other natural theologians believed that the basis for their reflections was in the careful observation of the natural world, rather than their own personal beliefs. In other words, they believed that theology was *secondary* to the empirical discoveries of science, rather than a way of shaping scientific work. Nonetheless, religious inspiration for science was certainly not limited to biologists. Many other scientists in the fields of physics, mathematics and chemistry believed that God blessed their work, even if theology did not appear to inform consciously the way they carried out their experiments. Robert Boyle, for example, spoke of divine guidance during his chemical experiments, God giving him the hints he needed to avoid dreadful explosions.[13] For the scientists of the seventeenth century, the wonder in science was not just a psychological state brought on by the excitement of the discoveries, but a feeling of deep religious awe. Johannes Kepler admitted as much in his confession that when he discovered the third law of planetary motion he was 'carried away by unutterable rapture at the divine spectacle of heavenly harmony'.[14]

Yet given that scientific practice may be infused with religious sensibility, it is worth asking in what way is science actually indebted to religion. Trying to disentangle the various cultural influences, including religion, on the practice of science is problematic. However, the portrayal of science following Darwin as fiercely hostile to religion does not do justice to the fact that the birth of modern science in the seventeenth century was deeply embedded in a much more religiously affirming culture. Whether science itself owes any of its specific *content* to religious presuppositions is much more controversial. At the dawn of modern experimental science it was relatively fashionable to include natural theology in the reports of scientific investigations. The church was a powerful force to be reckoned with, and some scientists who wished their theories to be taken seriously added theological language as a way of seeking approval. Robert Chambers, for example, writing in 1844, ascribed his law of development to the divine legislator, admitting in private letters that he did this to forestall possible antagonism from Christian believers.[15]

This raises the issue of how we know whether religious ideas have genuinely influenced the content of science. Clearly, simply finding religious language in the exposition of science is not enough, since it may be added on after the event for all sorts of social and cultural reasons. Finding a simple coherence between religious belief and science is not adequate either, since any thinker who is both a scientist and a believer would be expected to seek a degree of compatibility. Biographical details of the work of a scientist may show a hidden influence of religion. A good example

of the way religion has provided a source of inspiration is found
in the biography of the twentieth-century geneticist Barbara
McClintock, to be discussed in Chapter 2. An anti-religious
polemic may also influence the way science is described by scientists, and such a polemic clearly informs the work of Richard
Dawkins, also discussed in Chapter 2. The gradual secularization
of science has made any reference to God in contemporary formal
scientific journals unacceptable.

The synthesis of Pierre Teilhard de Chardin

A rather different way of approaching how science, in particular
biology, may become compatible with theology is to examine the
work of one of the early pioneers of science and religion, namely,
Pierre Teilhard de Chardin (1881–1955). Like the early biologists
of the seventeenth century, such as John Ray, Teilhard found that
his love for science matched his love for God and the church.
However, his was a deliberate synthesis following what he saw was
the splitting apart of Christian belief from studies of nature.
Teilhard was a scientist/priest who was deeply troubled by the
way science and theology seemed to operate in two different
cultures. His synthesis of science, especially evolution, with theological ideas made him one of the pioneers in the science and faith
debates of the twentieth century.

Teilhard's biography suggests that he was genuinely committed
to bringing theology into scientific discourse. For him science
without theology was like a head without a heart. He suggested
instead that both were needed for the body to function properly.
Evolution seems to be just as evident in his synthesis as the idea of
the final end-point of the universe, or Omega. However, as the
goal of the universe is also achieved through total identification
with Christ, or *Christogenesis*, in the end Teilhard does seem to be
giving prominence to Christ. The fact that he merged the idea of
evolution with his vision of Christ suggests an uneasy tension
between the two core myths in his theology. His metaphor for
nature was predominantly that of nature as like an organism. He
combined this idea with the metaphor of nature as a mirror,

showing forth the presence of Christ in the cosmos. His view affirmed God as divine designer, but this time the design was self-evident in the process of evolution. Hence he tried to turn on its head the criticism of design rooted in the theories of Darwin by finding in the idea of evolution a means for seeking not so much the autonomy of nature as the presence of Christ.

Teilhard constructed a synthetic view that sought to join evolutionary ideas with theology through a kind of pan-psychism. His theology, quite deliberately perhaps, was not formal from a systematic point of view; rather, it was a form of mysticism that stemmed from his commitment to both scientific investigation and Christian faith. His Catholicism ensured that he was not squeamish about natural theology, and for him the entire world was an expression of the activity of the divine. He viewed humanity not so much as at the centre of the universe but at the leading edge, the culmination of the evolutionary process. He saw the universe in dynamic rather than static terms, and sought to revise the action of God in the universe accordingly. He also had a strong notion of the cosmic Christ that 'divinises' the whole of creation by his incarnation.

Creation, incarnation and redemption are part of a whole process, a process of love in action, love that moves the stars as well as human beings:

Love is the most universal,
The most tremendous and the most mystical of cosmic forces.
Love is the primal and universal psychic energy.
Love is a sacred reserve of energy;
It is like the blood of spiritual evolution.[16]

Teilhard does acknowledge evil in the universe in that he sees original sin as an element within evolution and a denial of love that each and every person makes for himself or herself. However, overall it is still a highly optimistic synthesis.

Jürgen Moltmann is one among others who have severely criticized Teilhard for his identification of salvation history with the evolutionary process. In Teilhard's synthesis evolution itself becomes the Christification of the cosmos. For Moltmann, Teilhard has 'overlooked the ambiguity of evolution itself, and therefore to have paid no attention to evolution's victims'.[17] This leads Teilhard to justify both natural and human catastrophes, including both the First World War and Hiroshima as a price for the evolutionary process. Moltmann rejects such a move as theologically unsound as it ignores Christ's identification with both the victims of war and the victims of evolution. Hence the evolution of creation cannot be identified with its redemption or made equivalent, even if all are in some sense bound up together.

Some of the modern writers on evolution and theology draw heavily on the work of Teilhard de Chardin. *God's Ecstasy: The Creation of a Self-Creating World* by Beatrice Bruteau (1997) is an eclectic mixture of science, philosophy, theology and speculation that will be appealing to those who find the more traditional responses to issues in science and faith dissatisfying.[18] Her work bears some resemblance to that of Teilhard de Chardin in that it is an attempt at a synthesis between science and a mystical form of Christianity. However, Bruteau's theology appears to derive from the scientific data to an extent that is not so apparent in Teilhard's synthesis. While the language she uses is theological, it merely serves to develop icons, while finding their concrete basis in science and what science has discovered or is discovering. For example, the cosmos becomes a kind of incarnation of the Trinity, in such a way that it includes everything in the cosmos and thus does away with any concept of divine 'intervention'. Is the cosmos itself divine?

While Bruteau is careful to distinguish the infinite from the finite, her inclusion of the finite in the infinite leads to a version of the world as the 'body of God'. The distinction between God and creation seems to vanish further in her idea of the closing of the Trinitarian life cycle, such that the incarnate infinite is present simply in human consciousness and caring. Her theology seems to be based on images, which contrasts sharply with her more fact-laden scientific discourse. This visionary approach has the advantage of setting up powerful impressions, but they remain impressions that seem rooted more in science and far less in theological discussion. Instead of a genuine dialogue, theology becomes translated into a vague mysticism that is then moulded into the discoveries of science.

Bruteau's rehabilitation of Teilhard for the current engagement of science and Christian religion raises an important issue connected with Teilhard's work, namely, that it delineates a form of mysticism rather than any developed systematic approach to theology.[19] Such a mystical approach makes any engagement of science with the content of theology more difficult, even if it becomes more vivid in its presentation of religious experience. The difficulty in this case is that scientists would be apt to dismiss any such mystical renditions as spurious, not to be taken seriously in an objective, scientifically controlled world.

However, in order to explore the interaction between theology and the sciences it is not enough just to look at the influence of spirituality or religious beliefs. Rather, the *content* of that theology needs to be examined as well, for the direction of the synthesis achieved may or may not be helpful from the perspective of Christian theology. Yet, even if the religion of the scientist is considered to be heterodox, it still needs to be taken seriously as a possible influence on scientific practice. One temptation is to ignore its influence by dismissing it as outside the bounds of orthodoxy. However, an equally important temptation that strikes me as being even more prevalent today is to ignore the content of that theology altogether.

If forms of pseudo-science are imported into theology in order to justify particular accounts of creation, as in creation science, equally forms of pseudo-theology may be imported into science as a way of bringing in an invalid spiritual dimension. Just as scientists will quite properly reject such accounts as non-scientific, theologians need to be careful to discern what are appropriate modifications of religious beliefs. Of course, the criteria for theological validity are much more fluid compared with the practice of science, but I suggest that any reformulation of theology needs to be carefully justified from a theological and philosophical perspective.

Conclusions

I have attempted in this chapter to give a survey of some key issues
in the historical interpretation of the natural world. This acts as a
backcloth against which I will discuss the two principal concerns
of this book, namely, the contrast in approach to nature that
we find in genetics and ecology, and the implications of this for
theology. I have suggested, however, that we should not confine
ourselves to thinking of nature simply as imaged as either organic
or mecha-nistic. Rather, some interesting relevant issues surface
once we explore *other* images of nature in the history of interpretation, namely, nature as symbolic, mirror and autonomous. It
was only once the idea of nature as symbol had been discarded in
the sixteenth century that modern science could flourish in the
seventeenth. Those scientists of the seventeenth century who saw
nature as mirror to God perhaps became too entranced in their
own physico-theologies to be aware of its possible difficulties.

The view of nature as autonomous gradually took hold, and I
suggest still dominates the practice of science. How might we respond to this shift? Historically there are two possibilities open to
us as pioneered by early writers of the twentieth century. One, following Charles Raven, is to re-examine the work of those seventeenth-century authors such as John Ray and attempt a synthesis
in this way. Another, following the work of Teilhard de Chardin, is
to deliberately seek to combine evolutionary ideas with Christian
mystical theology. Both approaches have their problems. While a
return to the work of the seventeenth-century writers may give us
some clues, their work was conducted in a very different cultural
framework from our present context. For these writers the church
still had considerable influence on institutions of society, to such
an extent that some writers even added in theology to make their
science more acceptable! Such a situation no longer exists now, with
theology and the influence of the church effectively marginalized
from scientific practice. The framework in which biological science
is practised today forms the subject of the chapter that follows. The
alternative that Teilhard suggests is attractive in some respects, but
it has its problems in that identifying evolution with Christ tends
towards an overly optimistic vision for the evolutionary process.

2

Probing scientific practice

Both science and religion find common ground in the search for truth. Has the domination of scientific modes of truth weakened the specific content of theological truth? An exploration of scientific method has traditionally formed the basis for science's claim to authority. Textbooks on science and religion commonly include a discussion of scientific method understood through processes such as induction, deduction and falsification.[1] An investigation of methods in science and religion debates is mediated through an analysis of the philosophies of science. In this chapter I will begin by offering a social science critique of the values in science in order to enlarge our understanding of the way science really works in practice. I will be asking how far the search for truth in science aids or hinders the dialogue with theology. I will explore the presentation of science by the geneticist Richard Dawkins as an example of the way his own anti-religious philosophy influences his perception of science. The career of Barbara McClintock presents a very different picture of genetics in the twenty-first century that is far more empathetic with religious ideas. Furthermore, I will show how the latest developments in ecology do not fit either the current fashion of using ecology to support a more holistic philosophy or preconceived traditional ideas of scientific method, such as falsification.

Values in science

One of the central claims of science is that it is value-free and objective in its approach. When the French postmodern writers started using the mathematical formulae of theoretical physicists to support their philosophical views, the scientists involved were horrified. They insisted that their work was 'abused' and 'distorted', enlarged to support philosophical speculations that were completely unrelated to the original ideas. They even went as far as publishing a hoax article in an American journal called *Social Text*, deliberately offering a parody of the new physics as simply a linguistic construct.[2] The scientists had a point. The French theorists were quite unjustified in their use of science. But what were the reasons for the hostility of the scientists? One possible explanation is that it broke what has for a long time been a sacred code for the practice of science, that facts must be separated from values and that science is purely objective. The deliberate use of certain mathematical facts to support a particular value system seemed to go against the cultural root of science itself, namely that science is value-free.

Ironically, perhaps, the fact/value distinction is itself beginning to break down with the advent of quantum physics. Those attuned to this new physics recognize that all our observations affect, in some way, what is observed, and that the world is one of probabilities rather than rigid factual certainties. Nonetheless, for practical purposes we still operate according to a Newtonian system; the laws of gravity and motion still have relevance to our everyday existence. An argument can be made for an *expansion* of Newtonian physics to include more recent research rather than a simplistic replacement of one by another. In this sense the mythology of the split between facts and values survives, albeit in a more muted form.

But why do many scientists still try to hold on to the ideal of value-neutrality? There are four dimensions to this that are worth exploring here. However, the mythology of a purely objective science remains and is rooted in some powerful precedents:

The ideal of theoria

This is based on Aristotelian principles that science must be detached from practical affairs. Science is value-free when it is focused on theory rather than practice.

Scientific method

A core goal of scientific method was to achieve objectivity, with no traces of influence from 'bias' that might be caused by moral or other qualities, such as religious beliefs. Such beliefs would, it is argued, distort any knowledge gained.

The nature of value

Before the Copernican revolution, the ancients believed that value is God-given, built into the structure of the cosmos. The idea that value is created by human agency, rather than in raw nature, is presupposed by most scientists. They assume an instrumental approach to value, in other words, that value is measured by its usefulness to humanity. Accordingly, the world of nature becomes value-free, or 'disenchanted', and no longer organized according to natural harmonies. Science is neutral because nature is neutral; it is just an exploration of the efficient causes of laws in nature, without any reference to the idea of purpose.

The security of knowledge

The idea of secure knowledge relates to freedom from politics and ethics. Francis Bacon believed that knowledge of nature was neutral and that a Christian understanding of the Fall is related to the knowledge of good and evil. He identified knowledge of nature as 'safe', but moral knowledge as 'dangerous'. The longing of many scientists for purity of knowledge has continued, especially in the universities.

Yet even from the beginnings of science there is good evidence to suggest that the claim for value-neutrality based on the above precedents was not as solidly rooted in actual scientific practice as scientists would have us believe. As discussed in the last chapter, Francis Bacon was a champion of the idea of the utility of science for human benefit. This tended to weaken the distinction between theory and practice in a way that continues even today. In other words, it becomes much harder to sustain a model of freedom from value once science is applied in particular ways. Modern genetic engineering is a case in point.

In spite of his protestations of neutrality, Bacon also envisaged science as the herald to a new utopia on earth, as indicated in the last chapter. By the nineteenth century science was specialized and fragmented into numerous sub-disciplines. Such fragmentation has continued into the twentieth and twenty-first centuries, making any grand vision for science difficult to sustain. Following such fragmentation we now have competing claims for 'pure' knowledge by different groups of opposing scientists, such as those engaged in current debates between ecology and genetic engineering.

How could this ideal of value-neutrality serve to promote the interests of scientists? Scientists insist that in providing a detached approach to the problem this could be of service in arbitrating between opposing groups in legal or social disputes. The fact that science itself may be used in a political way, such as in the current disputes over the genetic engineering of crops by both Greenpeace and the biotechnology industry, is clearly undermining this ideal of science as secure knowledge. Further-more, it is clear that just because nature is neutral does not mean *necessarily* that the practice of science is neutral. The values of scientists will inevitably influence the priority given to some scientific work over others, even if the research itself aims to be as objective as possible. Classical portrayals of scientific method through models such as induction and deduction miss this point altogether.

The search for truth

Given that science can no longer be thought of as totally neutral, it is worth asking what values in science might be consistent with the theological task. One good example is to explore the claim by scientists to search for the truth. The strength of the scientific enterprise has gradually weakened the confidence of theology to such an extent that truth in our present culture still tends to be associated with scientific 'facts' rather than religious insight. Even back in 1970, Langdon Gilkey declared that the most important change in our understanding of religious truth in the last centuries – a change which still dominates our thought today – has been caused more by the work of science that by any other factor, religious or cultural.[3]

In this scenario theology was forced to see itself as describing 'symbolic' truth, rather than divinely revealed concrete truth. Gilkey suggested that traditional religious language carried both propositions, that is, factual elements and transcendent elements. Only in the last few hundred years of human history have these religious factual propositions been challenged. The source of this challenge is the rising strength of science. In the seventeenth century the relevance of science for current discoveries and truths was acknowledged, but any reflection on either the beginning or the end of the universe was left to religion. Gilkey suggests that is was only when Darwin and others began to see the world as a *story*, that is, as having a history, that science could enter with boldness into the realm that had been previously occupied by religion. The uncovering of historical errors in the biblical account, by archaeology, physical anthropology and so on, forced theologians to reconsider the nature of biblical truth. From then on no one has claimed to be able to establish anything relevant to the realm of scientific knowing by theological reflection alone, that is, by interference in scientific inquiry.

I suggest that the search for truth in science is a double-edged sword as far as theology is concerned. The claim that scientific truth has greater worth than theological truth needs to be strongly resisted. All forms of scientism, as I will show in the section below, tend to distort the claims made by scientists. Yet the search for truth, where it is genuine, is surely something that theologians will want to affirm. In a culture that is becoming dominated by postmodernist sensibilities, any claim for truth by any group tends to be viewed with suspicion. Postmodernity, in rejecting universal authority, has seemed to undermine the claims of modernity, including the validity of the search for universal truths.

Richard Dawkins points out that for scientists fiddling data or lying about the results is, in scientific practice, the one unforgivable sin. For him there is 'something almost sacred about nature's truth'.[4] However, before the search for truth is dismissed through a postmodern critique, it seems to me that such ideals, however misplaced, were necessary in order to foster science's achievements. As Michael Polanyi has reminded us, science involves a personal, committed way of approaching the world that bears some resemblance to a faith commitment.[5] I have my doubts whether scientists, or theologians for that matter, will entirely conform to the drift towards postmodernity and jettison the quest for truth entirely. Rather, theologians and scientists can find common ground in their search for universals. I will suggest later in this chapter that in other respects postmodernity may be a welcome companion to the dialogue process, in that it serves to break open the dialogue between science and religion so that both can be viewed in more contextual ways.

While political and social pressures on contemporary scientists will certainly diminish their interest in seeking truth, it is important to acknowledge the strength of their claim to seek truth. Hanbury Brown, for example, describes science in the following way:

> it acts as our essential link with reality and if we fail to maintain this link, then there is no longer any 'nature's truth', nor is there 'public truth', there is only 'your truth' and 'my truth' and we are in danger of losing the distinction between fact and fiction and science and magic.[6]

Brown's claim that science is an arbiter of truth may slide into a form of scientism, which is that the only possible truth is discoverable by science. Yet a check on such a development emerges in the more recent discoveries of quantum physics where it is clear that nothing is ever precisely definable because of the way an observer will have an influence on what is observed. This does not lead to the opposite extreme of subjective truth. Rather, any objectivity needs to be qualified and not claimed to be final in any sense. Arthur Peacocke and others have called this type of search for truth 'critical realism'.[7] It is 'critical' as it recognizes the provisional nature of our presuppositions, and that they are always subject to improvements and refinements. It is a form of 'realism' as it assumes that there is objective knowledge 'out there' that we can discover; in other words, it is not simply an illusion of the human mind. This leads to more searching for what David Deutsch has described as the *Fabric of Reality*.[8]

Pope John Paul II suggests that every truth presents itself as a universal claim, even if it is not the whole truth. He even defines the human being as 'the one who seeks the truth'. Furthermore, for scientists it is the personal confidence that an answer can be found that spurs on the search.[9] The euphoria of the nineteenth and early twentieth centuries about the unlimited possible benefits of science has now faded, but few would wish to live in a world without the clean water, electricity, antibiotics and medicines that make human life possible. The search for truth in the theological sense is related to answers to ultimate questions, but also is set in the context of a human community of faith. While the ultimate truth for a Christian is revealed in Jesus Christ, this is not opposed to the truths found in the natural order of things discovered by scientists. However, not all claims to truth in science are compatible with the Christian vision of truth. The discernment of the level of compatibility between competing claims for truth is one way of approaching the dialogue between science and religion.

Richard Dawkins: a case study in scientism

It is now worth asking whether the search for truth in science can come to so dominate the intellectual landscape of some scientists that other ways of seeking truth become effectively eclipsed. Richard Dawkins is a good example of a contemporary biologist who has vehemently rejected all religious ideas as against the 'rational' discoveries of science. In other words, his search for truth is limited to scientific experimental data alone. However, he seems to have imported value-laden language into his biological explanations. His notion of *The Selfish Gene*, for example, declares that we are simply survival machines for our genes. To use his words:

They are in you and me. They created us, body and mind; and their preservation is the ultimate rationale for our existence. They have come a long way, those replicators. Now they go by the name of genes, and we are their survival machines.[10]

That this is a materialistic and truncated view of persons is rather obvious to those of religious faith. Dawkins explicitly denies that he is advocating selfishness as a way of life. Rather, the selfishness refers to the *conservation* of particular genes. Nonetheless, I suggest that the *language* that he uses sounds metaphorical, and so easily lends itself to possible misappropriation. Dawkins is also vocal about his hostility towards religion of any sort. He has become the champion against religion, insisting that it has 'no more solid basis than the fairies'.[11]

Dawkins suggests that while religion may try to answer our search for meaning, that is, the answers to the 'why' questions, in many cases it is quite simply inappropriate to search out for such an explanation. He gives examples, such as why does the universe exist or why does Everest exist. However, such questions are not just the concern of theology; many physicists have been equally concerned with the question of origin. Furthermore, to assume that theology just answers the 'why' questions becomes a way of dividing it from the practice of science, so that science and theology no longer have anything to say to each other. Many theologians today would not wish to put religion in such a straitjacket.

Yet Dawkins's philosophy of science is not as coldly objective as we might expect from a cursory glance at the titles of his more popular books, such as *The Selfish Gene* or *The Blind Watchmaker*. He insists, instead, that while nature is fully autonomous, there is still wonderment that we can discover in the intricacy of its mechanisms. Furthermore, for him, the purpose of finding wonder in the natural world is so that other bases for such wonder will be seen in relative terms as unsatisfactory. For he suggests that while the wonder encouraged by science is based on facts, that encouraged by religion is based on spurious superstition. Yet, on the other hand, the wonder in science coheres more easily with the wonder experienced in music and poetry. Indeed:

The feeling of awed wonder that science can give us is one of the highest experiences of which the human psyche is capable. It is a deep aesthetic passion to rank with the finest that music and poetry can deliver.[12]

Alongside this development we find authors such as Matt Ridley offering a purely naturalistic interpretation of all human values, including the capacity for religion. In his book, *The Origins of Virtue*, Ridley suggests that we have natural instincts for cooperation that are biologically determined. In its original form Darwinism portrayed individuals of a species competing against one another and other species for survival. This played down the cooperative instincts that are equally characteristic of the social life of many creatures, such as that demonstrated by the behaviour of insects, for example, ants. Such cooperative activity arises through the processes of evolution and natural selection, like any other characteristic.[13] Ridley suggests that human society should be built in such a way that we can draw out these cooperative instincts to work for good.

Dawkins would agree. He believes that the behavioural responses to reward and punishment that we find in animals are primitive forms of so-called *primary values*, as they imply goal-directed behaviour. Such values evolve through a process of Darwinian natural selection. However, while natural selection led to the emergence of humans with large brains, our ability to think and have foresight means that we can act against what might seem to be the dictates of our genes. Dawkins introduces another concept, namely, that of 'memes', which are cultural constructs passed between members of the human community. Such memes compete for survival and, like genes, only some survive. He calls this the 'science of values', that is, a particular biological way of interpreting how values are passed from one generation to the next.

Even if biological research suggests that there is a biological component to altruism, religion or even values, this is not necessarily incompatible with Christian belief. We might chose to challenge its *scientific* basis by pointing to the fact that values emerge in a complex and intricate way in human culture in a manner that only has a very tenuous link with genetics. Memes, in particular, sound like an over-extrapolation of what is known in evolutionary theory. But it is when sociobiology is claimed to be the *only* explanation that it becomes particularly dangerous. While Richard Dawkins refuses to accept that he gains his values from science, he denies the possibility of any religious experience as having any value at all. It seems to me that to be logically consistent he would have to admit this as being a possibility, especially as according to him both science and religion have left us in an 'ethical vacuum'.[14]

However, Dawkins is not content merely to affirm the scientific explanation of nature as the only possible explanation worth serious consideration. He seems to wish science to actually take over some if not all of the functions previously held by religion. Rather than seeking to find an explanation in metaphysical reality, Dawkins believes that science can take over where religion has failed:

> And it's exactly this feeling of spine-shivering, breath-catching awe – almost worship – this flooding of the chest with ecstatic wonder, that modern science can provide. And it does so beyond the wildest dreams of saints and mystics. The fact that the supernatural has no place in our explanations, in our understanding of so much about the universe and life, does not diminish our awe. Quite the contrary. The merest glance through a microscope at the brain of an ant or through a telescope at a long-ago galaxy of a billion worlds is enough to render poky and parochial the very psalms of praise.[15]

Such a truncated view of wonder as coming from science in a way that excludes the wonder possible in religious experience is suggestive of an arrogance that points back to human aggrandizement rather than anything more sublime. Dawkins even suggests that although science is not a religion it should be given some space in religious education classes.

The way science attempts to take over and offer itself as an explanation for all aspects of our lives is known as *scientism*. It is as if in removing religion formally from our lives, science has come in and filled the void. Such a trend is worth considering here for a number of reasons. The first is that such extrapolations are not justified from a scientific point of view. The second is that by discovering such a trend its failure from a religious point of view becomes more apparent. The third is that by pointing to the misuse of religious ideas the way can open up for a more genuine dialogue of theology with science. It highlights the fact that values are embedded in science, and science is both a shaper of and shaped by cultural factors.

Mary Midgley's book *Science as Salvation* is relevant here.[16] She suggests that science has become so powerful, has such a hold on our lives, that it can itself take on the character of a myth. If the main anthem for science is one of praise, it is bound to express a confidence that envisages science as a spiritual power. This over-confidence may give way to a counter-reaction that rejects any influence at all of science on culture. Midgley suggests that while the official language is still one of modesty, very large claims still appear in much popular science writing. Many look to science as their source of meaning, their salvation.

The highly influential physicist and writer Stephen Hawking, for example, believes that when a satisfactory cosmology has emerged we will be able to answer the question of why we exist. In his highly popular book *A Brief History of Time*, he cannot refrain from using theological language to describe this potential achievement. For 'it would be the ultimate triumph of human reason – for then we would know the mind of God'.[17] Yet the answer to the question of why we exist by a physical explanation alone represents a very one-dimensional view of the purpose of the universe. The mind of God seems to be identified with physical causes, physical constants. In this case science itself has seemed to take the place of religion and left little room for genuine dialogue.

Scientism may take other shapes as well. A common one is that science is the ultimate source of knowledge. Peter Atkins, for example, claims that 'there is no question whose answer is not attainable by science'.[18] Dawkins also holds this view, as does the physicist David Deutsch. Deutsch, like Dawkins, argues that the basis of life is molecular, so that the organism is simply the environment of the replicators known as genes. For Deutsch life is a 'side effect' of the macroscopic physical processes operating at the molecular level. However, he cannot bring himself to believe that life will ultimately be meaningless, as the logic of such a view might imply. Rather, if we assume a closed universe, that is, a universe ending in a 'Big Crunch', we are only a tenth of the way through history from the early 'Big Bang'. Hence there is still time for us to find meaningful ways of expressing life.

Barbara McClintock: a case study in holism

Dawkins argues that biological science and religious belief are incompatible, even while subscribing to a strong commitment to science that in itself becomes a belief system known as scientism. Such a trend makes any dialogue with theology more difficult, if not impossible, since any claim of religion to be a source of truth is excluded and dismissed. There are, thankfully, other examples of contemporary geneticists who show a very different portrayal of the practice of biology. The career of Barbara McClintock is an excellent case study that raises a number of interesting issues worth exploring in the practice of science.

Barbara McClintock was born in 1902, and her life spans the emergence of modern genetics as we know it today. After a successful start to her career she made the radical suggestion that transposable elements exist in the genome of maize. She found parts of chromosomes break free during certain stress cycles, attach themselves to other chromosomes and exert control over their expression. That the instruction came from the entire cell, perhaps even from the environment, seemed to go against the dogma that information flow is from genes to environment and not the other way round. This presupposes a scientific method known as *reductionism*, whereby we can understand a biological process through reference to processes at a 'lower' level, that is, at the level of chemistry, physics and mathematics. It is these critical processes at the molecular level that affect the function of a living system.[19] The idea that the environment might influence gene function raised the ghost of Lamarck, long since thought to have been laid to rest by Darwin's theory of evolution. Furthermore, the genetic structure of DNA discovered by Watson and Crick in 1953 held to the central dogma that DNA was a molecule of fixed structure, passed down from one generation to the next without alternations, bar mutations from radiation and other sources.

Given the existing dogma of DNA, initially McClintock's discoveries were met with derision and disbelief. Furthermore, her work used relatively simple staining techniques and careful observations of maize. These methods seemed archaic compared with the much more sophisticated emerging techniques of molecular genetics that relied on simple, rapidly reproducing systems such as the phage virus or *Escherichia coli*. The story does not end here, however. Eventually transposable elements were discovered in other organisms.

The importance of McClintock's work for genetics was that now the genome could no longer be thought of as a static system. It was a dynamic system that responded to stimuli in different ways. Eventually, in 1984, she was given the Nobel Prize for Medicine, many years after her early experiments on maize. The story of Barbara McClintock illustrates in a clear way the grip of scientific reductionism as a scientific method in the genetics research of her time.

One of the reasons that McClintock was so successful was because she was prepared to consider the system as a whole and refused to assume scientific reductionism. However, her own description of how she made her discoveries is of value in the exploration of the practice of science. This is the opinion of her biographer:

> She herself cannot quite say how she knows what she knows. She talks about the limits of verbally explicit reasoning; she stresses the importance of her 'feeling for the organism' in terms that sound like those of mysticism. But like all good mystics, she insists on the utmost critical rigor, and, like all good scientists, her understanding emerges from a through absorption in, even identification with, her material.[20]

McClintock believes passionately that you have to 'hear what the material has to say to you', have the openness 'to let it come to you'. Reason itself is not, then, adequate to describe the vast complexity, even the mystery of living forms, such that 'Organisms have a life and order of their own that scientists can only partially fathom.'

Even more suggestive is McClintock's comment that 'You were sure in what I call a completely internal way. So you work with so-called scientific methods to put it into their frame after you know.'[21] She admits that it is the mysticism of the East, in particular Tibetan Buddhism, which gives her inspiration. Many other physicists have similarly been drawn to Eastern ideas. It is noteworthy that for McClintock there is no attempt to engage with Buddhist theology in a systematic way, rather her particular appropriation of its spirituality informs her philosophy of science. While she is prepared to admit that this informed her writing in private, in the public world of science she does not show her particular religious colours. It is this ability of science to disguise itself in a value-free, objective method that influences other interpretations of how science emerges. The religious aspects, where they exist, thus remain far removed from public scrutiny.

McClintock's biography raises another issue that is worth considering a little more here, namely, the place of intuition in scientific research. This is related to Polanyi's idea of tacit knowledge.[22] Tacit knowledge is the sense by which we become dimly aware of the direction in which we must seek for a solution, before its formulation. Perception comes from sense organs, and Polanyi suggests that even worms have this ability to reach forward and try and make sense of the world around them. In other words, tacit knowledge has evolved from small beginnings. He also understood it to refer to the acquisition of basic skills, such as riding a bicycle or cooking. Even though the detailed processes are not possible to specify exactly, it is still knowledge. Added to this is the idea of caring, of commitment, hence we have to believe that there is something to know. Tacit knowing is the everyday experience of ordinary people, but Polanyi suggests it is also the root of scientific knowing as well.

Polanyi's concept of tacit knowing goes some way towards recognizing that the practice of science is a very human activity that has its roots in everyday experience. Like the narrative and biographical approaches, it serves to remind science of its origin in human insight and perception, rather than giving it any more grandiose status. Nonetheless, there are some problems with his views. He seems to suggest that as long as there is commitment and caring, then accurate perception of reality automatically follows.

The unfolding science of ecology

The story of the changing face of how ecology is done gives us another window into the practice of science. The shifts that have taken place in ecology are far less well documented in the literature on science and religion than changes from, for example, Newtonian to the new physics. Early on in its history the fledgling science of ecology derived its name from *oikos*, or home of the earth. Ecology gave us some understanding of the way different species related to one another in a common home. In the early part of the twentieth century ecology was hailed as a guide to a future motivated by a conservation ethic.[23] This view persists in the public consciousness even today, so that ecology creates a sense of positive regard for the environment. Even those who use ecology for political or philosophical purposes, such as the radical left or the exponents of deep green philosophy such as Arne Naess, still rely on the vision of ecology as a system of stable interconnections. The equation of ecology with equilibrium, stability and order and harmonious interrelationships persists and influences cultural activity outside that of the science itself. Yet, on the other hand, ideas of harmony and order are reflections of our human culture as much as ecology.

The view of ecology in the early twentieth century was in terms of a dynamic succession of plant communities appearing one after another until a final stable climax was reached. The method of ecology then was to search for this succession of plant communities as a habitat or home for other species. Yet, as ecology progressed after the Second World War, shifts in thinking took place. Ecologists now looked for interrelationships between species in terms of energy exchange and flow through thermo-dynamic systems. The word 'ecosystem' became popular, and all parts within the eco-system contributed to the dynamic whole. The overall strategy for ecology then seemed to be to produce as large and diverse an organic structure as possible within the con-straints of the system. In the end we arrive at a state of order and equilibrium, where the nutrients stay in circulation instead of leaking out. The methodological approach to ecology now was to look to systems of energy exchange, but the overall presupposition was that order would be discovered in the system. The implication is that if the ecosystem was interfered with in any way there would be a loss of nutrients and the system as a whole would be damaged.

A more radical version of the same sort of methodological approach is found in James Lovelock's global Gaia hypothesis, which I will return to again in Chapters 7 and 8. Both James Lovelock himself and the ecologists would agree that too much human interference would lead to destruction of the life support system on which we all depend. Of course, there are different scientific interpretations of Gaia, which will be examined in Chapter 7, some of which would not be consistent with this model. I could qualify this by adding that such a view could be used to support technological intervention, for as long as we know the threshold of any likely damage, it might seem we could go ahead with impunity. More persistent is the view that delicately balanced ecosystems can be disrupted by wanton human inter-vention.

But if we look at the science of ecology today, another very different voice is beginning to make itself heard. Now the science of ecology is not so much about stability as about chaos. Any view of a final stable state is now being challenged, and instead of a stable ecosystem we have an erratic, shifting mosaic of different species, all competing against each other for survival. Instead of finding balance in nature, ecologists are finding natural disturb-ance, among the most prevalent of which are fire, wind, pests and drought. Now we find researchers, such as John Bissonette, whose main interests are looking at effects of habitat disturbance and fragmentation of species.[24] Instead of an ecosystem, as championed by the earlier ecologists, we have a fluid landscape of patches of different environments, loosely assembled together and never staying the same. Now we find differences based on the particular observation set in question, as will be discussed in further detail below.

Is this alternative view simply a result of the growing influence of population biologists, trained to track with mathematical precision the life histories of individual species? Or is it the resistance to holism with its political overtones and replacement by a new form of social Darwinism? While both possibilities may be partial explanations, a more intriguing one is that this coheres with a wider scientific trend towards discovery of chaos. The natural world as a perfectly predictable, controllable phenomenon is only one way of describing its reality.

Overall the history of ecology shows that any rigid definition of scientific methods is inappropriate as a way of describing the way science works. Rather than the paradigm shift that is apparent in the narrative of the new physics, here we have a quiet revolution, one that emerges gradually over time. This shift perhaps reflects the model of changes in science according to Imre Lakatos, whereby a progressive research programme eventually takes over a degenerative one and becomes dominant.[25] Furthermore, the resonance with chaos theory in physics suggests that ecology is sensitive to wider cultural movements in science as a whole. The search for stable systems is replaced by a more open, receptive stance – one that is not necessarily at home with equilibrium states, but is more prepared to consider life in its full complexity. In addition, the new ecology challenges previous assumptions about the philosophical basis for scientific method.

This greater sense of the fluidity of scientific method should be heartening to theologians. Theology necessarily draws on a wide variety of different approaches. I could analyse trends in contemporary theology in much the same way as I have done for trends in ecology. However, the very variety in theological discourse makes drawing generalizations fraught with difficulty. As an approximation, I think it is fair to suggest that the immediate post-war years of the 1950s were influenced by a reaction against the liberal compromises of the pre-war years. Theology sought to redefine itself by asserting the dogmatic basis for belief in terms of revelation, epitomized in Karl Barth's infamous *Nein* to natural theology. The problem with this approach is that while it gave theology a clear identity, it seemed to leave aside wider issues of society.

However, since then theologians have struggled to find a method that relates more to the practical issues of the time. Praxis approaches define theory by practice and through reference to that practice. Liberation theologies of all kinds have emerged – be it black theology, feminist theology, green theology, urban theology, and so on – all with a particular context in mind. As mentioned earlier, the cultural shift from modernity to post-modernity has undermined the status of statements of universal truth.[26] However, it seems to have allowed alternative positions to flourish: as long as the *context* is defined, then any approach seems to be justified. Has this trend been part of the wider movement towards chaos that we discover in both physics and ecology?

Before I address possible responses to this question, it is worth exploring in a little more depth how the changing methods of ecology have led to the emergence of a rather different philosophy of science. Such a philosophy coheres with those models of theology that stress context as central to theological method.

A newly emergent philosophy of ecology

Karl Popper's principle of falsification, commonly cited as a key method of modern science, does not fit with the way ecological science is generally conducted.[27] The falsification theory was based on the idea that theory could be built up around a series of mathematical statements. This worked reasonably well for the Newtonian style of physics, where universal laws governed by simple causes applied. If any exception was found, then the law could not be true. However, in the case of ecological studies single causal falsifications do not apply unless very small scales are used.

Ecological systems are characterized by multicausal factors that are far more complex than could ever be described in terms of simple falsification theory. This is complicated even further by the fact that every organism has a history, which in turn influences the results.

Ecologists have responded to the lack of fit between falsification theories and ecology by arguing for a new philosophical basis for ecology. This philosophy is more open to theory taking many different forms, including the possibility of *multiple causality*. Such a theory is not simply controlled by laws, but includes looser boundary concepts, such as frameworks, concepts, assumptions and generalizations. The possibility of this more fluid approach to theory is considerably removed from the reductionist approach to science.

Ecologists are now beginning to recognize, more so than they did previously, that the scale of their measurements over time and space will influence their results. Small time scales, over a matter of minutes, are used where measurements are made with small spatial scales, such as the leaf. For example, the openings in leaves that allow gas exchange, known as stomata, open and close in response to daylight and other conditions. The rate of stomatal opening and closing can be measured over a matter of minutes. On the other hand, the largest-scale boundary is appropriate where the landscape itself is being monitored: here it is necessary to measure changes over years, rather than minutes. More intermediate-scale boundaries extending between leaf and landscape are those of tree or canopy, then patch or stand, then forest or community.

The larger scales in particular need to consider the influence of the way the observations have been carried out in terms of scale, or *domain*. The term domain alerts the reader to the fact that time and scale boundaries are important in defining the particular purpose of a given ecological study. Other ecologists define domain in much broader terms to include the boundaries of discourse between ecological concepts and the practical realities to hand.[28] For example, the domain of ecological succession includes the specific characteristics of the species, sites of species interaction, effects of particular disturbances, and so on.

Another idea closely related to that of domain is 'hierarchy theory'. Hierarchy theory takes special account of the particular way the observations are taken in any given 'observation set'.[29] The particular space–time scales that are used in any given observation set need to be taken into account. Observation sets include the consideration of the particular techniques used for both measuring and analysing the data. The difference between domain and observation set seems to be one of emphasis. Whereas the *domain* sets up the relevant parameters for the approach used in any given ecological study, the *observation set* is a specific set of results found in a given study. Both domain and observation set are sensitive to the particular scale of space and time used. Hence, ideas such as equilibrium, local, global or stability are all relative to the particular scale adopted. In this way ecosystems may be described as static or dynamic, fluctuating or in steady state, integrated or a collective of individual components.

The complexity of natural systems is overlooked when the domain is not properly defined or just one observation set is used. Different interpretations based on different domains and observation sets are bound to arise. Apparent discrepancies in results when these are not taken into account can lead to some acrimonious theoretical debates within ecology. This conflict shows the importance of defining adequately the methodological parameters in any scientific study. The lack of mutual understanding between ecologists is complicated still further by the fact that different scales of ecological study use both different languages and different methods. Differences arising from a different use of language and method are particularly important in ecological theory, where rigid laws do not apply in the same way as they do with Newtonian physics. One example of difference in language use is the concept of ecological fitness. In ecological genetics fitness refers to the frequency of the presence of particular genes. However, for evolutionary biology fitness refers to how often that gene comes to be expressed in a given environment, or phenotype.

Given the complexity that exists between the different scales of investigation of ecology, be it the leaf, canopy and so on, how can patterns that emerge at one level be interpreted at another level?

This is not just an issue of reductionism or holism, but concerns the whole tapestry of how the questions are posed and the information gathered. The same process may appear to change when moving from one scale to another. These changes reflect what is known as *emergent properties*, which only appear higher up the scale. Such properties cannot be explained by reference to the interaction of the individual components, defined further down the scale. It is a good example of how the idea of emergent properties is relevant, not just between different disciplines, such as biochemistry, physiology and so on, but even within one sub-discipline of ecology. Some ecological models assume that a population response is the same as the average individual response. However, the scales used to measure accurately the individual response are very different from those used for the population, and new properties are evident further up the scale. A similar problem exists if we move from population to community or community to ecosystem.

Debates exist over how we should define emergence. Is it simply that the property of the whole is qualitatively different from the parts but is still the sum of its components? In this case emergence is still defined by bottom–up causation, that is, its component parts can explain it. Or, more radically, is the emergent property never predicted by the sum of the components? In the latter case some effect on the property by an influence further up the scale may be inferred, that is, top–down causation. The idea of emergence seems to me to make sense if it is based on top–down causation, rather than bottom–up causation, though in living systems we are likely to have a combination of both operative simultaneously. An increase in scale within one level will increase the cumulative effects of the individual components on a particular property. However, once a new hierarchical level is reached then other factors come into play. The idea of emergence as *vitalism* is strongly rejected by most ecologists, even if they support the idea of top–down causation. Emergent properties are still accessible to scientific investigation.

Ecofeminists have welcomed the move towards a greater appreciation of particular observations as it concurs with their own emphasis on specific context. However, they have renamed this 'observation set theory', in place of 'hierarchy theory', which they find offensive because of the implied idea of domination. The theory suggests that the context of observations is crucial in coming to certain conclusions in ecological theory. Furthermore, to envisage the natural world as either totally disordered or ordered is a mistake, because the complexity of the system is such that both aspects are apparent, depending on the perception of the observer.

Conclusions

I have argued that in order to probe deeper into scientific practice we need to be aware of the values of science, in particular the reasons why scientists have found it necessary to claim to be value-free in their method. There are some characteristics of scientific practice that seem at first sight to align science with theology. One such alignment is found in the common search for truth. Theology cannot ignore the pressure of science to be the ultimate source of propositional truth, effectively squeezing religion into the symbolic realm. Moreover, where science claims to be the sole arbiter of truth, it can exclude all dialogue with theology. Such a strong claim for science as the ultimate and only truth, as we have seen, is found in the work of the biologist Richard Dawkins. However, Dawkins is not content just to limit science to this claim, and he believes that in engendering feelings of wonder, science can take over where he believes religion has failed.

Fortunately, not all biologists are convinced that science needs to proceed along the lines he suggests. Barbara McClintock's career is a good example of how the domination of reductionism as method in science led to a failure by her contemporaries to listen to a new possibility emerging from her work that seemed to go against the current dogma in genetics. While she wrote her papers in the classical scientific language that presented her results according to the mechanistic approach to science, her own experience tells a different story. McClintock is ready to admit to her biographer that it was her contact with Tibetan Buddhism that inspired her to become more in tune with the organisms that she was investigating.

The historical development of ecology is also salutary in that it shows how different philosophies have come to influence the practice of ecology, and vice versa. Ecology and culture are thus in dynamic relationship, one with another. Of particular significance was the shift from an understanding of ecology as a single, dynamic system, to a more fluid approach that recognizes the possibility of the unexpected, a patchwork of influences that bears some resemblance to the science of chaos.

The philosophy of ecology has moved beyond the classic methodology of science, such as Popper's falsification theory, and become instead far more sensitive to the idea of multiple causality. Furthermore, the different scales used in different ecological experiments influence the way the results are interpreted, leading to competing ideas. What emerges is a far more complex picture of ecology than a simple one of a single dynamic system. Instead, we have new properties emerging at different levels of organization, with effects on both higher and lower levels. Such discoveries have a resonance with the stress on context in some philosophies of theology, such as those found commonly in liberation theology or feminist theology.

This understanding of ecology is worth bearing in mind when considering the practice of genetics, since it helps to put in perspective any claim of genetic science to determine the nature of an organism. I suggest that the claim to control nature through genetic manipulation needs to be set in the *biological* context that all organisms are part of complex and fluid ecosystems. It is to the science of genetic engineering and its possible applications that I will turn in the chapter that follows.

3

Genetic engineering:
the science and its applications

While it is possible to speak about the practice of science in general terms, I suggest that another way into understanding the philosophy of science is by looking more closely at the science itself. One example was given in the last chapter through consideration of the practice of ecology. Much of the language of scientific investigation seems so wrapped up in jargon that it is inaccessible to anyone outside the discipline. This is as true of biology and genetics as it is of physics and mathematics. How can we begin to demystify the scientific processes themselves? Popular books on science tend to be of two types: more journalistic books aim to expose the hidden agendas in science, while other books, written by scientists themselves, are keen to propagate the public worth of science against perceived hostility and public suspicion. This chapter aims to examine the practice of genetic engineering as a way of informing the theological and ethical debate in subsequent chapters. I intend neither to dismiss the scientific enterprise nor to promote it, but rather to offer a critical analysis of the scientific possibilities as well as the risks.

Every living creature, including bacteria, plants, fungi, animals and humans, contains genes, which are basically the carriers of information. Genetic engineering means moving genes from one organism to another, for example, from one plant to another type of plant. Traditional breeding of animals and plants achieved some of these results, but the process was relatively slow and laborious. For example, the first wheat plants were cultivated about eleven thousand years ago in the area around Canaan. About ten thousand years ago potatoes and beans were cultivated in Peru, while rice was first grown in Indochina and pumpkins in the middle Americas. Throughout the centuries farmers have tried to select the healthiest and most productive strains of plants and animals.

How does traditional breeding differ from genetic engineering? I suggest there are at least three important distinctions:

- Traditional breeding always involves a cross between two closely related species. Genetic engineering, however, permits movement of genes between completely unrelated species.
- The process of genetic change in traditional breeding is laborious and slow. By contrast, genetic engineering takes a matter of weeks or months.
- Genetic change through breeding was confined to a relatively small number of species of plants and animals. By contrast, genetic engineering has far wider scope, involving not just those plants and animals that give us food but also genetic change of organisms used in sewage disposal, pollution control and drug production.

Genetic engineering in practice

The biological basis of genetic engineering

What about the science of the genetic engineering itself?[1] Living cells contain a nucleus, which controls the activity of a cell, rather like a brain controls human actions. Chromosomes are found in the nucleus, and these contain the genes, the carriers of genetic information. Even as early as 1944 scientists knew that nucleic acids in chromosomes were responsible for carrying information from one generation to the next. But it was only when the structure of the nucleic acids was discovered in 1953 that genetic engineering became possible. James Watson and Francis Crick are given the credit for this discovery, though Rosalind Franklin and Maurice Wilkins provided vital experimental data.

The particular type of nucleic acid they described is called deoxyribonucleic acid (DNA). The structure consists of two strands of sugars and phosphates that are associated together in the famous double helical arrangement. Attached to the sugars we find four possible bases, known chemically as adenine, cytosine, guanine and thymine (A, C, G, T), which pair with particular bases on the other strand. These bases are structured in such a way that each base always pairs with just one other base out of the three available, rather like a key in a lock. A always pairs with T and C with G in a way that stabilizes the double helical structure.

The structure of DNA is important as the base pairs act like a code to determine the information carried by particular sections. We can think of it rather like an alphabet with four letters of A, C, T, G instead of our 26 alphabetical letters. When the nucleus is active in translating information, the double helix unwinds, and single strands of another nucleic acid known as messenger ribonucleic acid (RNA) pair with just one strand of the deoxyribonucleic acid. The sequence of base pairs is exactly the same, except in RNA the base *uracil* replaces *thymine* found in DNA. This RNA is like an intermediary in the process of protein synthesis. The messenger RNA then moves from the nucleus to the main body of the cell, that is, the cytoplasm, where protein synthesis begins.

Particular sequences of three base pairs code for a particular amino acid, carried by another intermediary, known as transfer RNA, that has three base pairs attached. This transfer RNA pairs with the single-stranded messenger RNA and allows particular amino acids to assemble in a particular order. Once these 'three-letter' words are strung together in a particular way, the sequence of amino acids is fixed. Mutations can occur by a single change or multiple changes in the DNA bases. A base is either replaced, deleted or inserted. A deletion or insertion is the most serious as it will lead to a string of further changes to the three-letter code subsequent to the alteration. These changes in turn lead to a different sequence of bases for the messenger RNA and altered sequence of amino acids.

Particular proteins consist of particular sequences of amino acids. The proteins may be enzymes that speed up particular reactions in the cells. There are twenty different amino acids that are coded for by the RNA. A gene is made up of a section of deoxy-ribonucleic acid that codes for a particular protein. Different organisms carry different genes and so can make very different proteins. Some DNA in non-bacterial species, known as *eukaryotes*, does not code for any amino acids; where this occurs *between* genes it is known as 'junk' DNA. In other cases it appears *within* genes, and in this case the 'nonsense' DNA is actually inserted into a messenger RNA sequence. This sequence of non-sense DNA, known as an *intron*, is cut out of the messenger RNA before it moves into the cytoplasm for protein synthesis. The remaining messenger RNA that codes for the protein itself is called an *exon*. Surprisingly, researchers have found examples in humans of mutations in the intron DNA that still lead to an altered protein structure. In this case a mistake is made in the excision of the intron, leading to an altered amino acid sequence. Hence not all the DNA consists of 'genes', but it still seems to play an important role in some cases. There are many scholarly debates about the possible function of these 'nonsense' sequences, though no clear consensus has so far been reached.

Genetic engineering is the term used to describe the range of techniques whereby pieces of DNA from different sources are joined to form what is known as *recombinant DNA*. In most cases this will involve moving sections of the DNA that are known to code for particular proteins or genes. By far the largest application of genetic engineering is in biological and biomedical research. Most biological laboratories presently use genetic engineering in one form or another for research purposes. The structure of DNA is such that by unwinding it can form another strand of DNA alongside each of the other strands and hence replicate itself. This is an essential attribute of the DNA in addition to the ability to act as a template for protein synthesis described above. This ability of DNA to replicate itself is vital if the organism is going to be capable of carrying information from one generation to another. Moreover, it means that any changes to DNA through genetic engineering are, bar further mutations, carried through to succeeding daughter cells following cell division.

Replication takes place during normal growth through a process

known as *mitosis*. All cells that are derived from the genetically
altered cell will carry the genetic information in its new
form. The situation is similar in the case of sexual reproduction,
which involves a process known as *meiosis*. In higher organisms
specialized cells known as *gametes* carry the information from one
generation to the next. These cells carry just one set of chromosomes, rather than the two sets found in all other cell types. When
the DNA of gametes is changed, then, following fertilization, *all*
the cells of the next generation carry the genetic change.

Transfer of genetic material

As mentioned earlier, the normal barriers that prevent, for example,
a sheep crossing with a mouse, or human with a pig, can be
bypassed in genetic engineering. Genes can quite literally be
transferred from almost any organism to another. One of the key
facts emerging from the study of genetics is that genes from
different species have a surprising similarity to each other. From
a geneticist's viewpoint distinctions between species are blurred
or even non-existent. As noted above, only a percentage of the
total DNA present in any chromosome forms particular genes,
which are the sequences coding for particular proteins. In practice
it becomes possible to move genes from almost any species to any
other. It is this ability to move genes across species that cannot
normally interbreed that marks out genetic engineering as
critically distinct from other forms of biotechnology, such as
cheese making or brewing. However, the techniques used to introduce the new genes are not perfect. As will be discussed below,
methods used to achieve this are relatively crude.

Methods used in genetic engineering

Isolation of the protein that is coded by the gene is perhaps the
hardest step of all, and can take researchers many months or years.
Once the protein is isolated, then the gene coding for it can be
identified. This is usually done by finding out the amino acid
sequence of the protein, synthesizing the RNA that corresponds

to the protein, then adding a radioactive marker to track the location of the genes in the chromosomes. However, isolation of the gene is not usually sufficient for success in genetic engineering. In addition, genetic engineers add to the gene what is known as a promoter sequence, which controls the expression of the gene.

There are two possible methods that genetic engineers can use to insert the isolated genes into the chromosomes of the recipient organism. Often these cells will be growing in what is known as a tissue culture, derived from a particular plant or animal organ. The first method is direct transmission, which has three principal subdivisions. One uses a 'gun', where DNA and tungsten are literally shot into the plant cells. The tungsten makes holes in the cell membrane and hence encourages the absorption of the DNA. Problems include possible damage to the cells, and only a small proportion of foreign DNA is absorbed. In the electroporation method, cells are placed in a solution containing the foreign DNA and an electric charge is applied, which puts holes in the outer membrane of the cell and allows DNA to be taken up. In the chemical method, silicon carbide crystals are added, which create small holes in the cell membrane, again allowing DNA to be absorbed.

In all these cases the outer cellular membrane is made more permeable in order to allow the DNA to be taken up by the cells. However, there is no real certainty of *where* the new DNA will recombine with the existing DNA of the 'host' cell. Thus there is an inherent uncertainty built into the process. It seems to be largely a matter of trial and error which cells take up the new DNA and synthesize the new protein, some conditions favouring the process more than others.

The method of micro-injection into a fertilized egg is only appropriate for the genetic engineering of animals. Eggs are normally obtained from the ovaries of animals that have just been slaughtered. Following maturation and fertilization in a laboratory, a very fine needle is used to inject the foreign DNA into the nucleus. Only about one in a hundred eggs injected incorporate the new DNA and become genetically transformed.

The second main method used by genetic engineers to insert

selected genes into chromosomes is by using vectors. A vector is an organism that can carry genetic material from one species to the next. The foreign DNA is attached to that of a vector, which then infects the species to be engineered. Vectors normally recombine with the 'foreign' and host DNA in particular places, which improves the specificity of the genetic change.

Another technique that is particularly successful in combination with vectors is the use of restriction endonucleases. Genetic engineers have identified enzymes that cut the DNA at particular points. One bacterial enzyme known as *EcoR1* 'looks' for a particular sequence, namely, GAATTC, paired with CTTAAG, cutting between the adenine and guanine in both strands. The two single stranded 'sticky ends' attach to other single strands with the sequence TTAAG or GAATT. In order to facilitate transfer genetic engineers can use the same restriction endonuclease to cut out the gene they wish to transfer, with exactly the same 'sticky ends' at each end of the gene sequence. When the 'sticky ends' begin to recombine, some of the cut DNA will take up the new gene. Another enzyme called *DNA ligase* will repair the damage and join up the broken ends.

Bacterial vector transmission proceeds as follows. Bacteria have DNA in a circular chromosome and also in smaller circular fragments known as plasmids. These plasmids normally function to transfer genetic material between different bacteria. Genetic engineers have taken advantage of this simple system to use plasmids as carriers of particular genes from other sources. The restriction endonuclease first cuts the circular plasmid DNA in order to open up the ring. The same enzyme is used to excise a particular gene from the donor species. Both the new gene and the bacterial plasmid DNA will have 'sticky ends' with free-floating sequences, as described above. When the two are mixed together a new bacterial circular plasmid forms, containing the foreign DNA. This bacterial plasmid is then used to infect the recipient organism.

A good example of this technique is the use of bacteria known as *Agrobacterium* that causes crown gall in some plants. Genetically engineered forms of *Agrobacterium* can be used as vectors to carry material from one species to the next. The galls are the result of the bacterial DNA inserting itself into its host. Genetic engineers found mutants of *Agrobacterium* that failed to induce a tumour, but still inserted themselves into the host DNA. These mutants are then used to facilitate the transfer of genetic material.

Marker genes, such as those that code for antibiotic or herbicide resistance, help to track the passage of the gene into the host cells. As expected from the above summary of the methods, the actual incorporation of the new gene into the host is very low, as little as 0.1%. An antibiotic marker gene helps keep track of the gene being transferred, as only transformed cells will be resistant to that antibiotic.

Possible applications of genetic engineering

Diagnosis and treatment of disease

Genetic engineering of humans

The Human Genome Project, which began in 1990, aims to find the complete DNA sequence that makes up human chromosomes. The original projected date for the completion of this project was 2003. However, the completion date is likely to be before this, since the first draft of the complete human genome sequence was announced earlier than expected, in June 2000. Knowledge of the full sequence of DNA in all the chromosomes will act like a reference library for research workers. This library will be useful in the development of both the *diagnosis* of human genetic diseases and *therapies* for particular diseases. At present it is illegal in the UK to conduct what is known as *germ-line therapy*. This is alteration of the sperm or egg cells that encode the genetic material for the next generation. Scientists believe that germ-line therapy is far too risky to justify at this stage. It also raises a number of ethical issues, to be discussed later.

Couples undertaking treatment of infertility through *in vitro* fertilization (IVF) may have embryos screened for genetic diseases prior to implantation in the mother's womb. At the time of writing, the use of IVF to help couples who are particularly vulnerable to genetic disease is not widespread, though it is used in some cases. However, it is likely to become more widely accepted for those families with a history of severe genetic disorder, such as cystic fibrosis or Huntington's disease. The low success rate of IVF at just 17.5% means that it is likely to be tolerated as a method of treatment only in the case of families with severe genetic disorders.

Some genes, such as that for Tay-Sachs disease, are always fatal. Other genetic diseases, such as that for phenylketonuria deficiency, can be treated at birth. Other genes predispose offspring to developing disease, for example, a gene called BRAC1 is involved in breast cancer. The genetic disease known as Down's syndrome is more common in older mothers. The use of genetic tests on human embryos for a number of genetically inherited diseases is routine, but only after pregnancy is achieved. In these cases abortion of the foetus that may be at a fairly late stage in development is the only medical intervention offered. I mentioned above the use of IVF for screening of embryos at a much earlier stage of development. The marketing of user-friendly diagnostic kits for expectant mothers who are known to have propensity for particular genetic diseases is likely to become more widespread. However, there is always a margin of error as genetic tests always work with *probabilities*, rather than show absolute certainties.

At present it is legal in the UK to use what is known as *somatic therapy*, that is, treatment of the cells of the human body. Somatic gene therapy has been used to treat cystic fibrosis. In this case the practical problem is how to transfer the genes into the cells of the patient. St Mary's Hospital Medical School has developed a technique whereby cystic fibrosis genes are carried in membranous cellular structures known as liposomes. This technique has been used in clinical trials. Unfortunately, as the cells in the lining of the lung shed very rapidly, repeated treatments are needed, and thus the technique remains very expensive.

Genetic engineering of animals for human benefit

While genetic engineering of animals can be directed towards treatment of animal diseases, the bulk of the research effort has been towards using genetic engineering of animals to facilitate treatment of particular human diseases, for example, through the production of medicines. The disease of emphysema, for example, frequently triggered by exposure to cigarette smoking or to other airborne irritants, is caused by defective production of alpha-1 antitrypsin (AAT). Treatment is the administration of 200 grams of AAT a year. A team based in Edinburgh succeeded in transferring into sheep embryos a copy of the human gene that encodes AAT. The result is that AAT is produced in the ewes' milk.

Bacteria could not be used in this case to synthesize the human protein because AAT needs to have a sugar attached, by a process known as glycosylation. This reaction happens naturally in mammals and humans, but not in bacteria. It is technically not possible to add the sugar to AAT produced by bacteria. In addition, genetic engineers are able to add a control gene along with the AAT gene in order to make sure that AAT is *only* produced in the mammary glands and nowhere else.

Nonetheless, only very small percentages of sheep embyros take up the AAT and control gene, and reach maturity. Genetic engineers were keen to find alternative ways of genetically manipulating sheep that had a higher success rate. This search was the driving force behind the effort to clone Dolly the sheep. Cloning, if successful, could produce unlimited numbers of genetically altered sheep.

Other animals genetically engineered to produce particular proteins for pharmaceutical purposes include mice, rabbits, goats and cattle. These may be used to treat human disease or for veterinary purposes. Other, more controversial genetic manipulations include the genetic engineering of animals so that they mimic human diseases. Mice have been genetically engineered to mimic, for example, the following diseases: cystic fibrosis, muscular dystrophy, cancer, sickle cell anaemia and Alzheimer's disease. The Harvard oncomouse that carried the human gene for propensity for cancer was produced in laboratories in Harvard and patented in the USA in 1988.

Another example of the use of genetic engineering is the development of the use of pig hearts for human transplants. Pig hearts can now be genetically engineered so that they produce human proteins like a coat or film around their heart. This is thought to prevent rejection after transplantation. Clinical trials have already been carried out.

Other experiments aim at boosting food production in animals, for example, by inserting genes carrying growth hormones. Chickens have also been engineered to stop them feeling 'broody' by deleting the gene that makes prolactin, with the overall result that there is a 15%–20% increase in their egg production.

Genetic engineering of bacteria and plants

One of the cheapest ways of producing pharmaceutical products for treatment of human disease is though genetic engineering of bacteria. For example, the production of human insulin by genetically modified bacteria has brought considerable benefits for diabetics. There is an unfortunate drawback of the use of human insulin in that it may lead to a loss of awareness of hypoglycemia, which was not the case when the bovine form of insulin was used for treatment. Other examples of bacterial modification include the bacterial production of human growth hormone. Older techniques, which used hormones extracted from cadavers, ran the risk of contamination with blood-borne diseases, such as hepatitis.

As in the case of animals, novel human genes can also be introduced into higher plants that then synthesize the product in question. This may be achieved by the vector method, using bacteria or viruses that normally infect the plant, or by direct ballistic methods discussed above.[2] This method of human protein synthesis is deemed much safer than other methods of extracting the protein from donated blood, which run the risk of being infected with hepatitis or AIDS.

A more important point, perhaps, is that those who support

genetic engineering believe the real potential benefits are, as yet, unrealized. Carrier bacteria or viruses can have a particular 'vaccine sequence' attached, so that antigen proteins for the anti-body are actually produced in the plant tissue. This technique, then, offers a way of producing hormones, edible vaccines, anti-biotics and blood-clotting factors and therapeutic proteins such as anti-HIV or anti-cancer agents.

Another possibility of genetic engineering for human health is through the removal of food allergens. Those genes coding for proteins responsible for causing human allergy to nuts, for example, could be identified and removed in genetically modified nut plants. In addition, genes coding for vitamins such as Vitamin A could be added to the genetic library of those staples that are not normally rich in this vitamin, such as rice or potatoes. A recent press release suggested that a Swiss scientist has now developed rice genetically modified so that it is rich in Vitamin A. Vitamin A deficiency is a common cause of blindness in poorer communities.

The special case of animal cloning

The puzzle for animal development

Cloning, that is, the reproduction of an individual without the normal method of sexual reproduction, was originally thought to be possible only in plants. Gardeners are well aware of the ability of plants to mature from grafting a single leaf, for example. However, researchers in Cambridge then discovered that it is pos-sible to clone tadpoles, though the cloning of frogs proved more problematic. Their interest stemmed from a particular concern with processes of development. When cells differentiate to become bone, skin and blood, for example, what happens to the DNA in each cell? Is some of it irreversibly switched off, so that only those genes that are relevant for that cell are active? Or is it possible to reprogramme the cell so that it becomes capable of making other types of proteins found in other cells? The ability to clone animals seemed out of reach. Hence the developmental scientists assumed that somehow the genetic material in the adults was selectively switched on and off in an irreversible way.

Cloning for drug production

Biotechnologists at the Roslin Institute in Scotland believed that it was well worth trying to clone sheep even against the odds. If it were successful, then genetically engineered sheep could be produced at will, avoiding the rather hit-and-miss genetic engineering processes, as described above. Ironically, the desire to clone Dolly was not so much for the purpose of countering scientific dogma as for very practical purposes, namely, production of particular drugs by genetically engineered sheep.

Cloning is also known as *nuclear transfer* as applied to animals. The egg cells first of all have their nuclei removed. Egg cells contain a single copy of chromosomes that is normally complemented by the chromosomes from a sperm cell. All other cells contain two sets of chromosomes. Ian Wilmut, at the Roslin Institute, led a team that discovered it was possible to insert the genetic material of a sheep's udder cell into an 'empty' egg cell that had its nucleus removed.[3] In the case of Dolly the sheep a nucleus from an udder cell was introduced into the egg cell using a very fine pipette. The egg containing the new nucleus was moved carefully between two electrodes and then subjected to a short burst from an electric current of about 25V. This pulse of energy mimicked aspects of fertilization.

In most cases hybrid cells failed to survive. The critical factor in ensuring success was discovered by Keith Campbell, one of the scientists working on the project. He found that if *both* the donor egg and the cells of the donor nucleus were in a resting state known as *quiescence*, less damage to the DNA occurred. Even then only a very small fraction of eggs with an implanted nucleus developed into an embryo, which was then implanted into a surrogate mother. It took 276 attempts before a normal lamb was born. The others had a range of abnormalities and were generally enlarged in size, posing a risk to the mother. Note that, strictly speaking, this is *nuclear cloning*, since a maternal egg contains *some* extra-nuclear DNA in organelles known as mitochondria that is different from the DNA in the nucleus. True cloning would only result if the cells for the donor nucleus came from the same maternal line as the donor egg, where both had the same mitochondrial DNA.

Polly, produced just six months later, was genetically engineered with some unnamed human genes. This allowed production of the human blood-clotting protein Factor IX in transgenic cloned sheep. Factor IX is necessary for the treatment of haemophiliacs. The level of production was 60 times that from human extracts.

Cloning human embryos for therapeutic purposes

At present cloning human embryos is illegal, even to address fertility problems. However, in the UK the Human Genetics Advisory Commission and the Human Fertilisation and Embryology Authority are pressing for the use of cloning to treat certain diseases.[4] Legally this would involve modification of the Act that controls experimentation on human embryos.

The medical argument in its favour relates to the treatment of severe degenerative diseases. Following fertilization, embryos remain in an undifferentiated state up to about seventeen days, when what is known as a primitive streak appears, where the 'head' and 'tail' end become recognizable. Prior to this development undifferentiated cells known as stem cells have the capacity to develop into a number of different kinds of cells, such as bone, blood or lung tissue. Embryo experimentation is legal up to fourteen days old. Scientists argue that use of cloned embryos that are less than two weeks old for their stem cells will offer the means of curing otherwise incurable diseases, such as wasting diseases of the bone marrow. These cloned cells would not run the risk of being rejected by the patient, as long as the patient was the source of the nuclear component of the cells.

So far cloning of human embryos has been attempted in both the USA and South Korea. In the USA an egg cell from a cow was used as the 'host' egg, along with the nuclear material from the salivary cells. The research was stopped soon after the cells in the host egg started to divide. In the Korean case an egg from a mother known to have fertility problems was used, though once again the research was stopped after the four-cell stage. In both cases the researchers realized that their work invoked a number of ethical issues that they claim led them to terminate their research. Even this research was met with hostile public protests. However, the fact that the research was possible and also showed signs of life demonstrated that human cloning is technically feasible. It seems highly probable that this research has continued 'underground'. The use of mice in cloning experiments is particularly significant, since mice have a rapid gestation period. This allows far more research to be carried out on refining the techniques of cloning.

The use of human cloning to treat human fertility, while illegal at present, may happen if there are sufficient financial rewards. Dr Richard Seed, a self-professed biologist in the USA, has offered the technique of cloning to volunteers who have tried and failed using other methods of fertility treatment, such as IVF. He has even offered to clone himself. It seems only a matter of time before someone, somewhere in the world will succeed in cloning a human being to full maturity. There are clearly ethical, social and theological issues at stake, which will be discussed in subsequent chapters.

Agricultural applications

The use of animal cloning

Cloning has also been used to try and improve the quality of meat from farm animals. However, so far it has not proved to be commercially viable. Granada, the American Company that sponsored this research in the 1990s, abandoned the attempt to use cloning as a way of producing genetically uniform cattle.

Genetic engineering of crop plants

The first genetically engineered tomato, known as FLAVR SAVR, may soon be on sale in the UK. This tomato was launched in 1994, in a wave of publicity in the USA, as the first genetically engineered whole food. In this tomato the gene that leads to softening is 'scrambled', so that the tomatoes ripen without going squashy. The engineered tomato allowed companies to transport tomatoes long distances following ripening, instead of artificially ripening green fruit. This was to the commercial advantage of the producers.

The very recent proliferation of the production of genetically modified (GM) crops is quite remarkable.[5] This is particularly evident in the USA where the global area of GM crops expanded from 1.5 million hectares in 1996 to 8.1 million hectares in 1997 and 20.5 million hectares in 1998.[6] The USA has also dominated the overall global market of GM crops, with 74% of the global acreage, followed by Argentina and Canada. By 1998 more than a third of the American soya bean crop and 45% of the Canadian oil-seed rape crop were genetically modified. Such changes impinge not just on those living in these countries but on all exports as well, including processed food, thus entering the global food supply.

Soya beans make up over half the total acreage of GM crops. At present most of the acreage comes from crops genetically engineered to tolerate herbicide, produced by the manufacturers, who also have patent rights over the genetically modified seed. Plants that have been engineered to be tolerant to a particular herbicide allow farmers to grow crops with no ill effects of herbicide on the crops. The herbicide and the hybrid seed are sold as one package to the farmers. Roundup Ready soya bean is a good example of this. Other examples include plants genetically engineered to contain a particular insecticide. Genetic engineering in this case seems to be for the commercial benefit of the producer.

Crop development through normal breeding methods has allowed farmers to select crops that give the highest yields or that are resistant to pests. Genetic engineering in this case is simply a way of enhancing this process and moving genes between different varieties. Those who are supportive of genetic engineering argue that it is simply an extension of normal plant breeding and cultivation that has been going on for years.

Genetic engineering allows genes to be modified so that the plant produces novel products. Oil-seed rape plants, for example, can be genetically modified so that their oil is very similar to that normally produced in the southern continents by palm and coconut trees. The UK currently imports 400,000 tonnes of palm oil and coconut oil, hence locally produced genetically modified oil-seed is likely to be a commercial advantage depending on particular economic conditions.[7]

Genetic engineering can also be used to render plants more tolerant to frost. For example, some bacteria that grow naturally on the surface of plants produce a particular glycoprotein that encourages the formation of ice crystals. If bacteria are genetically engineered so that they are no longer able to make this protein, there is an increase in the plant's frost tolerance.

Other experiments are under way to enhance the tolerance of crops to a range of unfavourable conditions, including high acidity, high aluminium, drought and high salt conditions. Drought and salt tolerance in crops is complicated by the fact that these attributes are coded for by many different genes. However, the genetic basis for salt tolerance in fungi is simpler and has recently been discovered to reside in just two genes. The intention is to try and introduce these genes into crops to see if they enhance salt tolerance.

Industrial applications

The first patent given to a life form was issued in 1980 by the Supreme Court in the USA for genetically modified bacteria. Normally we associate patents with particular novel products that are manufactured. A patent exists in order to protect an inventor from unfair exploitation by others who wish to use the same technology for commercial gain. The ability of scientists to transfer genes between species and use this for commercial purposes has led to patents being granted for particular gene sequences.

Genetically modified bacteria are commonly used to control pollution. Industrial pollutants, such as chlorinated hydrocarbons, pollutants from munitions factories and unwanted pesticides are all potentially degradable by genetically modified bacteria. The bacteria are genetically modified so that they capable of absorbing particular pollutants and degrading them to less toxic chemicals. Genetically modified bacteria can also be used to absorb heavy metal pollutants in contaminated land.

Risks associated with genetic engineering

Possible risks to human or animal health

In a report published in May 1999, the British Medical Association noted the real uncertainty associated with the release of genetically modified organisms (GMOs) for public health. The BMA stated that 'we cannot at present know whether there are any serious risks to the environment or human health involved in producing GM crops or consuming GM food products'.[8] For example, while genetic engineering in theory sounds very precise, in practice the techniques may lead to a number of unexpected difficulties.[9]

In order to monitor the passage of a gene into a new species or variety scientists have used marker genes, which include those coding for antibiotic resistance in some cases. The actual risk to human health is unknown, though the use of antibiotic marker genes is now discouraged. The risks to animal and human health are summarized by the points below:

- The possibility exists that humans will have an allergic reaction to certain genetically engineered products, which could occur as novel proteins are introduced.
- There are also possible effects of consumption of genetically engineered products on human health. Dr Arpad Pusztai claimed that his experiments on feeding rats with potatoes that had been genetically modified with the snowdrop gene for lectin production showed damage to rats' immunity. The media storm that ensued, followed by counter-claims that the results were not scientific, served to raise the levels of public anxiety still further. The results released so far do not give us any conclusive evidence for damage to the health of rats.[10] Even so, the fact remains that sufficient detailed tests have rarely been carried out in order to check possible *indirect* adverse reactions of single or multiple genetic modification(s). It is not sufficient, for example, to assume that just because the gene product itself is not directly toxic there are no indirect toxic effects caused by possible changes in gene expression or biochemistry.

- There are known to be considerable risks to animal health in some genetic engineering experiments. This leads to concern over animal welfare. For example, human growth hormones have been introduced into pigs to stimulate their growth rates. However, when this was done pigs became arthritic, went blind and had other abnormalities. The regulation of the gene was uncontrolled, illustrating the unpredictability of genetic transfer, even though this continues to be an area of active research.

Possible risks to the environment

Many believe that the risks associated with the technology itself are not adequately acknowledged. Part of the problem seems to be that monitoring of risk associated with novel foods is not, at the moment, nearly as stringent as that for new pharmaceuticals. Moreover, while there is a growing acknowledgment that environmental risk must be monitored, there is a lack of clarity about what would be unacceptable environmental damage. The risks to the environment can be summarized as follows:

- An important question is the specificity of action claimed for the gene introduced. For example, scientists have introduced the bacterial gene from *Bacillus thuringiensis*, which expresses an insecticide, into maize plants. Bt-maize is marketed by Novartis on account of its specificity to the corn borer insect, which attacks maize. However, subsequent research has since shown that lacewings are also vulnerable. More recently *pollen* from GM maize has been reported to be toxic to caterpillars of rare Monarch butterflies. Although there have been some counter-arguments against the validity of these experiments, the possibility of risk remains while there are still conflicting reports. Bt insecticide sprays would, of course, have the same effect. However, the claim that Bt maize is more environmentally friendly seems to be called into question.
- Another ecological issue relates to the creation of unwelcome new plants. Environmentalists are concerned that genes, such as those coding for herbicide resistance, could find their way into

the wild population of weeds and create new 'superweeds' that would be impossible to control. Oil-seed rape, for example, will cross with wild mustard. One of the problems facing environmentalists is that it is difficult to conduct adequate assessment of ecological risk from GMOs. In particular, the ability of oil-seed rape to cross with wild cabbage, hoary mustard, wild radish and charlock has only recently come to light. Hence, in the case of oil-seed rape, the spread of genes to other species is more likely than had previously thought to be the case.[11]

- The possible disruption of the food chain is of particular concern to ecologists. For example, if insect-resistant genes were transferred to wild varieties, insects would be denied food, and this would have knock-on effects down the food chain.

- The loss of biodiversity is another area of risk that is particularly important in assessment of the environmental impact of GM crops. One way loss of biodiversity might occur is through use of broad-spectrum herbicides on crops that have been engineered to tolerate them. These herbicides would eliminate all the wild varieties of plants and grasses in the areas where the crops are grown. While the manufacturers argue that use of such crops leads to a reduction in total herbicide use, its effectiveness in reducing weeds is so striking that many ecologists are worried about a loss of biodiversity. Environmentalists fear that this would lead to a further reduction in wildlife through loss of natural habitats. The organization English Nature has called for a moratorium on commercialization of GM crops.

- Another relevant risk is the possible ecological invasion by genetically modified organisms. Introducing new varieties into areas that were unknown to a particular species has, in the past, led to ecological problems. Rhododendron, introduced into Britain some years ago, has now become a major weed. Similarly, pests could develop from GM crops. Professor Mark Williamson, an ecologist and former member of the government Advisory Committee on Releases into the Environment (ACRE), suggests that pests are most likely to be created from salt-tolerant or frost-tolerant plants and those engineered to be insect-resistant.[12]

Exploitation of patent rights

There are a number of differences between the USA and European
patenting systems, which have important practical outcomes. In
Europe the first to file the application is given the patent. No
public disclosure is allowed, hence all research must be kept secret
until the patent is released. In the USA an inventor is given a year
after news is first released for the patent to be filed. However,
patents are settled according to the actual dates of invention. This
can lead to acrimonious battles between rival groups. Patents are
considered to be necessary by the biotechnology industry in order
to ensure a return on their investment in research and development. The high cost of patents leads to expensive royalties, which
means that poorer nations are denied access to the technology.

Lawyers who are involved in patent law consider that patents
are there simply to protect the rights of the inventor, rather than
giving an assessment of the acceptability of a particular process or
product. However, patenting cannot be detached from social and
political issues so easily. The ethical good in patenting might
include the free access of information and benefits to society, the
reward for particular inventiveness and a principle of justice so
that others do not exploit the invention unfairly.

As one might expect, patent rights may be misused in those
cases where one company gains a monopoly on a particular genetic
transformation. Alternatively, the royalties given for some patents
may not reflect the actual benefit gained. In their search for new
sources of genetic variation researchers have discovered that the
oldest strains of crop plants that have the greatest genetic diversity
are confined to the poorer nations of the world. The payments
given for the use of the genetic potential of these crops do not
reflect the advantage gained by the commercial companies. The
social and political risks associated with genetic technology will be
discussed in subsequent chapters.

Use of genetic engineering in warfare

The use of genetic technology as a tool for weaponry is a
subject that many scientists are reluctant to discuss. Details of the

development of any biological weapon are surrounded in secrecy. Until these weapons are used in actual warfare, the possibility that this is taking place can only be gained from journalistic reports. However, this investigative journalism needs to be taken seriously in the absence of more reliable sources of information. One such report is that of a genetically engineered antibiotic-resistant variant of anthrax produced by the Russian Federation.[13]

Part of the problem in detection of biological weapons using biotechnology is that the technical processes are identical to those used to produce beneficial agents. For example, viruses processed to make vaccines in small-scale plants can just as easily be produced for biological weapons. Given the global spread of biotechnology, at least a hundred countries have the capacity to make biological weapons. Furthermore, information about how to make biological weaponry is freely available on the Internet.[14]

The Human Genome Project offers the possibility of obtaining the information needed to develop a range of medicines and understand more fully all kinds of diseases. However, this additional knowledge will also help in the development of new and more lethal forms of biological weapons that attack the human genome in specific ways. The possibility that microbes could be genetically engineered to attack specific ethnic groups might seem far-fetched, but the British Medical Association considered it to be a real possibility in a report published in 1999.[15] While genetic differences within populations are just as striking as those between populations, there are some gene variants, or *alleles*, that are more common in some populations compared with others.

Only fairly small changes in the structure of microbes are necessary to change them from benign to highly virulent forms. Very rarely we find forms of influenza virus that are lethal for humans. However, some avian flu viruses are lethal to 90% of the birds that they infect. Japanese scientists have managed to genetically engineer the structure of a highly virulent turkey virus so that it becomes benign.[16] It is entirely plausible to engineer human flu viruses so that they become more, rather than less, virulent. While the legislation of most countries would prohibit such a development, terrorists would ignore any such prohibitions.

Given available biotechnology, it would also be relatively cheap and easy to produce such weaponry.

There are other examples of how genetic engineering could be used to enhance pathogenicity. For example, many bacterial pathogens are light-sensitive and are destroyed by the sun's radiation. The genes that code for light resistance are known in non-pathogenic bacteria. It would be relatively easy to transfer light-resistant genes to the pathogens, and hence enhance virulence. Other characteristics, such as the ability to withstand desiccation, could be transferred in a similar way. Bacteria and other organisms can be engineered so that they synthesize toxins that are normally produced by other organisms, in much the same way as the production of pharmaceuticals in general. This type of transfer has been used to human advantage. For example, the gene for scorpion toxin has been added to a virus that normally attacks caterpillars, leading to a deadly insecticide. Other regulatory proteins that control different physiological functions could be altered and used in warfare, for example, to change moods and lead to disorientation.

Genetic engineering could also be used to produce more virulent diseases or toxins lethal to specific animals and plants. A more indirect method of attack through endangering food supply is one that has been used before, for example, in the Vietnam war.

Conclusions

The ability to transfer genetic material from one species to another engenders in a unique way the opportunity for major shifts in the evolution of species, even the evolution of our own species. Furthermore, the recent technique of animal cloning opens up the possibility of even greater human intervention in the reproduction of species, including humans. As long as the focus of application of genetic science is on medicine and the treatment of disease, then this seems to be a positive attribute of the new discoveries. However, many scientists are genuinely worried about the negative consequences of genetic engineering, including effects on human health, the environment and its potential use in biological warfare.

The science of genetic engineering shows us something of human ingenuity, namely, that through a particular mechanistic approach to science the possibility of profound changes in the nature of life itself comes into view. In addition, the dominant image of nature is that of a mechanism to be manipulated for particular ends. I suggest that genetic engineering would be more difficult if a different image of nature compatible with experimental science were to be adopted, such as that of a mirror into the divine mind discussed in Chapter 1. For a mirror implies that God has created the creature and that it can only be interfered with at our peril. The only possible justification in this case would be to assume that the mirror has in some way become tarnished by natural or human evil, and that this imperfection can then be corrected by human intervention. This may be one reason why medical applications of genetic engineering have more widespread public support than other uses. The image of nature as autonomous is also more difficult to entertain. In this case nature itself would have its own *telos*, or direction, so that to interfere with it might seem to go against what is part of nature's own processes. Another way that such alternative images of nature might be used to support genetic engineering is by focusing the idea of nature as divine mirror or autonomous on humanity alone, thus justifying human intervention. The theological issues associated with genetic engineering will be examined in detail in Chapter 5 and the ethical issues in Chapter 6.

It is also clear that there is too much at stake in genetic engineering that is of public importance to leave decisions about its future to scientists alone. The need for a clear public debate on the issue has been widely recognized by many Christians in different churches who have actively contributed to this debate. It is important to keep these debates in view before considering more detailed theological or ethical positions. The response of different churches to questions surrounding genetic engineering is the subject of the chapter that follows.

4

The church and the new genetics

It was argued in the last chapter that genetic engineering presents us with the possibility of fundamental genetic changes to the natural world. Such changes have clear beneficial applications, but also entail risks to both human health and the environment. The purpose of this chapter is to first of all to survey some of the ways the church as an *institution* has responded to the challenge posed by genetic engineering. I will show that its response has been mixed, and more often than not comes from a particular perception of science. Moreover, there has been a strong tendency to focus almost exclusively on the implications of genetic engineering as they relate to humans. The survey of the responses of the different churches is intended primarily to be *illustrative*, rather than *exhaustive*, within the limited scope of this chapter. I will suggest that a way forward in ecumenical dialogue is through a recovery of the Wisdom tradition, as developed in both Eastern and Western traditions of Christianity. This forms a framework for the discussion of subsequent chapters where the theological and ethical issues raised by specific examples of genetic engineering will be considered in more detail.

The response of the World Council of Churches

The World Council of Churches (WCC) is a multi-church organization consisting of the major Christian churches, including Anglican, Protestant and Orthodox. Roman Catholics have acted as observers in some of their meetings, but generally have stayed on the fringe. Statements from the WCC are not binding on its members, but are taken seriously by a large proportion of its membership.

Problems in human genetics were first mentioned in 1968 in consultations around the general issue of 'Experiments with Man' and in the 1970 consultation on 'Technology, Faith and the Future of Man'.[1] The first most sustained consultation to address the issue of human genetics was 'Genetics and the Quality of Life' in Zurich in 1973. Nineteen papers were prepared on genetic counselling, caring for genetically handicapped children, public discussion of the prevention of genetic defects, foetal diagnosis and abortion, and eugenics. Most recommendations were of a highly practical nature, examining the ethical issues arising out of use of artificial insemination or egg donation for correction of genetic defects, genetic counselling and genetic services in general.

The 1979 conference on 'Faith, Science and the Future', held at MIT, Cambridge, Massachusetts, took the debate further. Nine hundred participants attended. One session entitled 'Ethical Issues in the Biological Manipulation of Life' included in its agenda sections on eugenics, genetic engineering, behavioural control, justice in the allocation of scarce resources and experimentation on both humans and vertebrates. Unlike previous statements, this document was far more suspicious of genetic engineering, fearing that it could be used to support eugenics. It suggested that the 'closest scrutiny of the social and economic conditions . . . will be continuously required to ensure that such technologies contribute to a just and partici-patory society'.[2] The document also drew a sharp distinction between somatic and germ-line genetic engineering, arguing that no individual could give consent to the genetic engineering of a subsequent generation. Any such decision had to be in a broader social context.

Following the 1979 conference a working group was established to advise the churches on the ethical implications and social consequences of genetic technology. In 1981 scientists and theologians met at Vogelenzang in the Netherlands to discuss 'Ethical and Social Issues in Genetic Engineering and the Ownership of

Life Forms'. They made recommendations on a number of specific topics, such as the role of churches in the work of national regulatory committees. Biotechnology in the Third World became an issue that attracted some discussion as well.

However, the 1982 document, 'Manipulating Life', was much more positive about how faith can learn from science. Anthony Dyson suggests that one reason for this shift to a more positive appraisal may have been that many members of the working party were also scientists. He notes that 'This view differs greatly from the initial reactions of some Churches, which have been of fear, distrust and even calls for prohibition of these new developments.'[3] For the working party the main danger was the possible *misuse* of the technology once it gets into the wrong hands. It was the inequitable distribution of power, influence and knowledge that opened the floodgates for possible abuse. The document supported the possibility that future generations could have an altered genetic make-up, especially if deleterious genes were removed. While it emphasized the role of human freedom to transcend nature, it also cautioned against substantial alteration of genetic make-up.

The 1988 WCC meeting in Bossey considered 'Science and the Theology of Creation'. The documents produced by this meeting showed the mixed reaction to science that seems to underlie the ambiguity felt towards the new genetic technologies. On the one hand, there was the strong influence of scientists themselves. The eminent physicist and priest John Polkinghorne was influential in supporting the role of science in human affairs. He rejected the philosophical model of the world as a mechanism or an organism. Instead he favoured something in between where openness and newly emergent properties came through interplay of chance and necessity. He suggested:

> the world is no mere mechanism. That it has a flexibility, a suppleness within its processes. That I think affords a threefold freedom. A freedom for the whole universe to be itself, a freedom for us to act within that universe of which we are a part, and also I think that it is reasonable to suppose that God

has not only given freedom to the whole world and to human-kind but also has reserved some freedom within the subtleness of process for its own action. I think we begin to perceive a world, not only of which we can see ourselves as inhabitants, but also a world which is not closed to the providential action of God, a world in which a scientist can pray with integrity.[4]

The fact that openness exists within the world's processes meant that the future was in some ways open:

> God does not know the future. He does not know the future because the future is not there to be known . . . I think that involved in creation was not only a *kenosis* of God's omni-potence, but also a *kenosis* of God's omniscience. God knows all that can be known, but the future cannot be known.[5]

The underlying philosophy of an open future as far as God is concerned seems to open the way for human intervention and indeed endorse it. Polkinghorne did recognize the possibility of evil, but seemed to regard freedom in the natural world as a neces-sary corollary to human freedom, 'even though it involves genetic malfunction'.

On the other hand, included in the conference proceedings we have a rather more cautious approach to science and technology that is much more aware of the social and political issues. Günter Altner, for example, suggested that the current debate between theology and the natural sciences was not just theoretical. Rather, 'technological civilisation and life on earth are on a collision course directly related to the appropriateness of scientific and technological reason, and its limits and results'.[6] Altner put scientific progress in the context of negative developments of technology, as in environmental devastation and the nuclear threat. Furthermore, the manipulation of life in modern molecular biology seemed to go against the openness to change and development inherent in the new physics or in the evolution-ary process itself. The comparison with nuclear technology stressed the point further:

> Although physics and biology have got beyond mechanistic

thinking and have re-discovered the factor of time in the general process of becoming, the technologies they have produced (nuclear and genetic technology) are an objectifying manipulation of nature in the classical sense . . . In view of the extent to which destruction has proceeded, the task to which both partners (*i.e. theology and the natural sciences*) must be committed is the endeavour to preserve the integrity of creation on earth . . . Modern technology is epitomised by a blindness which must be replaced by a symbiosis in the shape of a kind of general metabolic exchange between humanity and nature.[7]

There are still no signs that biotechnology is becoming more widely accepted in WCC circles. A report produced in 1989 entitled 'Biotechnology: Its Challenges to the Churches and the World' once again highlighted the possible dangers of the new technology. The report dealt with human genetic engineering, reproductive technologies, patents, environmental effects, military applications and the impact on the Third World. Recommendations included:

- Prohibition of genetic testing for sex selection.
- A ban on experiments on genetic engineering of the human germ-line, but ethical guidelines for the future. Strict control on genetic engineering of the somatic line.
- A ban on patenting of animal life forms.
- Strict international control on release of genetically engineered organisms.
- Ban of research into use of genetic engineering for biological or chemical warfare.
- Consultations between churches, scientists and international organizations to reflect on the politics of biotechnology and its impact on global justice.

In this case the positive benefits of genetic progress tended to be subordinated to the negative consequences, such as military use and environmental dangers and possible negative consequences for the Third World. The degree of support for genetic engineering may reflect how far scientists have influenced the debate, compared with more social/political interests.

The response of the Anglican Church

One of the Anglican Church's first reports, entitled *Personal Origins*, produced in 1985 by the Board of Social Responsibility, examined human embryology, rather than genetic engineering as such. However, it showed the same kind of ambivalence that we find in the WCC's reports. Some participants welcomed change and accepted the need for new knowledge, with a strong rebuttal of any claim that we are prisoners of our genes. Others felt that the boundaries of natural law could be lost as well as God's purposes for creation, leading to an overestimation of our human abilities.

More recent statements produced by the Board of Social Responsibility seem to be much more positive with respect to approving new advances. The submission to the House of Commons Science and Technology Committee's Inquiry into Human Genetics is worth considering in some detail as it shows the positive framework in which it offers its critique. This states:

> the Board welcomes advances being made in the understanding of genetics in relation to human beings, and the possibilities which these afford for preventing birth defects and treating genetic diseases. Christians engaged in scientific work have seen themselves as unravelling the mysteries already known to God and work on the human genome project should be seen in the same way.[8]

The positive statement was qualified by caution that knowledge should not be abused, for example, through the stigmatization of those with a specific genotype. The board insisted that genes alone do not fully define what it is to be human. It was also anxious to distinguish between genetic intervention to help disease and that to 'improve' certain characteristics considered to be desirable, such as body height or intelligence. It suggested that the real reason to oppose germ-line intervention was that the science was as yet still too imprecise to predict the consequences. This contrasts with the earlier WCC reports that rejected germ-line intervention in principle.

The board also rejected use of terms such as 'playing God',

believing that this merely served to heighten emotive reactions to the issues in a way that did not help discussion. It suggested that the media had biased public awareness against genetic technology. The role of the church was now one of endorsing 'proper' communication of information. One example of improper use of media coverage was through the publicity around certain 'behaviour genes', which led to an oversimplication of causes of behaviour. It suggested, further, that even if a genetic component was found, it should still not be used as an excuse for certain types of behaviour.

The board did express some anxiety about the possibility of a genetically disadvantaged underclass. It suggested that we need to provide adequate counselling services for those diagnosed as having a genetic disease. It recognized that those who are disabled might become marginalized if all the funding went into the prevention of inherited disability conditions. However, it still endorsed the use of genetic screening as long as it was 'properly regulated'.

The statement finished on a very positive note about the Human Genome Project (HGP), which 'is enormously worthwhile, it will be the threshold of a new age of discovery about humans'.[9]

The response of the Science, Medicine and Technology Committee of the Board of Social Responsibility to the Nuffield Consultation Document on genetically modified foods was drawn up in August 1998. Once again it was very positive about the new technology, seeing few disadvantages as far as the church was concerned. The first theological issue raised was how far humanity can legitimately interfere with the natural world. The committee suggested that two broad attitudes were held by Christians: one was a sense of being apart from the natural world, and one was being a part of it, with a move towards the latter in more recent thinking. The committee suggested that the idea of responsible management of nature, or stewardship, was very widely accepted. It found no evidence in the Christian tradition to oppose genetic modification in crops.

The second theological issue the committee raised concerned uncertainty. It suggested that campaign groups and others had distorted the evidence in such a way that politicians were less honest than they could be. It argued that the Christian tradition is one which accepts uncertainty as a given, but in spite of uncertainty we begin to act with prudence. Prudence for them was defined as the means by which principles are put into practice in an imaginative and moral way. 'Applied to technological advances, prudence would allow us to judge whether such advances should be banned or used.' It acknowledged that uncertainty about long-term impact was always going to be present with genetically modified food. The committee argued that the appropriate response was not to resist change but to come to terms with uncertainty. It was also dismissive of possible harmful effects of the new technologies, even though the public perception of risk was much higher. The committee agreed, nonetheless, that we need to gain further information on the possible risks involved and take appropriate action, while erring on the side of caution.

The committee did recognize that genetic modification of food raises particular issues for the developing countries of the world. However, it appeared to be reluctant to discuss this in any detail, admitting that this was a complex issue where regulation was problematic. It suggested that companies have no additional responsibilities with genetically modified food compared to any other foodstuff. It endorsed a 'reasonable' level of patenting, while admitting this might have negative consequences for developing countries. It suggested, further, that the current regulatory bodies were satisfactory; rather it was the public perception of these structures that needed attention.

Overall, this document is a remarkable endorsement from a Christian perspective of the programme to introduce GM foods. Public anxieties are dismissed as out of touch or unscientific, or explained as media distortions, while concerns about the Third World are marginalized as too complex really to be of concern for the UK context. I suggest that this approach is an unfortunate oversimplification of the issues around the genetic modification of food, and one that fails to take into account a number of theological and ethical concerns. Furthermore, it seems to be out of touch with the grassroots opinion of the Anglican Church, where there is far more ambivalence associated with the new technology. These concerns will be taken up up further in subsequent chapters.

The response of the Roman Catholic Church

In 1983 Pope John Paul II gave a lecture to the Pontifical Academy for Life on the Human Genome Project. He issued a stern warning on the possible abuse of knowledge as power over others, rather than for human good. He insisted that the human genome had anthropological dignity, so that any intervention must be for the good of the person concerned. He also argued strongly against any discrimination against those people with genetic defects. He welcomed the use of therapeutic advances in genetic engineering, where this could help in the treatment of disease, but warned against diagnostic uses that then lead to abortion.

He mentioned the possible genetic intervention in other species in the following way:

> To tell the truth, the expression 'genetic engineering' remains ambiguous and ought to become the object of genuine moral discernment, for on the one hand it covers adventurous attempts aimed at promoting I know not what superman, and on the other salutary efforts aimed at correcting anomalies, such as certain hereditary maladies, not to mention beneficial applications in the fields of animal and vegetable biology which can be useful in food production. In the latter cases, some are beginning to talk of 'genetic surgery' so as to show better that the physician intervenes, not in order to modify nature, but to help it to develop along its line, that of creation, that willed by God. In working in this obviously delicate domain, the researcher follows God's design. God willed man to be king of creation.[10]

Such words imply that in principle the Pope supports genetic intervention as long as it is 'following God's design'. How we might discern what this might be is left vague.

The Pontifical Academy for Life has also produced documents on Roman Catholic teaching on human genetic intervention, including the Proceedings of the Fourth Assembly of the Pontifical Academy for Life, held in 1998, entitled *Human Genome, Human Person and the Society of the Future*.[11] This book contains a wealth of information on the science, as well as the religious implications, of human genetic intervention from an official Roman Catholic perspective. Overall, the Human Genome Project is only welcomed in as far as it contributes to the healing of human diseases. Any attempt to patent sections of the genome or use it as a diagnostic tool for human genetic disease leading to abortion is roundly rejected. The focus of ethical discussion for Roman Catholic documents tends to be pro-life, and hence is particularly cautious about any genetic engineering that could endanger human life, from the very first moment of conception. A discussion of the Roman Catholic position on human cloning will follow in a later chapter, but the suspicion of the abuse of the power of science in this respect sits rather uneasily with the affirmation of the autonomy of science in Vatican II documents.[12]

In Britain the Catholic Bishops' joint committee on bioethical issues produced a report entitled *Genetic Intervention on Human Subjects* in 1996. Much of this discussion relates to the Catholic prohibition of abortion or use of foetuses for experimentation. The bishops suggested that the attitudes of others are influential in making disability a handicap in society. Hence, they seemed to have some awareness of the possible social consequences of genetic intervention. For them, genetic counsellors need to be those who speak on behalf of the disabled.

While they welcomed somatic therapy, they could not condone germ-line therapy, as it would almost inevitably involve use of *in vitro* fertilization and the destruction of some embryos. Curiously, perhaps, they accepted germ-line therapy through the screening of gametes, that is, the egg and sperm cells, if normal sexual reproduction took place. They emphasized that this is particularly the case where there is a real possibility of eliminating genetic diseases. They rejected the use of germ-line therapy as a means of improving cosmetic characteristics. In particular, they were worried about the possibility of parents viewing their children as raw material for their own intentions.

More recently the Pontifical Academy for Life has produced a short book on the implications of genetic manipulation of non-human species.[13] This book is, in general, affirmative of genetic manipulation of animals and plants, as long as sufficient attention is given to ecological responsibility. However, the degree of attention this subject has received compared with the exhaustive tome on human genetics emphasizes the priority shown by the Catholic Church towards issues relating to the human species, rather than the created order as a whole.

The response of the Church of Scotland

The Society, Religion and Technology Project (SRT) of the Church of Scotland is interesting, not least because it is one of the few church-based bodies to respond in a thorough way to the genetic engineering of non-human life. The book arising from this consultation, entitled *Engineering Genesis*, includes a review of different Christian responses to genetic engineering. For example, does it represent the use of our God-given gifts, or is it symptomatic of an inevitable loss of a right relationship with God and nature after the Fall? Leaflets produced by the SRT Project state an intermediate position, so that:

Our awareness that we do not match our technological achievements with good judgement about their use, implies acting with caution and humility in using the inherent power in genetics, rather than an absolute prohibition.[14]

The SRT Project did not reject the cloning of animals as long as this was restricted to the production of proteins of medical value in milk. However, it did argue against any routine cloning of animals for meat or milk production. It was significant perhaps that Ian Wilmut, often considered to be the 'father' of animal cloning, was also a member of the SRT Project. The project rejected the idea of cloning humans as

this would violate a basic aspect of the dignity and uniqueness of a person made in God's image. To make a genetic copy of an existing human being is quite different ethically from the unpredictable occurrences of twins of unknown genetic type in the womb.[15]

Another significant contribution was over the issue of patenting. While it allowed for patenting of a novel gene sequence, the project rejected the idea of patenting of whole life forms. It also rejected any idea of patenting sections of the human genome following the research of the HGP.

Part of the brief of the General Assembly of the Church of Scotland in 1998 was to urge the European Commission and European Parliament to amend a draft directive on the Legal Protection of Biotechnological Inventions, to ensure that living organisms and material of human origin could not be patented. They used theological and ethical arguments to support their case. For them, it is

> unwarranted to have invented something which is part of God's creation, or a product of nature. What we have really invented is not the animal but the new sequence . . . To extend patenting from industrial artifacts to living things in themselves is to violate a normal ethical distinction between what is alive and what is not. They are not just another industrial commodity.[16]

Engineering Genesis contains very little theology as such, rather it is ethics done in a way that is conscious of Christian principles. The chapter on risk/benefit is interesting in that it shows how different levels of risk are acceptable to different groups. Broadly speaking, there are those who assume technology will benefit society, and so regulation is on the basis of what can be foreseen as the result of past evidence and experience. For the supporters, if we hold back because of unknown dangers, then we are responding to unnecessary fears.

An alternative approach is more distrustful of technology and claims that experience shows we should not take risks at all unless there is good justification for so doing. This is known as the precautionary approach. In this case the ethic is one of cooperation with the created order in which a sense of humility towards the created order is stressed. Furthermore, an awareness of those groups likely to be put at risk by the technology is highlighted, along with the Christian principle to support the disadvantaged.

Engineering Genesis is also critical of the membership of regulatory bodies, believing that the views of non-scientists are rarely taken seriously. Another concern is the global nature of the new technology and how regulation will be achieved in some parts of the world, such as China, where hundreds of releases have already taken place. In the USA there are even fewer restraints on both patenting and release of genetically modified organisms. Pressure to relax laws still further intensifies through lobbying groups of powerful biotechnologists such as the Senior Advisory Group on Biotechnology.

The response of the Methodist Church

The Methodist Church has produced a series of leaflets on genetic engineering, but these are mostly on the ethics of experimentation with human embryos.

One leaflet entitled *Human Genetic Engineering: Good or Evil?* by David Hardy covers genetic modification in general and is broader in scope than the title suggests. Overall Hardy is positive about genetic engineering, while insisting on the need to respect creation as belonging to God. He has some hope that genetic modification will become the way a new creation can be brought into being through human intervention. At the same time he recognizes that genetic engineering may lead to even greater exploitation. He is cautious about our own ability to use the knowledge for good. He comments: 'Whether or not we have the necessary Wisdom to handle for good the knowledge that we can acquire, is a very important question.'[17]

Hardy does acknowledge positive aspects of genetic engineering in the treatment of certain diseases, such as cystic fibrosis. For him there is no essential difference between using a gene from an animal to help cure a disease through somatic gene therapy and using animal organs for human transplantation. In common with most other churches, as a Methodist he rejects the idea of genetic therapy for enhancement of non-essential characteristics. He suggests that the HGP may be the final threat to the idea of human uniqueness and what it means to be made in God's image. He also recognizes possible problems with the HGP in that what is considered deviant can be codified genetically, so that other factors influencing behaviour are dismissed. In general he is cautious about any possibility that Christian opinion will make much difference. Hardy concludes:

I think it is fair to say that Christians have lost much of their influence with regard to moral issues in our society. This is perhaps not surprising when we find it hard to come to a 'common mind' about many issues and when we are often busy with internal Church matters to give serious time and thought to them. No one wants an arrogant dogmatism, but often we are so unsure ourselves of the right course of action in a complex moral dilemma, that we fail to give any credible moral lead at all. However, I believe that God is a moral God and that it is our calling to discern, in humility, what we believe his will to be in every situation, however complex it may appear.[18]

In 1998 Andrew Fox gave a lecture to the annual Methodist conference entitled *Whose Life is it Anyway? God, Genes and Us*. Fox was far less cautious than Hardy. He was particularly positive about the possible use of cloning technologies to treat Parkinson's disease. Does cloning run counter to the idea that we are made in the divine image? For him the fact that twins are genetically the same as clones supported the principle of cloning. Unfortunately, Fox's account lacked theological depth and was more like a description of what happens scientifically, followed by a reference to what Christians might think with one or two biblical texts quoted out of context.

Nonetheless, the Methodist Church has contributed in a significant way to making genetic issues more accessible to church congregations in the publication of more popular leaflets and study packs, such as *Making Our Genes Fit*.[19] Unusually, perhaps, this study pack contains a balance of information on genetic engineering of all species and their implications. The biblical texts that accompany the study pack might encourage a rather simplistic theological analysis, though it is probably realistic to include this as the pack is intended for use by Bible study groups.

Taking the ecumenical response further

The above survey of the literature shows that the church as a whole is generally ambivalent about genetic engineering. The degree to which individual denominations support or reject it seems to depend on how far individual representatives are supportive of science. The WCC reports were more aware of global issues and the possible effects of the new technology on the poorer nations of the world. The official statements of the Anglican Church were surprisingly positive, as were more recent statements from the Methodist Church. The Church of Scotland has gone some way towards presenting a range of possible views on the issue, speaking out specifically against cloning of whole organisms or parts of the human genome.

It seems that the church wants to take a lead in moral affairs, but is often uncertain how to do so. The reluctance to speak out against the practice of science may come from amnesia associated with the perceived historical record of the church as an institution that unjustifiably blocked scientific progress. Overall the framework for theological and ethical discussion seems to be missing, other than a vague reference to the idea of stewardship. In the section that follows I suggest that we need to develop a stronger ecumenical theological vision from which to make ethical judgments. Apart from the deliberate corporate effort of the World Council, the statements of the churches on genetic engineering seem to have been conducted in isolation. So far the official response of the Roman Catholic Church, in particular, appears to have bypassed serious consideration of the issues associated with non-human species and tended to reduce the theological complexities of genetic engineering to a pro-life dogmatic standpoint.

I hope to show that one way that the debate can move forward is by exploring the church's Wisdom traditions. Indeed, it is through seeking Wisdom that the church will have the courage to face the new developments in science that will inevitably follow in the new millennium. I think we can even go further and suggest that it is through an exploration of Wisdom traditions that the church can make a significant contribution to the debates around the new biology.

Does science have its own Wisdom? The answer to this question is, of course, 'Yes'. However, over the years the nature of its task has so changed that it no longer is necessarily capable on its own of answering all the issues it raises. The idea that science is distinct from philosophy, which means literally the love of Wisdom, is relatively new. Science used to mean all kinds of knowledge and was equivalent to philosophy, but by the end of the nineteenth century science had become just one kind of knowledge.

According to the Aristotelian tradition, Wisdom is the crown of scientific knowledge and cannot exist apart from science. Yet even in this view knowledge *as such* was not identified with the highest achievement possible in the human mind. The notion of divine Wisdom *as gift* developed into the Augustinian tradition, where Wisdom becomes the foundation for science. Thomas Aquinas takes up the Aristotelian notion of Wisdom as emergent from science. The clash in the ways of relating Wisdom and science becomes clear: is Wisdom learned through science or given by God? Is it an achievement or gift? If God gives us all our Wisdom, then the danger is that we ignore science altogether. On the other hand, if Wisdom is only achieved through science, then our searches may finish with science and not move on to Wisdom.

In practice we face both possibilities today. If the church seeks her own Wisdom in ignorance of science, then the two areas remain split apart and separate from one another. On the other hand, modern scientific research rejects any requirement to seek higher Wisdom. Mary Midgley suggests that the problem we face goes even further in that the specialization and fragmentation of knowledge is such that it seems to have screened out all other ways of knowing as having any validity.[20]

The church and Wisdom

One of the difficulties in defining our task to seek Wisdom is that the understanding of what Wisdom means in the church is multi-faceted and escapes any clear definition. However, by highlighting themes from different traditions I hope to give some indication of how these traditions can offer rich resources for issues in the new biology facing the church today. It seems to me that above everything else Wisdom is a dynamic resource for reflection in different church traditions. In this sense it can help build up an ecumenical community, extending perhaps even wider to faith traditions other than Christianity, though they will not be dealt with here. I will focus, instead, on biblical Wisdom as the resource for all the churches, but also look at Thomas Aquinas' contribution and that of Sergii Bulgakov.

Biblical Wisdom

I will start with a brief introduction to biblical Wisdom, before exploring the notion of Wisdom as discernment in Aquinas and sophiology in Russian Orthodox thought. This can only be a brief sketch, but I hope it will give a map of ways in which Wisdom can act as a resource for reflection.

In the biblical tradition, Wisdom is rooted in the concrete experiences of human beings. But Wisdom also links human experience with the wider natural environment, so that a practical Wisdom could emerge, even though knowledge of what we call natural sciences was very rudimentary. While there was a clear sense of the responsibility of humans, belief in God as the creator of the world was assumed and there was no distinction between faith and reason. Reason is valued, but not overvalued. Hence, the close observation of the natural world characteristic of much Wisdom literature is less about finding evidence for God than celebrating God's creative activity.

While the Old Testament sages were sensitive to regularities in the world, it seems unlikely that this represented a quest for a cosmic order, as in Greek philosophy. The natural world was less an 'object' to be analysed than a celebration of life. Wisdom came from observation of the natural world, but also as a gift from God. Perhaps the image of seeing is too closely bound up in our own culture with that of control and manipulation. If true, then it would be more appropriate to speak of the relationship between humanity and the natural world in the Wisdom literature as a kind of hearing. Some Psalms even hint at the relationship like a voiceless word. In Psalm 19 we read:

> The heavens declare the glory of God,
> The vault of heaven proclaims his handiwork;
> Day discourses of it to day,
> Night to night hands on the knowledge.
>
> No utterance at all, no speech,
> No sound that anyone can hear;
> Yet their voice goes out through all the earth,
> And their message to the ends of the world. (Psalm 19.1–2)

Wisdom's place in creation is elaborated in Proverbs 8.22–31. Proverbs 8.22f. suggests that Wisdom is associated with the beginning of creation: 'Yahweh created me when his purpose first unfolded, before the oldest of his works.' In Proverbs 8.30 we find: 'I was by his side a master craftsman, delighting him day after day, ever at play in his presence', although the Hebrew word for craftsman may possibly mean foster child.

The idea of Wisdom is rooted in life, in contrast to the special knowledge of the gnostics, where Wisdom is a mysterious gift for the elect. Having said this, the Wisdom literature does become more specifically theological in its personification of Wisdom as feminine divine. Ben Sira, for example, portrays Wisdom as an attribute of God, personified as female. Like the books of Job and Ecclesiastes, for Ben Sira Wisdom is ultimately a mystery known only to God. All human strivings after Wisdom are only partial reflections of the divine reality. As such Wisdom instills a spirit of humility that applies equality to theological reflections on creation. The opposite of Wisdom is arrogance (Sir. 10.7–22); hence it is through humility that humans are given the task of rulers of the earth.

The replacement of arrogance by humility through Wisdom is a theme worth pondering in the modern environmental context, including the commercialization of life through genetic patenting. Furthermore, Job 38 reminds us that the care of Yahweh for creation goes beyond concern for the welfare of human life. The metaphor of humanity as king over creation means that humanity has vice-regal responsibility over creation. However, there is no divine mandate for autonomous human rule over creation. There are always limits to the ability of humans to influence the earth. Recognition of human limits to understand and change the natural order is one of the characteristics of traditional science. In the light of the new possibilities now on offer in genetics, the challenge to science and technology goes further than simply limits protected by either the limits in the technology itself or legislation alone. Instead, a greater humility is called for so that biotechnology will direct its future in a way that is in tune with consequences for the whole of creation.

What are the many faces of Wisdom as portrayed in the biblical literature? At least three could spring to mind, namely, human, social and cosmic. The quest for Wisdom includes a plural outlook on the world that takes into account its full complexity and diversity. Wisdom becomes a way of looking at the world in its wholeness and fulness, but without ignoring detail. Yet Wisdom portrayed as human Wisdom remains aware of its limitations; human actions show propensity to evil and injustice. The sage was concerned with the way people behave, with *ethics*. The sage also took an interest in human skill and achievement, especially in the life of the family, but also looking more widely to the skill of the craftsman or politician. Wisdom deals with the social relationships of people everywhere, in particular pointing to instances of injustice between nations, without necessarily always referring to particular political events.

As applied to science today this would encourage a much broader approach that is fully aware of its human and social context. Yet it would be too simplistic to suggest that we can draw a line from biblical Wisdom to ethics in our contemporary society. In other words, the kind of ethics Wisdom includes is a matter for careful scrutiny, given the specific problems we face today. However, a broad approach that takes into account *both* the *goodness* of the creation and the particular human, social and environmental *consequences* of human action is in continuity with the biblical Wisdom tradition. This leads to a further face of Wisdom, namely the cosmic. The cosmic scope of Wisdom refers to the emphasis on the human and natural environment considered as a whole rather than in any dualistic sense.

In the New Testament Wisdom becomes identified with the Logos and thus with Christ. Parallels in origin and function of *Logos* (the Word) and *Sophia* (the Greek word for Wisdom) are characteristic of John's Gospel. For example, the role given to the Logos in the prologue to John's Gospel echoes that of Wisdom in Proverbs 8.22–23. Both the Logos and Wisdom existed in the heavens before the world was formed, and both share in the creative process. James Dunn has explored the relationship between Christ, the cosmos and Wisdom in Colossians.[21] The church becomes a mirror or microcosm of the divinely ordered cosmos. Hence 'as the creative power of divine Wisdom is now defined in terms of Christ, so the cosmos of divine purpose can (should) now be defined in terms of the Church'. The paradox of the claim of this early Christian community is 'that the Wisdom behind and permeating the universe is most clearly seen and its character most clearly perceived in the cross'.

Wisdom in Thomas Aquinas

The strand of biblical tradition that associates Wisdom with right action is developed in the theology of Thomas Aquinas. Aquinas believed that the true end of all the virtues is goodness, and, loosely speaking, we can think of prudence as the means of attaining this end. The task of prudence becomes discerning through the use of reason the right course of action to express a particular virtue, both for the good of the individual and the good of the community. It is part of the human condition to possess Wisdom in various degrees and thereby its counterpart, foolishness.

Aquinas' idea of prudence so far seems to be following

Aristotle's treatment of *phronesis*, sometimes translated as 'practical Wisdom'. Aristotle suggests that *phronesis* has the following three components, namely, to take counsel, to judge what has been discovered and to act in a certain way. Where actions are those of prudence, the desire is to attain a true good. However, Aquinas goes further than Aristotle in that he translates his *philosophical* notion of prudence into a much more *theological* concept of Wisdom. For Aquinas the virtue of prudence will never reach its desired aim of goodness through human effort alone because of the distortions of human sin.

How may we achieve prudence in a way that is aligned to God's Wisdom? For Aquinas this is only possible through the gift of the Holy Spirit, engendering the theological virtues of faith, hope and charity in addition to that of Wisdom. These virtues come as a gift from God, so that it is *love* that is the supreme means through which humanity can know intuitively the mind of God. However, this is not simply an unthinking response to the Spirit. As John Mahoney points out:

> From a consideration of the many texts in which Aquinas writes of this internal teaching of the Holy Spirit we can see how important for him was not only the activity of the Spirit but also the activity of man's own intelligence under the influence of the Spirit.[22]

Above all, Christian Wisdom rooted in the love of God allows the individual to discern God's Wisdom in practical contexts. Such Wisdom leads to an alignment of both heart and mind to the will of God through the Holy Spirit.

Aquinas also develops the notion of community discernment. Exercise of Wisdom in a community allows it to conform to the ordering in the universe that for Aquinas is an expression of the divine Wisdom. While he saw this ordering through the lens of medieval cosmology, it was no static fixed realm but still open to the creative work of God. The task of humanity was not just to accept the order given by God, but to bring order into it through active cooperation with God. For Aquinas, it is in the church, through the Holy Spirit, that Wisdom comes to find its fullest expression in both individuals and community. While not all individuals are given the same degree of Wisdom, they are part of a community of the church, and it is in this community that some are given a gift of Wisdom for the benefit of all the others.

Wisdom in Russian Orthodoxy

As noted earlier, one strand of biblical Wisdom is more theological, reflecting more specifically on our understanding of the divine. A more cosmological and explicitly theological approach to Wisdom finds full expression in the sophiology of Sergii Bulgakov (1871–1944).

In the second and third centuries of the church, the image of Christ as Logos became dominant, obscuring the earlier Wisdom Christology. Yet the idea of Christ as the Wisdom of God persisted in the Eastern Orthodox tradition. After the council of Ephesus in 431, where Mary was proclaimed Mother of God, a common tradition of associating Sophia with Mary developed. In the Russian Orthodox tradition we find varied representations of Sophia by the late seventeenth century in addition to that associated with sophianic representations of Christ and the Mother of God. First, there is the Novgorod type in which Sophia is portrayed as a fiery-faced angel. Second, in the Kievan type a woman of the Apocalypse stands for Sophia. Third, in a representation based on an allegory of Proverbs 9.1, Wisdom has built her house. Finally, in the Iaroslavl type a crucifix, surrounded by seven gifts of the Holy Spirit, stands for Sophia.

Bulgakov saw it as his task to formulate a theology that took into account these images and one that he believed was fully Orthodox. His book, *The Unfading Light*, developed the idea of the cosmic Sophia as the intelligible basis of the world, the Wisdom of nature. Creation becomes a theophany, a manifestation of God through Sophia. Bulgakov believed that one of the legacies of the Reformation was a split between anthropology and cosmology. He insisted that Wisdom is characteristic of all persons of the Trinity. Wisdom is the very being, or *ousia*, of God, made visible through the workings of the Son and Spirit. Sophia is the means through which the divine ideas become reality, expressed both as the *truth* of the Logos and the *beauty* of the Spirit. Divine Sophia becomes creaturely Sophia in the creation, at the first act of God 'in the beginning'. There is also a shadow side to creaturely Sophia, her 'dark face', that corresponds to woman Folly of the biblical accounts.

Wisdom and the new biology

Aquinas' emphasis on Wisdom as discernment reflects the practical Wisdom of the sage. The choice is held up between contrasts – Wisdom or Folly – yet both the Pauline account of Wisdom and Aquinas' interpretation of Wisdom indicate that the Wisdom of God can at times seem like Folly to human beings. However, the ability to make choices is one of the crucial tasks for science today. How far should we be allowed to become co-creators with God in engineering crops and animals for our own benefit? How far should we take transgenic experimentation, especially that relating to human beings? Should there be a moratorium on all human cloning? How do we distinguish one research project from another in terms of its likely risk and benefit for humanity and the earth? Who is responsible for measuring these risks? In order to begin to answer such questions we need a well-developed sense of Wisdom as discernment.

Bulgakov's understanding of Wisdom as related to the very being of God necessarily complements the more practical approach of Aquinas. While the Thomistic notion of the Spirit of Wisdom coming to its fullest expression in the church is a reminder that Wisdom is a gift as well as something that we can learn, it is the Eastern tradition of sophiology that develops most fully the theological tradition of Wisdom. Its significance for our present discussion is that is helps us to realize that Wisdom is not an option for a few, but elaborates more fully who God is and the means through which God becomes manifest in creation. Furthermore, unlike the creation spiritualities that have flourished in much contemporary theology, a theology of Wisdom serves to unite themes of creation and redemption by identifying Christ the Redeemer and the divine Logos with Sophia, the Wisdom of God involved in the creation of the world.

Such a theme of redemption reminds us that the world as we know it has not yet reached perfection, but is still in some sense unfinished. However, this does not necessarily mean that we can take on lightly the task of becoming arbiters of the future evolution of creation. The Christian concept of redemption is a reminder of the real possibility of human sin and distortion of motives in all human activities. In the light of the glory yet anticipated we can ask ourselves whether the changes we are making to creation through genetic engineering in any way reflect the future glory of the coming kingdom. This anticipated future glory shows nature to be not just a faded mirror to the divine mind, but the possibility of the immanent presence of God as glorified Wisdom in the new creation. We find hints of this presence of the Wisdom of God in the natural world as we experience it today. It is only in the context of the present and anticipated participation of creation in God that our minds become sufficiently clear to make the kind of wise judgments that will be required in this new millennium.

While it would be unrealistic to suggest that all scientists become Christians, the church still can play a part in its witness to the Wisdom of God. As Bulgakov suggests:

> As the receiver of the outpouring of the Spirit's gifts, it is the Church, and so too the mother of the Son who was incarnate from the flesh of Mary by the outpouring of the Spirit into her – Mary, the heart of the Church; and as such Sophia is also the ideal soul of creation, Sophia is beauty . . .[23]

Yet it is not by human creative powers alone that the world will be transformed into the image of Sophia. Instead, 'It will be achieved by the creative act of God, bringing to ripeness the "good fruit" of creation – by the outpouring of the gifts of the Spirit.'[24]

How might this Wisdom tradition contribute to theological and ethical reflection on specific instances of genetic engineering? Possible answers to this question form the subject matter of the following two chapters.

5

Theological reflection on current issues

I suggested in the last chapter that Wisdom could become a way of rediscovering a joint response to genetic engineering by all Christian traditions. I intend to explore the Wisdom motif further in this chapter, especially in contrast to other alternatives, such as the notion of stewardship or co-creation. I outlined in Chapter 3 the spread of possible applications of genetic engineering, from the modification of bacteria in industrial waste management through to genetic modification of humans in medical interventions to applications in warfare. Some of these developments, such as the use of genetic engineering in eugenic-directed warfare, seem abhorrent in a much more obvious way than other applications. While it is important to keep such applications in mind in order to glimpse the possible horror of genetic engineering, I suggest that more interesting cases to consider for theological and ethical reflection are those where there could either be a positive or negative response. A more subtle approach is required in such cases in a way that shows up the adequacy or otherwise of different theological alternatives. The focus for this chapter will be in two areas of current debate: the genetic modification of food and the cloning of animals, including the possibility of human cloning. While this is far from comprehensive, given the swath of possible applications of the new genetic technologies, I suggest that it does give us a starting-point in thinking theologically about other complex issues in genetic engineering as they arise.

Theological issues in the genetic engineering of food

Theological arguments in favour

One of the most controversial areas for debate from both a secular and religious perspective is the use of genetic engineering of food for human consumption. Two theological perspectives that can be marshalled to support this development are the ideas of stewardship and co-creation.

According to the stewardship ideal, the biblical creation story in Genesis 1.26–30 gives humanity dominion over the earth. Humanity, in acting as steward of creation, is encouraged to use all creation for human benefit, including genetic engineering.[1] Secondly, we can view humans as co-creators. This is based on the idea that as *imago Dei* we are entitled in some sense to assist God in the creation of the world. This leads on to the notion that human-ity is *improving* nature by using genetic engineering, a concept that is particularly popular among American theologians. Philip Hefner pioneered use of the term co-creator, and by inserting the prefix *created* to co-creator believes this highlights human subordination to God and hence avoids the problem of hubris.[2] Ted Peters also believes that we can become co-creators with God.[3]

Ronald Cole-Turner writes in a similar vein, though he does seem to acknowledge, especially in his later writings, that the term co-creation brings with it a highly optimistic epistemology.[4] In order to correct such a view he suggests that we join the idea of creation with redemption. However, it seems to me that in this context introducing the concept of redemption is also somewhat ambiguous. While on the one hand it could serve to remind us of our own fragility and tendency to sin, on the other it could *also* lead to the idea that we are somehow party to the redemptive processes in the natural world. The suggestion by Peters, for example, that we might be able to undo some of the negative effects of the Fall, bears remarkable similarity to the positive views of science expressed by Francis Bacon at the dawn of experimental science in the seventeenth century.[5] The crucial question in this case is whether human beings can become agents of redemption of the natural world. Our anthropology is critical in this context. If we believe that human nature is basically good, but only tarnished by human sinfulness, then such a possibility does seem to be realistic. On the other hand, if we have a more pessimistic view of human nature, then appropriating such a task of improving creation to humanity would seem to be fraught with difficulties.

Cole-Turner's other way of dealing with the possible problems associated with the idea of co-creation is to examine more closely what it means to understand in a metaphorical way God as Creator understood in terms of human technology. He describes God as the 'first gardener', a metaphor for the creative acts of God.[6] Hence the practice of agriculture is thereby sanctioned and blessed. Yet he takes a step further than this and suggests that not only does this sanction the literal act of gardening, but:

> God is authorizing human beings to create in the natural order. Indeed, by understanding the vegetation as partly dependent upon agriculture, the Yahwist sees the human work of tilling the ground as something upon which God's own creative work depends. God as gardener depends in part on human gardeners to till and keep the garden.[7]

The logic of such a position is inevitable as applied to genetic engineering. Our work and God's are seen as intermeshed, the only difference being that God is creating out of nothing, while we are limited by the constraints of the medium in which we work. If this is the case, then it could suggest that the biological and human technological limits to human creating are the *only* limitations imposed on human activity. Human activity begins to carry divine significance. Cole-Turner admits that there may be times when we cannot see God in a technological project, but he fails to clarify how we might *recognize* this for ourselves. In other words, it is not obvious how we achieve the Wisdom needed to discern the presence of God in a project. Further, he suggests that if we fail to see God in our new technologies we are alienating God from them in a way that refuses God a place in the new science. He says that God's involvement in genetic engineering is not fundamentally different from any other creative process of evolution, since both use the 'natural' processes of genetic recombination that have existed for several billion years.[8] Yet it seems to me that any such justification for genetic engineering is just as flawed as arguments against it on the basis that it is 'unnatural'. I will return to this issue again below. Cole-Turner also suggests that God uses genetic changes wrought by humans to achieve God's purposes. Of course, this assumes that we know what God intends; in particular, it assumes a certain eschatological position in favour of the new technologies.[9]

It seems doubtful whether Cole-Turner's metaphorical alternative to co-creation is any more successful in dealing with the problem of relating human intentions to those of God. Both alternatives seem to suggest that such forms of knowing will be transparent, that it will be obvious when genetic engineering is of God and when it is not. Indeed, it relies on a consequentialist approach to ethics, which will be considered again in the next chapter.

The idea that humans might become co-creators through genetic engineering is not confined to Protestant theologians. However, Roman Catholic discussion so far in this vein has been limited to genetic engineering in humans. There is every reason to suppose that a similar position would be taken on the genetic engineering of crops. As long as genetic engineering is directed towards healing and promoting human intelligence, then American theologians Benedict Ashley and Kevin O'Rourke view such human activity as a way of becoming co-workers with God in the incomplete evolutionary process.[10] While they do not use the term co-creators, they insist that such activity allows human beings to share in God's creative power. Much more controversial from an ethical point of view is the fact that they not only endorse the use of genetic engineering to treat genetically inherited diseases, but they also do not rule out the possibility of the *improvement* of the human species through genetic engineering. They view this as an exercise of good human stewardship of human creativity and resources, while admitting, only in passing, the possible danger of eugenics. Their admission that it may be difficult to decide which characteristics of humans should be promoted as being 'superior' seems a very weak response to the real problems associated with eugenics.[11]

Some of the theological arguments used to support genetic engineering are counter-attacks on any hostility, especially among religious groups, towards genetic change, especially those that view the world as sacred. While the counter-attack is often against hostility towards the patenting of genes, it is also relevant to the general commercial applications of genetic engineering in the development of novel foods and products. Ted Peters, for example, believes that our fear of genetic engineering is based on a false sense of genetic determinism. He argues that giving humans more freedom does not take away God's freedom.[12] He suggests, further, that if genetic engineering can be used for good, then it becomes a sin not to use it. The moot point, of course, is how far genetic engineering of food can be considered to be a good. This raises more complex issues associated with the economy, politics and ethics of food use.

Another counter-argument is based on objections to genetic engineering as 'unnatural'. Supporters of genetic engineering argue that such objections are based on the philosophically dubious and romantic equation of the 'good' with the 'natural'. Theologians who support the idea of natural law do so on the basis that this is a particular interpretation of the natural world rather than a simple blanket affirmation of all that is. For example, few would object to the eradication of the smallpox virus, even though this was part of the natural creation.

We can ask ourselves at this juncture if any of these theological models take into account the ambiguity in our relationship with the natural world. Those who support genetic engineering do so in the belief that it is no more 'unnatural' than any other human interventions in the natural world.[13] The dilemma is where, if at all, we draw a line in human intervention. The difficulty with the theological models suggested thus far is that they do not help us to make decisions in this matter. The idea of stewardship, for example, can easily slide into the view that the natural world is simply a resource to be managed. The idea of co-creation, again, can seem to baptize all genetic engineering and so becomes hubris.

While the Roman Catholic interpretation of humanity as co-workers in genetic engineering is within a pro-life perspective, theologically it seems to affirm genetic engineering as long as it is within a consequentialist ethical perspective. The ethical issues will be revisited in the following chapter.

Theological arguments against

Those who object to genetic engineering tend to view the relationship between God, humanity and the natural world in a more holistic way, compared with a more traditional hierarchical approach. If the idea of stewardship is used, it is now couched in terms of our Christian obligation to *participate with nature*. More often the stress is on the love of God for all creatures and the goodness of creation as beloved of God. The idea of covenant is particularly significant, stemming from the promise of the Noahic covenant that demonstrates the love of God for all creation, not just humans. In other words, we are called to live in a harmonious relationship with the natural world rather than simply manipulate it for human benefit alone.

Those who reject genetic engineering in general have a more pessimistic view of human nature. The idea of 'playing God' is often used in a derogatory way to imply unwarranted breaking of boundaries created by God, rather than in the sense of humanity becoming a co-creator. Are we 'eating the forbidden fruit'? A similarly pessimistic view of human nature underlies the belief that we cannot prevent the abuse of technology. Human arrogance leads to a false sense that technology will solve all our problems. While official church documents recognize the possible dangers of human genetic engineering, relatively few seem to have tackled the problems associated with agriculture. For example, the Church of England's response to the Nuffield Consultation Document on the genetic modification of food takes the view that it is the perception of risk in the public mind that needs to be addressed.[14] Nonetheless, it recognizes the possibility of abuses in the developing nations and the complexity of the political economy of hunger.

Another objection to genetic engineering draws on the Old Testament prohibition of mixing kinds, found in Leviticus 19.19. However, it is by no means clear whether the distinction of 'kinds' should refer to the biological species. For example, mules were accepted without objection in the biblical narrative, such as I Kings 1.38–39, even though they come from mating a horse with a donkey. It is also possible to argue that this law is simply ceremonial law that has now been superseded in the Christian faith by the coming of Christ.

Related to the above is how far it is justifiable to adapt the natural order represented by species. Those who support genetic engineering believe that moving a small section of DNA across species is not the same as creating a hybrid of two species. The MAFF report took this line, arguing that there could be no religious objections to transgenic organisms as long as the modified creatures still looked the same.[15] This is likely to be an oversimplified assessment of religious sensitivity to this issue.[16]

Objections to genetic engineering have come primarily from the grass roots of the Christian community rather than through official statements. It seems likely that this pressure has contributed to a shift in attitude in the Church of England, with more recent reports suggesting that the church commissioners will be refusing to let their land be used as trial sites for genetically modified crops. A logical extension of this would be to disinvest in companies undertaking genetically modified crop trials. The chairman of Christian Ecology Link, Tim Cooper, has specifically called for the church commissioners to disinvest in companies that are involved in GM trials, exploring opportunities for investment in organic foods instead. He rejects the idea that the Church of England had arrived at an agreed policy on this issue.[17]

Other objections to genetic engineering draw on broad Christian ideals of love, respect and justice between peoples. The long-term consequences of biotechnology to poorer nations lead to a consideration of issues of justice.[18] Nonetheless, any presumption on the part of the richer nations that genetic technology must be good for the 'developing' world needs to be called into question. The particular needs of the local communities must be taken into account. In this case a theology of liberation can become the basis for arguing against exploitative technological practices.[19] It is interesting that although the official Roman Catholic position on genetic engineering of crops is positive, liberation theologians such as Sean McDonagh are far more aware of its use in an oppressive way.[20] It is clear from the above that theological arguments against genetic engineering stress human vulnerability to sin, as well as greater emphasis on humanity as part of nature, rather than apart from nature.

The public response to the applications of genetics in agriculture showed a much higher degree of sophistication than has often been assumed to be the case by official regulatory bodies.[21] Furthermore, their responses showed that far from being divorced from religious issues, many of the respondents framed their arguments in a way that was implicitly theological. This is not to suggest that any kind of systematic theology could in some way be read from the public response to the issue. Rather, the kinds of issues that surface in the public debate are themselves theological in nature and require deeper theological concern. Areas worthy of theological and ethical analysis surfaced. Issues included, for example, whether it was justifiable to cross boundaries in the natural world, recognition of the prevalence of sins such as greed and selfishness, the mistrust of official sources of authority and the questioning of the motivation of those who develop the technology.

Religious issues associated with food

I suggest that genetic modification of food has far-reaching theological significance that is completely missed if we just think of food either in a mechanistic way as a resource or as an untouchable element in an integral creation. In many religions, including Christianity, sharing in a communal meal has profound religious significance, which also needs to be taken into account in theological reflection on the issue. I suggest that we need to become much more conscious of the way food functions in a religious understanding of reality in order to arrive at an adequate assessment.

The sacred symbolism of food and drink would come quite naturally to those sages well versed in the ritual laws of purity described in the book of Leviticus. Mary Douglas's classic text *Purity and Danger* tries to delve behind some of the reasons for particular designation of some foods as clean and some unclean.[22] She suggests that the taboos over certain foods were a way of imposing order on an otherwise chaotic existence. Certain animals were forbidden, as they did not fit into the classification of animals according to certain types, as typical of a cosmological world where land, air and water seemed very different spheres of existence. If we extend this argument, then deliberately crossing types that inhabited another sphere would render such a creature unclean.

However, the rules of purity were in all probability much more complicated than this. A pig or camel is not really anomalous, and the modern caricature of Jews as those who reject pigs for food does not take into account all the other animals forbidden under Jewish law. Another possibility is that animals that eat meat are somehow trespassing on the cultural world of humans, who alone are given warrant for meat eating after the flood narrative in Genesis.[23] However, this is unlikely to be the full explanation as some herbivores were forbidden as well. Animals that could be consumed by humans seemed to be limited to those that had both cloven hooves and chewed the cud. While the rationale for excluding some animals may be obscure, it is fair to suggest that for the Israelite eating reflected wider social and political worlds. The disciplined practice of excluding some food mirrored the social practice of excluding mixing with other nations through inter-marriage.[24] The boundaries drawn between the sacred and the secular led to some food being sanctioned as good to eat and some rejected.

The detailed stipulations in Leviticus on how to prepare food for sacrifice designate an even stronger religious significance for food. It is through offering of animals and cereals normally consumed that praise is rendered to God, sins are expiated and guilt pardoned. While an analysis of why sacrifice is offered is outside the scope of this chapter, we can say its purpose overall was to re-establish harmonious relationships between God, humanity and the cosmos. The sacrificial acts of the microcosm are symbolic of events in the macrocosm. In ancient Judaism food becomes integral to the religious, social and political worlds.

It might be possible to argue that, from a Christian perspective at least, the particular ceremonial and ritual laws as described in Leviticus have been superseded by the coming of Christ. The letter to the Hebrews, for example, spells out how Christ takes the place of the sacrificial lamb. The details of the ceremonial laws of eating could be ignored according to Christian tradition, as the account of Peter's vision in Acts 10.13 makes clear, where God declares all animals and birds of all kinds good to eat, even those previously rendered as unclean. It is interesting to note that Peter interprets this vision as a licence for a change in social relationships as well. Now Gentiles are not excluded from divine grace, since all foods are declared clean. This would support Mary Douglas's suggestion that the food laws act as a mirror for social activities between peoples as well.

However, I suggest that the Jewish background to the religious sanction of certain foods is important to bear in mind, even if the details are not adopted in Christian practice. The Leviticus narrative is an important reminder that food has particular cultural and religious significance. This is easily forgotten in a modern consumer society where there is an over-reliance on pre-packaged and processed food, divorced from the context in which the food was grown. It may be one reason why genetically engineered food seems to have been accepted by the majority of the public in the USA, with its even greater cultural reliance on processed products. However, leaving this aside, I suggest that the religious significance of eating and drinking has actually become even stronger in the Christian tradition.

Wisdom's banquet

If we return to motif of Wisdom, we find an explicit reference to eating and drinking in Proverbs 9. The particular invitation of Wisdom to her banquet seems particularly apt in the present context. After meticulous preparations, Wisdom, as portrayed in Proverbs 9.5, offers an invitation to 'Come and eat my bread, drink the wine I have prepared'. Those who decide to share in this meal leave the company of the 'fools', who are immature, the eventual goal being to 'find life'. Such an offer of life is normally made by Yahweh alone. We could interpret Wisdom in this context in various ways as a cosmic, cultic, prophetic or even domestic figure.[25] This is in sharp contrast with woman Folly in the verses that follow. Folly, like Wisdom, invites us to a meal of food and drink, but now 'Stolen waters are sweet, and bread tastes better when eaten in secret' (Prov. 9.17). So the drink that she offers is stolen, and we are told that it is sweet to the taste. Little preparation has gone into the meal, she merely announces her wares to the fools who are passing by. While Wisdom's offer of food leads to life, Folly's meal quite unwittingly leads to death.

The message is clear, that what appears to be good may not be the right path as it is the impulsive action of fools, rather than the life-giving celebration of Wisdom. While it would be otiose to try and pretend that this passage could be directly applied to our contemporary situation, the message is apparent. A lack of adequate preparation and consideration is the way of Folly, not Wisdom. The way genetic engineering of food has expanded without proper public consultation betrays certain foolishness. Yet Wisdom is known by her fruits. In particular cases of genetic engineering of crops we need to ask ourselves whether such an action is really going to be life-giving for all involved.

If we turn to Wisdom in the New Testament, we find that in John 4, 6 and 7 Christ invites his listeners to share in the bread and water of life. Such invitations echo the invitations of Wisdom to the banquet in Proverbs 9. Biblical scholars commonly acknowledge the close association of the person of Christ with Sophia in the Gospel of John. The offer of life that Jesus makes in John 4 goes beyond that of Wisdom in Proverbs in that it is eschatological; it is life that is everlasting rather than temporary. Ultimately we find this offer of Christ as life of the world extended in the Passion narrative, where Christ becomes the sacrificial lamb. Furthermore, at the heart of the Christian liturgy is the Eucharist;

here the daily foods of bread and wine take on a deeper spiritual significance as the body and blood of Christ. Such a meal resonates with the banquet of Wisdom.

The concept of altering food offered in the Eucharist with genes from another animal or even human species may be technically feasible, but is it desirable? If we feel a sense of abhorrence at the idea, then this reflects the ultimate challenge of genetic engineering of food. It seems to suggest that many of our human interventions are outside the limits appropriate to right relationships between God, humanity and the earth. Moreover, it seems to challenge what it means to be human. We are confronted with the fluidity of boundaries between species in a way that has never been possible before, so that everyday actions such as eating and drinking can become the objects of our own manipulations. Rather than restoring order, it seems to symbolize disorder and chaos, even while attempting to grasp control and power over the natural world.

In attempting to discern which, if any, genetic modifications might be justified, we need to develop a deeper sensitivity to Wisdom's invitation to the banquet. Rather than simply asking if the technology is possible, we need to question whether there has been adequate preparation and reflection on the consequences of such an action at the social and cultural levels. The promise of biotechnology is an ambiguous one, and it would be easy to reject all genetic engineering outright. However, in all cases to date there seems to be very little justification for genetic engineering of food. The figure of Wisdom is a reminder that our actions have to cohere with justice and goodness.

Where genetic engineering leads to deeper situations of injustice it cannot be justified from a Christian perspective. Indeed, I suggest that in all probability genetic engineering is only warranted when used to produce pharmaceuticals necessary to sustain human life, where no other alternatives are possible. The recent Food Ethics Council report argues that the genetic manipulation of food should adopt the precautionary principle in refraining from genetic manipulation through genetic engineering unless good arguments can be put forward in its favour.[26]

Nonetheless, while social and political factors were aired, the Food Ethics Council did not consider the possible religious objections to genetic manipulation of food.

So far the direction taken by much of food technology seems far from desirable as a global project. Even those projects that claim to be offering assistance to the poorer nations of the world, such as the introduction of Vitamin A in rice plants, seem like a technological fix that assumes a dubious model of development. Indeed, the political assumptions behind the call for a spread of the technology to poorer parts of the world betray a lack of real appreciation of the limitations of the 'development' models of the past. A fostering of respect for local communities and cultures might encourage a deeper Wisdom that is prepared to listen to the voices of those who are different culturally and who do not share the philosophical assumptions that have dominated the Western world. While we need to be realistic about the infiltration of GM foods into the global food chain, an appropriate theological response is called for as well. Such a response is one voice among many, but it harks back to the ancient religious tradition in early Judaism, where eating a meal is of supreme religious significance. When Wisdom invites us to the banquet we are promised wholesome food that she has prepared herself. In contrast, the impulsive and seductive voice of Folly offers another kind of meal, one that leads to death instead of life.

Just as Christ offers us life in the Eucharistic meal, so too, for Christians, sharing food takes on profound religious significance. It symbolizes not just our labour but also is a way of receiving and entering into the life of God. This sacred space seems to be denied if our basic foods become genetically modified. Wisdom calls and expects imitation, and we learn Wisdom by sharing in her meal. Yet in a Christian sense Wisdom cannot be separated from love and peacemaking. Such action requires boldness and courage on our part, but also sensitivity to the complexity of the culture in which we find ourselves, and also towards those of other cultures and religious traditions. Just as we need to give greater attention to the public voice in discerning the ways forward in our present culture, so too we need to give more attention to those who are on the receiving end of the technology in alternative cultures and communities in the global market. In a sense we are all indirectly implicated in the chain of events that has fostered the growth of such global biotechnology.

Theological issues in the cloning of animals and possibly humans

Much of the debate about the cloning of animals and possibly humans has been concerned with ethical issues. While it seems to me that ethical issues are of critical importance, theological analysis needs to be included as well. It is tempting to rush to a consideration of the particular ethical dilemmas without developing a theological basis for ethical judgments. The widespread public outcry against the idea of human cloning is quite understandable in view of the resistance to the use of any human genes in food and the much greater caution associated with manipulation of the human species.[27] Nonetheless, where genetic engineering could be used to prevent human suffering and death the public attitudes are more positive. Cloning animals is now technically feasible, and there seems little doubt that it will eventually be applied to human beings. Yet should we necessarily accept this development with resignation?

Issues associated with animal cloning

The cloning of animals raises theological issues about the human perception of animals, such as how far animals can be considered to be independent entities worthy of special treatment compared with other life forms or inanimate objects. In other words, cloning presents us with a particular challenge to develop an adequate theology of nature. It asks not only the ethical question about how far we are justified in our intervention in the natural world, but the theological question of our role in the future of nature and the philosophical question of the meaning of the natural. If cloning is simply part of the long progression of human treatment of animals, beginning with their domestication for human food in the earliest civilizations, through to greater and greater mechanization of agriculture and different forms of 'factory farming', then it could seem to be quite an unproblematic extension of human technology. On the other hand, if we view such developments in terms of a shattering of the close relationships between humanity, nature and the land, then cloning becomes anathema, a final symbol of all that has gone before in breaking down patterns of intimacy between humanity and the natural world.

This brings us back to the question for theology that is raised both by genetic engineering of food and cloning, namely, what kind of future do we want? If we see ourselves as co-creators, we enable the systems of nature to go beyond what is naturally possible. Even though Philip Hefner qualifies his idea of co-creation by suggesting that we are acting as created co-creators, the implication is that we have been given the freedom to make interventions in nature. This is not a retrograde step, rather it is an enabling of the systems of nature to 'participate in God's purposes in the mode of freedom'.[28] Non-human nature is exalted to participate in transcendence and freedom by the action of humans. For both Hefner and Peters, it is freedom that is the defining quality of being human. Through these processes we open up new futures for the whole natural world and ourselves. The eschatological view expressed here is clearly both optimistic and fully realized. For the

> purpose of human being and human culture is to be the agency for the birthing of the future of the nature that has birthed us – the nature which is not only our own genetic heritage, but also the entire human community and the evolutionary and ecological reality in which and to which we all belong – at least the nature that constitutes planet earth.[29]

This highly optimistic anthropology is embedded in an eschatology that is realized through human interventions and technology. While Hefner claims to reject scientism, it seems to me that his transcendent dimension arises out of science and seems to baptize its efforts in the transformation of nature.

It would be naïve to suggest that we can go back to an agrarian culture in ignorance of modern technology. However, I suggest that too great a focus on human achievement and human freedom obscures other theological principles, such as the mandate to give proper respect to the animal world. We tend to think of respect primarily as an ethical concept, but I suggest that it is also rooted in a theological perception of creation as fundamentally good. Given the intrinsic goodness of creation, how far are such manipulations really for the benefit of the creatures themselves? The promoters of Dolly the sheep went to great lengths to show that the cloned animals themselves were cared for and nurtured in a way that was responsible. The death of many animals in the development of the techniques and the suffering caused to many others were certainly not a way of showing respect. While I intend to return to the consequentialist approaches to this problem in the next chapter, if we ask ourselves whether animal cloning affirms the goodness of the creature, the answer must be in the negative. Instead, the creatures become instruments of human manipulation, however far we try to compensate for this by treating those animals that do survive with proper care and attention.

The only exception to this that is worth consideration is where cloning is used to perpetuate a species that is threatened with extinction. There have been press reports of this taking place in New Zealand, cloning a rare breed of seaweed-eating cattle that would not otherwise survive.[30] The scientists concerned suggested that 'Elsie' represented new hope for other endangered species, including the giant panda. Elsie, born in the summer of 1998, was at that time reported to be the first clone to be alive at the same time as her mother. She belongs to an ancient herd of short-horn cattle that was introduced to the sub-Arctic Auckland islands in 1850. Ironically, perhaps, it was human intervention that rendered the herd near extinction. A disastrous culling programme by the Department of Conservation rendered the whole herd extinct apart from a single survivor, Lady, who escaped their notice. Yet even in this case we might ask about the long-term good of the species. Cloning may give a temporary reprieve from extinction, but the subsequent lack of diversity in genetic make-up of the offspring would not bode well for the future of that species. Indeed, I suggest that even in these cases cloning represents a crude and ineffective way of trying to cover up the human interventions that allowed the species to become extinct in the first place.

For Moltmann none of the creatures of the earth have 'been destined to be "technologically manipulated"'.[31] Such false dreams of humanity lead to an aggressive ethic that is ultimately destructive. He suggests that a right attitude towards the natural world is one that respects the dignity of all of God's creatures. God's love for all creation, Christ's self-offering for them and the indwelling of the Holy Spirit in them all add up to confer on every individual creature rights in an all-comprehensive community of creation. However, it seems to me that conferral of rights on nature will do little to curb the growing impetus towards genetic engineering and associated technologies such as cloning.

The theological motif of stewardship could be used either to support or reject animal cloning, in a similar way to the genetic modification of food. As suggested in Chapter 3, animal cloning is often viewed as a convenient way of achieving a regular supply of genetically modified animals. The tension that exists in many cases is an ethical one, namely, can the perceived good achieved for humanity justify animal cloning? Some might argue that this does represent stewardship of resources given to us by God for human benefit. Certainly, the medieval view that animals were automata, having no rationality, would encourage such a development. Yet it does seem to be highly presumptuous to suggest that animals are simply there for human usefulness. Moltmann's idea of the dignity of all creatures, including animals, is relevant in this context.

If we turn again to the Wisdom motif, then a theology of nature based on Wisdom is one that allows Wisdom to be the source of all life, including animals. Judaic Wisdom relied on close observation of the natural world, not just for human benefit alone but as a source of wonder in celebration of the Creator. I have suggested elsewhere that Wisdom is one way of understanding how God interacts with creation, namely, that it is through divine Wisdom as agent of the creative process that the world becomes what it is intended to be.[32] An awareness of the importance of Wisdom in the creation of life fosters an attitude of respect – indeed, it is the necessary precursor for it. Moreover, humans are instructed by the ancient Israelite sages to seek Wisdom and get understanding. Such a message is as relevant today as it was in the ancient texts. Wisdom helps us to begin to articulate an answer to the question why we need to give due respect to all creatures. It was suggested in the last chapter that such Wisdom is cosmic in scope, and not restricted to the human community. On this basis animal cloning can be seen as only justifiable in rare circumstances for the production of medicines needed to treat life-threatening diseases, where human life cannot be continued in any other way.

Human cloning and imago Dei

The idea that humans are made in the image of God has developed as a result of a rich theological tradition. It is the theological basis for affirming the difference between humanity and other creatures. Yet it is also the basis for giving special value to human beings in and of themselves, as those who reflect God's image. The interpretation of the meaning of the image in the Thomistic tradition focused on human reason as distinct from animals. Of course, a simple focus on reason is no longer viable today, as animals too are known to have their own rationality, even if it is less developed when compared with humans. Another ontological basis for the idea of the uniqueness of the image focuses on human consciousness, especially self-consciousness, which is uniquely present in human beings.

The problem with all such categorizations is that they tend to flounder once science discovers such traits in closely related mammals, such as monkeys or dolphins. Indeed, the blurring of the boundaries between human biological nature and that of closely related animals only serves to undermine any naturalistic basis for human dignity and value. The genetic commonality between all species, especially those closely related to humans, reinforces this trend towards a weakening of the special nature of humans.

An alternative approach to the idea of image relies on a more functional understanding of what it is to be a human person. In this case it is the way humans *behave* towards creation that defines their nature as image-bearers. Some authors have even taken the idea of having dominion over creation in Genesis as being intricately linked with concept of the image of God.[33] Such a model of the image tends to stress separateness from the rest of creation and human privilege. This is very different from ideas of the image based on particular ontological characteristics of the human, such as reason. A functional model of the image might even become the basis for justification of animal cloning for the sake of human benefit.

I suggest that both models of image-bearing are in need of a deeper appreciation of the complex issues associated with human personhood. Persons cannot be reduced to raw natural character-istics, either in terms of natural qualities such as reason or crude patterns of dominion in relation to the earth. Instead, persons are persons in relation, not just with God, but with each other and the earth. In this scenario image-bearing is about becoming more con-scious of those interrelationships and a rejection of all images of the person that seek to truncate it to one or two characteristics. I suggest that being a person is far more than just defining genetic characteristics or finding the genetic basis for particular traits. Yet the way these genes interact with the environment, understood as both the natural environment and social environment, helps to delineate what is means to be personal. Such genes, like all other characteristics of human personhood, need to be treated with respect.

Why should we worry about cloning over and above changing other characteristics of the human person? I suggest that it is the radical nature of the change ensued by cloning that raises particular theological issues associated with image-bearing. The presumption in cloning is that we have a right to do as we please with human beings, to treat different cells and organs of human bodies as tissues for manipulation. I am not suggesting that a cloned human, should one be born, is in any way denied the possi-bility of bearing the image of God. Such a possibility is in the hands of God alone. Nonetheless, the possibility that a cloned human being could bear the image of God does not amount to its theological justification, in the way that Peters seems to suggest.[34] Even the Pontifical Academy for Life insists that a cloned individual would not share the same 'soul' as its physical donor, rather it is 'created directly by God', and in this the 'aura of omnipotence that accompanies cloning should at least be put into perspective'.[35] The Vatican statements take this further and argue that human cloning suggests an 'impossibility of involving the spirit, which is the source of human personality'.

I am less convinced that it would be impossible for the Spirit to be involved, but the opposite emphasis on human freedom is equally problematic. For Ted Peters the theological justification for human cloning relies almost exclusively on such an emphasis, for as humans are free creatures made in the image of God, human cloning simply reflects that God-given freedom. What Peters interprets as the desire for freedom, the Vatican interprets as an illicit desire for omnipotence. Certainly, some of the examples of the purposes for human reproductive cloning given in the Human Genetics Advisory Committee Consultation Document, such as the restoration of a dead relative, would veer on the side of omnipotence. However, in all such cases human personhood and freedom are narrowly defined in terms of an individual right to act in a way that ignores the concept of community. I suggest that we need to think also of what such a development means in terms of what we are becoming as persons in relationships. While the Vatican identifies the relationship between man and woman as that which is marred and defaced through cloning, it seems to me that the brokenness extends much further than this to the human community as a whole and to the relationship between humanity and the natural world.

Of course, the latest developments in artificial intelligence might suggest that there will come a time when it is impossible to distinguish ourselves from automatic machines.[36] If we follow this philosophy, then human cloning seems no better or worse than any other scientific development. However, I suggest that our genetic identity is to some extent reflected in who we are, even if we keep reminding ourselves that we are not solely determined by our genes. No one can deny the fundamental importance of our genetic make-up in setting the scene for what is to follow in human development. It is the basis for all embryonic and pre-embryonic diagnostic tests for human diseases. It seems that on this basis cloning represents a step too far; it is a step that negates human dignity by ignoring the relational aspects of human identity and personhood.

While therapeutic human cloning is heralded as the technology of the future, it seems that this is still a denial of human dignity. As Wisdom is also portrayed as woman Wisdom, humanity is given special dignity. The special place of Wisdom in the human community, unlike other holistic models of creation, allows for the distinction between the human and non-human community. Of course, a *conceptus* up to fourteen days old cannot be thought of in exactly the same way as a foetus in later stages of development. The ambiguities associated with use of this technology at this stage are more difficult and subtle. They relate to more general issues of how far we are justified in experimentation on early human embryos. Clearly, giving a *conceptus* identical rights to human persons is not appropriate – this forms the basis for justification of experimentation on embryos up to fourteen days old. Any emotive language that suggests therapeutic cloning amounts to using human persons as spare parts for the treatment of diseases is likely to encourage scorn rather than respect in the medical community faced with the real dilemma of human suffering.

Can we really assume when human life begins? Certainly, from the point of view of genetics life begins at conception, even if physiologically human life is only considered viable after implantation. It seems to me that our choice of defining life as worth saving after fourteen days is based on the knowledge that only a proportion of fertilized eggs will survive in the natural situation. However, of those eggs that are fertilized *in vitro*, how might we know which ones are viable? To assume that all life is dispensable prior to fourteen days old just because a proportion of fertilized eggs fail to survive in the natural state seems to be somewhat spurious. Furthermore, as suggested earlier, all human life, even cloned life, is worthy of respect. We need to ask ourselves whether such a development is a true reflection of our vocation to bear the image of God.

Conclusions

This chapter has focused on two particular examples of genetic engineering that have become the subject of intense debate, namely, the genetic modification of food and animal/human cloning. Both examples demonstrate that it is possible to present theological arguments either in favour or against such developments. The key theological issue of whether theologians support or reject genetic technologies seems to be their own presumptions about anthropology. A more optimistic anthropology will support genetic engineering in that humans are given the gift of science to improve the natural world. We become co-creators of the world and agents of evolution, even if qualified by an awareness of the possibility of human error. A more pessimistic anthropology suggests that human sinfulness is too pervasive to be confident that human intervention will be for the benefit of the whole earth, not just humanity. Moreover, once we see all of life as in some sense sacred, genetic manipulation of the earth takes on a sinister aspect where we are usurping God's place as creator of the world.

I have indicated both in this chapter and the previous one that a recovery of the Wisdom motif goes some way towards helping humanity to discern the boundaries and limits to genetic engineering and cloning. I suggest that Wisdom in the theological sense would not automatically either favour or dismiss the possibility of genetic engineering. Wisdom, on the one hand, affirms the special dignity of the human race, but the idea of Wisdom as agent of creation of the world shows that it is also cosmic in scope. Wisdom would, however, encourage caution on the part of humans rather than impulsive action. The speed with which the new food technologies has developed has allowed relatively little time for careful reflection and discernment. The link between Wisdom and justice is a reminder that global development issues are critical factors to be considered in any theological reflection on genetic modification of food. The issue of animal cloning, like genetic engineering, demonstrates the power of humanity to manipulate the world for its own benefit. The limits to this activity once again becomes important. The need to respect the creatures involved and the dignity of all human life, however it is formed, come to the fore. While human cloning is inevitably bound up with ethical questions, I suggest that the precautionary principle also applies, namely, that we need to be careful about coming to easy conclusions about when human life begins if the rationale is simply to facilitate experimental research.

In addition, the technologies need to be scrutinized by much wider public debates on the issues. Any assumptions, such as that the public have nothing to say or that this must inevitably represent a good, need to be challenged. Wisdom suggests a much deeper caution, which looks not just at the short-term consequences but also the long-term ones, which perceives the deeper motives in such an endeavour. Wisdom also asks what this tells us about our own humanity and the kind of people we are becoming in the twenty-first century. Is this really consistent with human justice?

John Polkinghorne, who has consistently affirmed the practice of science, is much more hesitant to endorse human cloning. He admits that scientists alone cannot be left to make the decisions. Rather, there must be other parties in the debate who give due respect for human life and to moral dignity. He suggests that any theological position must be consistent with ethical integrity.[37] It is to these ethical issues that I turn in the chapter that follows.

Ethical debates in genetic engineering

I suggested in the last chapter that theological arguments could be brought to bear either to support or reject genetic engineering and associated technologies, such as cloning of animals and humans. I argued that the theological basis used either to foster or criticize genetic engineering needed much more careful appraisal. A theological approach drawing on the motif of Wisdom seems to be a good starting-point for reflection, given the complexities involved. In this chapter I review the most common ethical approaches used in favour of or against genetic engineering, and suggest that these too need to be complemented by the development of Wisdom as an ethical virtue. I also discuss some of the ethical and theological issues associated with patenting of genetic material. Clearly, the development of an adequate ethical approach is of vital importance, given the mushrooming of new genetic technologies and how such processes impinge on every aspect of our lives.

Consequentialism and the new biology

The secular philosophical basis for or against genetic engineering is generally expressed through a consequentialist philosophical framework, namely, that the outcomes of a particular action are considered on the basis of whether there are more benefits than risks or vice versa.[1] A consequentialist approach makes no prior judgment on whether a particular action is good or bad and the notion of good is pragmatic, rather than an absolute.

Those who are in favour of genetic engineering highlight the possible benefits. The scientific basis for these changes was discussed in Chapter 3; here the likely benefits are briefly summarized.[2] They include the potential enlargement in food production, especially in those areas of the world where there are shortages. Associated with this is the increase in land use by allowing genetically modified (GM) plants to grow in nutrient-poor or dry conditions that would not have previously supported crops. In addition, supporters suggest that the total chemical input over the whole growing period may be less when GM plants are used. For example, in some GM crops insect infestation can be checked by internal production of insecticides. The overall efficiency of agricultural production goes up when GM crops are used, leading to higher yields and cheaper foodstuffs. This economic gain is one of the main reasons why this technology has expanded so rapidly in the USA.

Also, consumers are now given more choice in what they can eat, and the quality of foods may even be improved by genetic modifications. For example, in those areas of the world where there is high Vitamin D or A deficiency in humans, staple crops can be modified so as to prevent conditions, such as blindness, associated with such deficiencies. Furthermore, GM organisms can actually be environmentally friendly in other ways as microorganisms can be used to clean up pollutants, other wastes and toxins that would otherwise be very difficult to remove. In addition, the benefit to human and animal health through the development of new drugs actually saves lives and reduces suffering.

Overall, the growth of the economy through the development of the biotechnology industry creates jobs and improves the standard of living for everyone. The excellence in genetic research brings cultural benefits in raising the standard of scientific research at a national level and preventing the 'brain drain' to other continents, especially the USA.

Summarizing, I suggest that the possible benefits of genetic engineering fall into a number of different categories that are important to distinguish:

• Alleviation of human suffering at the basic level of food, either by feeding a starving population, improving nutrition or removing allergies. This might be thought of as a form of preventative medicine.

- Environmental benefits associated with growing modified crops or using microorganisms to control pollution.
- Medical benefits through the development of new drugs, which is related to therapeutic uses of new pharmacological products.
- Economic benefits through the creation of new wealth and employment.
- Cultural benefits in giving greater consumer choice and in achieving scientific excellence, thus preventing the most able scientists from leaving the country.

Those who argue against genetic engineering believe that the risks outweigh the benefits. However, it is not just a simple issue of pointing to the risks and drawing up a cost–benefit type of analysis, but also evaluating counter-arguments against the very benefits that are claimed for genetic engineering. Taking the same broad categories in turn, those against genetic engineering suggest:

- The belief that genetically modified crops will feed the world is a self-deception. Such a technological fix to the problem is neither desired by those in poorer nations, nor realistic. The problems of starvation and lack of access to healthy diets cannot be whitewashed by simple technological 'solutions' that cover up the underlying social and political causes of poverty.
- Far from improving environmental conditions, genetically modified crops lead to risks to the environment and potential damage to ecosystems and the food chain, as well as loss of biodiversity. More details of these risks were examined in Chapter 3.
- While some new drugs may be developed through genetic engineering, once it is applied to foodstuffs there is a potential health risk in consumption. Such risks to animal or human health include potentially fatal allergenic reactions or reduction of disease resistance through the consumption of antibiotics

introduced by means of genetic marker genes. Other risks specifically related to humans include the possible transfer of diseases from animals to humans in transgenic work, or the unknown effects of a gene product following transfer to a new organism, especially indirect effects on overall physiology and biochemistry. Such effects are very difficult to test or predict in advance.

- It is worth asking who is really to gain from the new genetic engineering products. In most cases it seems as though it would lead to an even further redistribution of wealth, to the detriment of poorer nations.
- The lack of adequate labelling of GM food actually reduces consumer choice and limits freedom. Furthermore, at a cultural level it is worth considering not only the possible benefits to the cultural wealth of richer nations but also the potentially damaging effects on traditional subsistence agriculture. Such traditional agriculture is likely to be far more sustainable in that it relies on less chemical inputs and artificial fertilizers.

Of course, those in favour can counter such arguments. They will cite examples where genetic engineering has brought economic benefits to those who are struggling to survive. To suggest that the whole economy needs to change in order to solve the problem of world hunger seems to them to be unrealistic and harsh in view of the immediate benefits possible through genetically engineered products. Secondly, environmental damage does not compare like with like – while genetic engineering may not be preferable to organic farming, it is certainly preferable to conventional farming that uses chemical methods. It is unrealistic to suggest that modern agricultural techniques are unnecessary to meet the world population's food requirements. The possibility of a return to organic farming is a myth that is ultimately destructive for those in need, and will spell starvation and death for many in poverty. Furthermore, it is a luxury that is only possible for those in the West who can afford to pay for organic alternatives.

Then, any risk to human health by consumption of GM food ignores the far greater risk posed by consumption of high levels of pesticides and other chemicals in the diet. Supporters may admit to the remote possibility that antibiotic resistance from marker genes used in genetic engineering of crops, for example, would be transferred to animals or humans. However, any antibiotic-resistant genes are now largely removed as useful markers in genetic engineering, so cannot be considered to be a threat to human or animal health. Furthermore, all new genetic products undergo rigorous testing procedures and hence pose no real danger to human health. The idea that humans may catch diseases from animals via genetic modification is quite simply ludicrous. Those who argue against genetic engineering on the basis of redistribution of wealth betray their own politically left-wing agenda that has little to do with the actual risk or otherwise of the new technologies. Finally, the labelling of GM products is improving all the time, but to insist that all products that have any derivation from GM crops be identified poses far too great a burden on the food industry.

Of course, it is quite possible to counter these arguments as well. However, rather than delineating the reply, I suggest that we need to reflect on the *process* of the debate. We seem to have reached *gridlock*, where there is no real empathy or understanding of the issues from either side. Both argue their case on rational principles of consequences, yet as these are in many cases as yet unknown, in terms of *both* the risks and the benefits, the debate ends in suspicion and misunderstanding. Hostility abounds on both sides of the argument. Those in favour accuse those against of being anti-science or, worse, attaching themselves to forms of romantic spirituality and 'New Age' ideology. Those against accuse those in favour of being culturally naïve and narrow-minded, bent simply on profits at the expense of the cultural goods of society as a whole. In the end it seems that hidden from view there are other reasons as a matter of principle for rejecting or accepting genetic engineering that then serve to influence the way utilitarian arguments are presented. I will be coming back to these reasons in the section on deontological ethics later in this chapter.

The special case of cloning

Those who are in favour of animal cloning generally argue on much the same lines, that the benefits outweigh the risks. However, unlike the situation for human cloning, many of the risks are known and quantifiable as the experiments have taken place. While, as discussed in the last chapter, the Vatican strongly resists human cloning, it gives qualified approval to cloning or genetic manipulation of animals or plants 'wherever it answers a need or provides a significant benefit for man or for other living beings'. This consequentialist approach is qualified by suggesting that humans have to bear in mind their responsibility to protect animal life and respect the biodiversity of all species.[3]

Those against animal cloning have a particular concern for animal welfare and animal suffering, and believe that the death and suffering of animals cannot be condoned even for the sake of the treatment of human disease. The medical argument in favour of animal cloning is certainly more convincing than any argument for its use for uniform food production, such as finding the basis for the ideal steak.[4] However, even from a consequentialist position, there are still difficulties in condoning animal cloning in those cases where drugs can be produced by alternative methods. The question we need to ask is whether such alternative methods also lead to animal suffering or have as many medical benefits.

The argument for the use of cloning or genetic engineering for the production of human blood products includes the safety aspect for human treatment of disease, namely, it no longer runs the risk of contamination with blood-borne diseases. Certainly, in the case of Dolly the sheep, the main purpose of cloning was to be able to produce more sheep that were genetically modified with human genes. Genetic engineering of fertilized eggs has a low 'success rate' in terms of survival of sheep embryos. In other words, questions relating to cloning in animals are part of a broad consideration of how far is it permissible to modify the embryos or egg and sperm of the animals concerned.

At the moment such techniques are fully legal in animals, and the idea of germ-line changes to animals is not usually challenged.[5] Yet the consequences for the animals themselves also need to be taken into account. Certainly, traditional agricultural breeding methods have always selected those animals that produce the highest 'yield'. Are cloning and genetic engineering of animals any different in their goal? From a purely consequentialist position, genetic engineering of animals does not seem to raise any new ethical issues compared with traditional breeding. Even if we take the *telos* or 'purposefulness' of the animal into account, breeding and domestication of animals challenges this as much as genetic engineering or cloning. Of course, we are still left with the more difficult issue of whether there are limits to the extent of modification, even according to a consequentialist framework. Those Californian scientists who managed to produce a chimera between a sheep and a goat in 1999 seem to most observers to have gone a step too far. This is a radical denial of the inner orientation of the creature to its own particular end, or *telos*. It also seems to serve no purpose for the benefit of humanity other than satisfying human curiosity.

Human cloning is even more complex in that potentially it can be used for either therapeutic or reproductive purposes. The scientific basis for this was summarized in Chapter 3. Most argue that the risks are far too high at present to warrant its application to humans for reproductive purposes. Human cloning for reproductive purposes is illegal, but those who are in favour argue primarily on the basis of likely positive consequences.[6] For example, it could give infertile couples the opportunity to have a child, where other methods, such as *in vitro* fertilization (IVF), have failed. The counter-argument in this case is that this reifies the desire of the parents as an ethical imperative, to the exclusion of consideration of the psychological needs of the child. Such a child is likely to be confused in its identity and would not have a clear perception of its place in a family. Of course, supporters believe that this is not necessarily self-evident, since at the time of writing no human clone has ever been allowed or has ever been known to survive to maturity. Yet for many the risk is simply not worth the benefit, and the complex social and psychological needs of the child should not become the subject of experimentation.

Even more controversial is the idea that human cloning might be used on the death of a child or a loved one. However, such arguments are faulty scientifically in that there is no reason why the clone should be similar in personality to the lost relative. The idea that any individual could be replaced by technological means is abhorrent for most, even among the supporters of the general idea of human cloning.

Many more are strongly supportive of the use of human cloning to treat human diseases, an application known as therapeutic cloning. Ian Wilmut, for example, who is known to oppose human cloning for reproductive purposes, is a keen supporter of the use of the technique to treat human disease. Certainly, simply on a consequentialist ethic the benefits seem obvious – the possible alleviation of disease and death by the use of stem cells. However, the arguments in favour also show up clearly the limitations of consequentialist approaches, since in this case any human identity of the growing human cloned cells is deliberately denied. The basis for this denial is purely a naturalistic one, namely, that human life recognized as differentiated life has not yet begun prior to fourteen days old. If the consequences for this life are taken into account, then it could be argued that it is not right to destroy life in order to let life persist. However, it could be argued even in this scenario that the ethical status of the growing embryo should not have the same weight as that of the adult or child who is dying, and who is a fully developed person.

In the end it is the assumptions behind the way cloning technology works that seem to lead to ethical difficulties with therapeutic cloning. I suggest that consequentialism alone offers a bias in its favour. As it is the most common approach adopted in secular ethical debates, it seems highly likely that the use of cloning for therapeutic purposes will become routine. However, there is always the possibility that other voices will be heard.

Human genetic engineering

Another area that will become of increasing concern in ethics is the use of germ-line therapy to treat human diseases. This is more likely to become widely available in the near future than any routine use of human cloning for reproductive purposes.[7] The consequences again seem clear enough – the treatment of debilitating human disease. However, the proportion of human disease that may be treated genetically in this way is small compared with the sum total of all human diseases. Even the Human Genome Project, which aims to map the whole of the human genome, can only identify *some* of the genes responsible for diseases in humans.[8] Locating genetic components for other diseases is likely to be a slow and laborious process, taking many years of careful scientific research. Even somatic gene therapy has suffered some recent setbacks, with the benefits not proving as inevitable as many scientists had hoped. For example, while somatic therapy has been used to treat immune deficiency, somatic therapy is still very inefficient and far from giving cures for diseases such as cystic fibrosis. It is these setbacks that seem to have set in motion a new drive towards germ-line therapy in the USA.[9] As far as the supporters are concerned, the consequences of evolution itself are 'damn cruel', so we should take evolution into our own hands.

The American Association for the Advancement of Science (AAAS) in December 1999 discussed the legal, ethical and technical aspects of germ-line therapy. Technically germ-line therapy might be easier than somatic therapies, but the optimism may be ill-founded. Moreover, practically speaking, there are only a very few genetic diseases that could be treated by germ-line therapy. In practice, couples who are at risk of genetic disease can opt for IVF treatment and hence select those embryos that do not carry the disease. Those who refuse such a method for other religious reasons are equally as likely to reject the idea of germ-line therapy. A theoretical exception to the IVF option might be where both parents have cystic fibrosis. Ronald Cole-Turner was present at the AAAS meeting, and admitted that he could not understand the aversion to germ-line therapy in Europe. However, even at this meeting discussion continued about the other possible uses of germ-line therapy for *enhancement* of particular traits, rather than simple treatment of diseases. Such a view was aired as early as the 1980s, as mentioned in the last chapter.

At the time of writing, twenty-three European countries have signed a petition for the prohibition of germ-line therapy. The European nations seem to rely on a deontological as well as a consequentialist approach, regarding germ-line therapy as an affront to human dignity. Those who draw primarily on consequentialist approaches cannot understand this view. Furthermore, enhancement of particular characteristics would be a negative step, since it finds echoes in the dark memory of eugenics and Nazi Germany.

Deontological ethics and the new biology

While the intrinsic worth of genetic engineering is unlikely to be used in open debate, those in favour of genetic engineering may have particular reasons for giving value to it quite apart from its consequences. I have hinted that these reasons may be a significant factor underlying the hostility in the debate, even though the argument is more often than not presented in consequentialist terms. For supporters the positive results of genetic engineering are obvious and precise, while the risks seem vaguer and less quantifiable. Furthermore, it is often tied up with an implicit commitment to science as such, which serves to render any objections to genetic engineering as 'unscientific' or even a form of 'romantic' mythology. Yet the assumption that the science is itself value-free seems to be left unnoticed and unchallenged. There also seems to be little real awareness of the philosophical, social and cultural setting in which the science is conducted.[10]

Deontological ethical arguments against genetic engineering include objections as a matter of principle, rather than simply because of unwelcome consequences. Some of these arguments may be framed in theological language, but others are from a purely secular perspective. Theological arguments both for and against genetic engineering were explored in the last chapter. One secular argument against is that genetic engineering is unnatural. While this is a weak argument from a philosophical perspective, as it equates the good with the natural, it is still commonly used. Another common argument against genetic engineering is the lack of respect that it implies. In all breeding methods there is a tendency to treat animals and plants as commodities. Genetic engineering allows an even greater detachment from the creatures in such a way that they can become highly vulnerable to exploitation.

Paul Taylor has suggested that respect for the natural world is a key paradigm in the development of a theory of environmental ethics. He insists that we are all part of a single biotic community.[11] The question is whether this recognition of mutual dependence constitutes a moral relationship as well. Robin Attfield argues against the idea that interdependence strengthens moral relationships, preferring the notion that all species that have interests have *moral standing*.[12] What does it mean for a species to have interests? This seems to be related to the idea of what constitutes respect. Immanuel Kant believed that if we treat people as a means to our own ends and do not recognize them as ends, we are failing to show respect. Genetic engineering has to treat living things in a mechanistic way in order to achieve its goals. There is a clear temptation to show lack of respect to all creatures so that they simply become means to our ends.

The idea of respect relates to the theological understanding of the worth of all creatures coming from the acknowledgment of God as creator of all things. Philosophers and theologians both acknowledge the idea of respect for all life. However, for secular philosophers, respect emerges from our recognition of mutual relationships, while for theologians it comes from our recognition of God as author of these relationships and as ultimately the one who creates, cares for and loves all creatures. Andrew Linzey has consistently argued against genetic engineering of animals from a theocentric perspective, describing it as a form of slavery. His ethic is also inclusive of the notion of animal rights.[13] This is a step beyond merely giving animals respect in that it implies a moral response that invokes justice between animals and humans. While rights language is not necessarily the most appropriate way to foster respect for animals, as rights and responsibilities are normally considered together, it does at least put the issue of our treatment of animals in the foreground of ethical debate.[14]

The case of human cloning

Those who argue from first principles for human reproductive cloning do so on the basis that there is nothing intrinsically wrong with using science to aid human reproduction. John Harris insists that cloning does not amount to an affront to human dignity, and supports the principle of human cloning[15] According to supporters, human cloning is no different from other 'artificial' techniques such as IVF. Furthermore, identical twins have identical genetic make-up, so cloning would be no different except that science has assisted the process. In a similar manner to the genetic engineering debates, arguments against cloning are deemed simply anti-science and irrational responses to unknown technologies. Furthermore, any suggestion that cloning could lead to psychological damage to the child is unfounded as it has not yet taken place.

Those who argue against human cloning do so on the basis that it is a denial of the uniqueness of the human person and human dignity. As this has a profound theological content, it was dealt with in some detail in the last chapter. Children need to be viewed not as a right of the parents, but a gift. Theologians in particular insist that a child has to be thought of as a gift from God, rather than simply meeting human desires. Another objection to cloning that, strictly speaking, is neither consequentialist nor deontological relates to an appreciation of the history of misuses of genetics. In this case the *memory* of eugenics is ever present and is enough to lead to caution about the future of the human race shaped entirely by our own manipulations. This issue will be highlighted again in the final chapter. Another objection is that human cloning simply panders to the myth that humanity is immortal and will go on forever. This brings us back to the question once more of how such technology is shaping who we are becoming as people in relationship to the natural world and each other. One way this is particularly brought into focus comes through consideration of the issue of patenting. In this case we seem to reach a central issue that appears in all deliberations over genetic engineering, namely, how far is humanity entitled to change nature into a form of art?

Are we entitled to reorder nature for our own ends? What does this say about ourselves as human beings?

Ethical debates in the patenting of life

Some of the ways patenting is justified from an ethical perspective were discussed in Chapter 3. One of the main ethical problems with patenting biological processes is how far scientists can claim to be creating an invention when they are a product of nature. Furthermore, if the invention is alive, what about subsequent generations? In the USA the patent rights have gradually extended, first to plants and seeds (1985), then to animals (1987). In 1988 scientists working at Harvard University filed a patent for a genetically engineered mouse with a much higher probability of developing cancer. There were vocal objections to this development, as an example of unnecessary suffering and the immorality of extending patents to animals. While there was a widespread public outcry at this development, the patent was still granted.

In Europe a patent has yet to be granted to the Harvard oncomouse, even though it was filed in 1990. In this case a range of protest groups including anti-vivisection, animal rights, environmentalist and church groups filed objections. In May 1998 a new European Directive on patenting was passed by the European Parliament. This allows all microbiological processes and products to be patentable, and all animals and plants that have been modified genetically. Lawyers believe that patents are there simply to protect the rights of the inventor, rather than giving an assessment of the acceptability of a particular process or product. Yet it is particularly difficult to isolate patenting from social and political issues in the way suggested by legislation. The ethical goods in patenting might include the free access of information and benefits to society; the reward for particular inventiveness; and a principle of justice so that others do not exploit the invention unfairly.

However, there are other philosophical and ethical assumptions in patenting life that account for the far more mixed public response. For the purposes of the patent the particular organism in question becomes a commercial commodity. Indeed, without this assumption patents could not be granted, and the biotechnology industry would be considerably weakened. Those who support the idea of patenting believe patents serve to protect the rights of the inventor rather than diminish the value of the creature. Those against patenting believe that it is morally objectionable to patent a living creature as it assumes it is like any other invention. Patenting by its nature seems to deny respect due to the creature as having intrinsic worth. In other words, patenting seems to reduce life to instrumental worth alone.

A clause does exist in patent law in the European Directive, which allows an invention to be refused patent protection if it is against public interest or morality. Examples might include a patent on animals that are genetically engineered for cosmetic purposes such as baldness or cloning of adult humans. As might be expected, the issue of patenting has led to a mixed response among theologians and church groups. In May 1995 a petition was presented to the US government signed by 180 representatives of eighty different faiths or denominations calling for a ban on patenting of genetically engineered animals and human genes. For some representatives the earth is *sacred* and should be treated as such. Jeremy Rifkin, a spokesman for the campaign, takes this stance, arguing that 'by turning life into patented inventions, government drains life of its intrinsic nature and sacred value'.[16]

The theologian Ted Peters has strongly attacked this statement on the grounds that its theology is vague and seems to assume that genes are in some way sacred.[17] He is scathing about the basis for the argument, describing it as a 'hoodwink'. Peters believes that it is human creativity that alters the natural state, but to consider this to be outside the realm of God's creative purpose is false. However, Peters's opponents would argue that their concern does not stem simply from a belief that the world is sacred, though for some this will be the case. Rather, it is the intervention in the natural order that has taken many millennia to develop that seems disturbing to the relationships between God, humanity and the earth.

The Church of Scotland's SRT report takes an intermediate

position.[18] It supports patenting of particular genetic processes used and the application of genetics for a particular industrial, agricultural or medical product. It strongly objects to the idea of patenting unaltered parts of a gene sequence. It also rejects the idea that living organisms of any kind can be patented. The report states that patenting living organisms denies their inherent significance, which sets them apart from mere 'products of industry'.

Developing Wisdom as an ethical alternative

I have suggested in the last two chapters that Wisdom can become a theological resource within the Christian tradition that is especially relevant to the issues facing us in the new biology. I argue here that Aquinas' understanding of Wisdom is particularly informative for reflection on the meaning of Wisdom as a virtue and as a basis for developing a Wisdom ethic.[19] For Aquinas Wisdom is one of the intellectual virtues. Reason is both speculative and practical. The three virtues of speculative reason are Wisdom, *scientia* and understanding. The two virtues of practical reason are prudence and art. *Scientia* is the comprehension of the causes of things and the relationship between them, while understanding means grasping first principles. Wisdom is the understanding of the fundamental causes of everything and their relationship to everything else. It informs both speculative and practical reason. For Aquinas the fundamental cause is God, so Wisdom is ultimately knowledge of God's nature and actions. Ultimately, then, the Wisdom ethic that Aquinas develops is a theocentric one, even though he does not deny the use of human reason.

I suggest it is this appreciation of the use of reason combined with an awareness of both practical issues and the intimacy of the presence of God that makes the Wisdom ethic particularly instructive in unravelling the dilemmas facing us in the new biology. For reason alone will tend to draw us to a consequentialist approach to ethics, in that it is the one favoured in the current secular climate. On the other hand, theological reflection alone is drawn more towards deontological approaches that perhaps lack a connectedness with the secular alternatives and so prove ineffective. Michael Banner seems to associate prudence with a consequentialist approach to ethics.[20] However, I suggest that while prudence is involved in the discernment of risks and benefits, it has the potential to go much deeper than this in that it is informed by the particular character or virtue of those making the decisions. The philosopher David Cooper also argues the case for a virtue ethic when dealing with the ethical issues associated with animal biotechnology, though in this case he focuses on the virtue of humility, especially that of humans in relation to other animal species.[21] I suggest that a Wisdom ethic includes humility, but also looks to an even wider picture of interconnectedness.

Aquinas believed that the true end of all the virtues is goodness, and, loosely speaking, we can think of prudence as the means of attaining this end. Prudence is a clear perception of reality and is required for the practice of all the other moral virtues, namely, courage, justice and temperance. However, in many cases we cannot separate the goal of a virtue from the action or practice of it. In other words, the means and the ends are closely intertwined. The task of prudence becomes what Aquinas describes as discerning, through the use of reason, the right course of action to express a particular virtue, both for the good of the individual and the good of the community.

Keeping the balance between the good of individual and community is particularly challenging when addressing issues in the new biology, as indicated earlier. It is important, too, to see prudence in alignment with justice, temperance and courage. For rational action without justice is not a real act of prudence. In considering the aims of genetic engineering we need to ask ourselves how far this coheres with issues of justice between peoples. Moreover, courage is needed in challenging those aspects of the status quo that go against the aim of justice. Finally, the notion of temperance, although perhaps unpopular today, is an important quality to align with prudence in that it implies self-restraint. It is far too easy to assume that the goods one pursues for one's own ends are self-evident, without proper consideration of how this might affect others in the community, both of humans and the natural world. Wisdom is a reminder of this polyvalence in goodness, that the good for the individual must be balanced with the good for a community as a whole.

While Aquinas did not extend his ethic beyond the human community, in our contemporary culture where our environmental awareness is such that we are conscious of the radical interdependency between all creatures, I suggest that such an extrapolation is justified. Again prudence is needed to balance the needs of the human community with those of the natural world. While it is tempting, perhaps, to return to a form of holism that no longer distinguishes the individual from the community of humans or the earth, it seems to me that such blurring of the boundaries is unhelpful in the search for Wisdom. Wisdom recognizes the connections that are present, without fusing all together in a form of monism that ultimately can only lead to passivity in our relationship with the natural world.

Prudence finds what Aquinas terms 'the mean' in moral virtues, since the virtue itself cannot determine what that mean might be. The mean of a virtue is based on reason. Prudence is the right choice of actions working for the good of the individual and community that together lead to a life of virtue. It is part of the human condition to possess Wisdom in various degrees, and thereby its counterpart, foolishness. While Aquinas frequently states that it is self-evident that good is to be pursued and evil avoided, it is only in the notion of prudence that he elaborates *how* this might come about. It is therefore an ethical imperative, in that it delineates in some measure how to achieve the theological good that is the challenge of Christian discipleship.

The right use of reason, then, is essential when it comes to consideration of possibilities in the new biology. Yet this is not the same as the belief that reason will automatically favour a particular narrowly defined scientific knowing. Prudence is subtler than this in that it is reason directed to a particular goal, namely, goodness for an individual and for a community. In discerning the way forward in genetic engineering the goal of the action becomes important, but this is not simply understood in terms of consequences, rather in terms of the motivation and basis for such reasoning.

Another aspect of prudence that emerges in the thought of Aquinas is the ability to have a clear perception of reality in a specific situation. This requires virtues that Aquinas names as allied to that of prudence, namely, memory of the past, insight into the present and shrewdness about the future, along with reason, understanding, openness to being taught, circumspection and caution. The need for memory of the past is both individual and collective, so that if either memory is suppressed or obscured, then insight into the present is impaired along with a distorted assessment of goals for the future. Prudence gives us the habit that allows us to compare any new situation with the old, and by noticing differences between them it allows us to act appropriately for the good. It helps us notice very subtle differences in situations, rather than simple application of certain rules and generalizations from past experiences.

Prudence, then, encourages flexibility in thought that is very different from the conditioned responses pre-programmed by past experience. I suggest that such subtlety is a much-needed quality in facing complex issues in the new biology. While we are reminded constantly of the newness of the techniques that are now possible, a historical appreciation of the ways new science has become used or abused in the past may help us to find ways forward. This is not the same as nostalgia about the past, but learning from past mistakes and past experiences. Wisdom relies on the sum of the cultural learning of past generations; it is an expression of maturity that is prepared to be patient, rather than automatically welcoming all that is novel and different. However, at the same time it reflects an attitude that is open to the possibility for the good. This means that a Wisdom ethic will not automatically condemn genetic engineering out of hand, but consider it carefully in the light of past experiences and the possibilities for the future.

Aquinas' idea of prudence as discussed so far seems to be following Aristotle's treatment of prudence, or *phronesis*, sometimes translated as 'practical Wisdom'. This was mentioned in Chapter

4. It was also suggested that Aquinas takes the philosophical notion of prudence further in that he translates it into a much more theological concept of Wisdom. For Aquinas the virtue of prudence will never reach its desired aim of goodness through human effort alone because of the distortions of human sin. It seems to me very important that this reminder of the real possibility of human weakness is not glossed over by over-enthusiastic approaches to the new biology.

For Aquinas, prudence can only become fully aligned with God's Wisdom through the gift of the Holy Spirit, engendering the theological virtues of faith, hope and charity in addition to Wisdom. In other words, while Wisdom may be acquired by use of reason and study, it may also come through the gift of the Holy Spirit inclining the individual towards a life of virtue. The seven gifts of the Holy Spirit are courage, piety, fear, counsel, understanding, *scientia* and Wisdom. Counsel is part of prudence, hence four of the intellectual virtues are analogous to the gifts of the Spirit. When virtues are acquired through the use of reason, they are intellectual virtues; when they come as gifts from God, then they are gifts of the Holy Spirit. The precise way God infuses such gifts into the mind is left obscure. It is love that is the supreme means through which humanity can know intuitively the mind of God.

Aquinas recognizes that the natural good is never realized in a human community because of sin, so that conflicts are always bound to arise. Given this limitation, Aquinas ascribes to love a unifying function, to which all the virtues are ultimately directed. For Aquinas, then, Wisdom in a community, like that in an individual, finds its fulfilment through love, understood as charity. Through the gifts of God's grace in faith, hope and charity, humanity becomes deified. Aquinas links the three gifts associated with the speculative intellect with two of the three theological virtues, faith and love. While understanding and *scientia* are linked with faith, it is Wisdom that is supremely linked with charity. Significantly, the beatitude associated with Wisdom is that of the peacemakers. Aquinas suggests that the friendship of charity is crucial, as it removes the clash of wills that leads to discord and instead promotes peace.

The opposite of Wisdom is Folly, interpreted as rooted in the sin of *luxuria*, or lust, that is, the absence of self-discipline in desires of this world. Moral evil undermines Wisdom by corruption of the intellect as well as the will. The one who has no Wisdom at all is a fool, characterized by a dull conscience, wrong standards and self-deception. Hence, for Aquinas the will is involved in the pursuit of Wisdom or Folly.

Aquinas' understanding of Wisdom as an intellectual virtue that is acquired by the *will* might seem counter-intuitive, as we tend to think of the excellence of the mind in terms of intelligence. For Aquinas the will desires the good by nature, but it is the task of the intellect to judge something as good. The task of judging is influenced by the passions, so that the passions, will and intellect act together to lead to certain actions. For example, under the influence of anger something may seem good that shows itself in a different light once the anger has subsided. Moreover, Aquinas suggests that the will influences the intellect, commanding it to adopt a particular belief. While such an idea may seem odd, closer reflection shows how this is particularly relevant in the case of those on different sides of the European debate over genetic engineering of crops. I suggest that it is the passion for science or the passion for the earth that seems to be influencing the rational judgments of the mind in its perception of the good. While both passions are worthy ones, Aquinas challenges us to look beyond these to a passion for Wisdom, understood as conformity to the Wisdom of God.

While Aquinas is certainly unaware of the social dimensions of existence that condition all our choices, the tendency today is to look for biological or social determinants of human action, instead of facing the real possibility of human freedom. If we recognize the influence of the will in informing our choices, then the real possibility of freedom becomes present. While the influence of our genetics on human behaviour, including our ability to reason, is undisputed, I suggest that this is just one component of being persons made in the image of God. I would fully agree with Ted Peters in his suggestion that human freedom is a real dimension to anthropology.[22] However, it seems to me that Wisdom as a motif qualifies this freedom in directing it in a particular theocentric way. Freedom on its own can easily become irresponsible, even though it is clear that this is not the way Peters himself understands freedom.

Other secular philosophers, such as Alasdair MacIntyre, have taken up and developed the idea of a virtue ethic.[23] In his early work Stanley Hauerwas also develops an ethic of character.[24] He considered this approach to be a way out of the sterility of utilitarianism, which focuses simply on the problem in hand. Significantly, Hauerwas seems to link his idea of character formation with the notion of prudence in Aquinas. In his later work Hauerwas shifts to consider the community dimension of moral discernment and speaks more in terms of narrative.[25] However, Aquinas' understanding of prudence includes this community aspect, especially that in the church, in a way that is much more difficult for Hauerwas' character ethic.

Aquinas' eternal law of God or Wisdom of God is imperfectly expressed in *both* moral laws and natural laws. In as far as the natural laws in creation participate in the Wisdom of God, they are expressions of God's Wisdom. For Aquinas the life of virtue was only possible through friendship, interpreted as charity. Such friendship enfolds the life of every Christian in relationship with God and others. Milbank suggests that our self-identity, once constituted by love and friendship has, since the Enlightenment, become replaced by the need for control and ownership in a way that extends from possessions to persons.[26] While feminists have argued that patriarchal cultures have always fostered a sense of control over women and nature, Milbank seems to be suggesting that this need to control has become so dominant that it has eclipsed all other ways of relating. Aquinas' idea of friendship is relevant in that it counters the trend towards control in contemporary society. I suggest that this sense of control is made explicit in the desire of humanity to intervene in nature through genetic engineering and cloning. Furthermore, once the idea of friendship is reinstated, this can then be extended to include friendship with all living creatures, even though the nature of such friendship will follow a different dynamic from that between humans.

Aquinas' understanding of friendship goes beyond that of Aristotle in that he suggests that our chief vocation is to be in a relationship of friendship with God. Such friendship is no easy romantic attachment, but a gradual transformation of the human heart so that we can enter more fully into the life of God. Our true and lasting happiness comes from discovering the good that God intends for us, and this can only ultimately be found in God. The ultimate good for Aquinas is not Aristotle's *eudaimonia*, a life of flourishing, but *beatitudo*, that is, partaking and reflecting on the beauty, goodness and holiness of God. This distinguishes human activity from that of other creatures. Such friendship is only possible by divine gift, given by the grace of God. Receiving such a gift heals wounds and allows us not only to love God but also to live a new kind of life that is in keeping with the desire of God. Moreover, such a life of friendship with God is inseparable from a life in Christ, who both mediates for us and is an example of perfect friendship with God.

How might a sense of friendship influence our attitude to genetic engineering? Clearly, human activity to be truly human, according to Aquinas, is to be in right relationship with God. Right and just relationships between human beings and all creatures follow from this fundamental transformation of right relationship with God. In the case of genetic manipulation of crops, the framework of friendship with all peoples of all cultures needs to be one of the most significant factors in qualifying such manipulations. The tendency for an anthropocentric restriction of issues of social justice in genetics to manipulations of the human genome misses out both indirect issues of social justice through the genetic manipulation of the non-human world and consideration of justice for the whole creation.[27] I suggest that a Wisdom ethic resists such anthropocentrism, while giving due respect to the particular worth of human beings. Although at the time of Aquinas the primary function of animals was thought to be in the service of humanity, he still insisted that we respect the inner purpose of all creatures as given by the Wisdom of God. Our knowledge of ecology is such that we can no longer think of creatures in isolation from one another. Hence genetic manipulation of crops needs to be considered in the light of changes to the goals and goods of all other creatures as well.

I propose that it is respect for the inner purpose of all creatures that allows us to enter into friendship with them. This is not the same as suggesting that humanity relates to all creatures in friendship to the same extent as friendship between humans. Rather, friendship includes charity, a love that goes beyond difference in identifying as far as possible with the particular inner goal of all creatures. Such identification will then qualify all particular manipulations through genetic engineering and animal cloning. Human interventions need to be considered on a case-by-case basis. We then ask ourselves, given our knowledge of this creature, is this change for its ultimate good or is it simply related to the desire for human benefits? In addition, while the principle of choosing the good for a creature can be upheld, a reference to consequentialism is also appropriate as an additional factor to be considered. In other words, a Wisdom ethic takes into account long- and short-term consequences, but is not simply guided by these factors alone. In the case of animal cloning, I have my doubts if any cloning represents the good for that creature. However, it may in some cases be necessary to qualify this in those rare situations where human life is dependent on the use of animal cloning. Where there are possible alternatives, then these need to be given preference.

Finally, friendship with each other as mirrored in our friendship with God will lead us to have a profound respect for the sanctity of life. Even secular philosophers have used the sanctity of life principle as a guide for particular ethical action in the case of humans.[28] Human cloning for reproductive purposes is a denial of what it means to be human in the denial of family relationships. Human cloning for therapeutic purposes is more problematic ethically, yet if we consider genetics, life has begun with conception. Of course, any such *conceptus* is not a person, but given the sanctity of all human life, however nascent, to use such products of human manipulation to treat diseases seems to me to be unacceptable. The tide is against such restraint as the possibility of helping those in pain through these techniques is held up as the ultimate goal to be achieved. No one can deny the basic right of human beings to care for those who suffer. However, it seems to me that we need to think much more carefully about alternatives. Can we presume that such human cloning is part of God's intention for humanity?

Conclusions

The issues raised by genetic engineering and other techniques of the new biology such as cloning present an ethical challenge that has become the subject of intense debates, from the perspectives of both secular and Christian approaches to ethics. The language of these debates is often cast in consequentialist terms, assessing the technology from the detached position of the observer of both risks and benefits. Nonetheless, a major drawback in all these debates is that the risks are often as yet unknown in real terms, and the benefits are also as yet unrealized. There are conflicting and confusing reports of both the possible risks and benefits. This confusion is not helped by the fact that behind the support or rejection of genetic technologies there lies first of all a blurring together of different categories. For example, the support for GM crops cannot be based on information about the medical benefits to be gained from genetically engineering plant species or somatic therapy in humans. There again, the fear of eugenics or risks to human health through consumption of genetically engineered food cannot become the basis for rejection of all kinds of genetic engineering.

I suggest that the debate reaches gridlock because behind the support for genetic engineering lies the presumption that to be against it would be somehow to deny science its claim on knowledge. Again, behind the resistance to genetic engineering is a feeling that power is now in the hands of those who are irresponsible in their attitude towards both people and the planet. Neither caricature is helpful, nor takes us very far in the debate. The claim for the intrinsic worth or otherwise of genetic engineering or associated technologies such as cloning also reflects this balance of loyalties.

Another possible alternative, which seems to be the official view of the Roman Catholic Church, is to condone all technologies that apply to the animal and vegetable world, with certain qualifications, but reject such technology where it interferes with human reproduction and procreation. However, such a view fails to appreciate fully the close interrelationship and interdependency between humanity and the natural world.

I suggest that theology has a more vital role to play in ethics than simply condemning those actions that impinge on an infringement of human dignity. Rather, an ethical position that draws on the Thomistic tradition of Wisdom as discernment can become the basis for a more subtle approach to the pressing issues facing us in genetic engineering. Of course, this does not necessarily exclude the possibility of considering consequentialist or deontological ethical alternatives. However, the fruitfulness of these positions alone may be limited. Wisdom is helpful in that it does not deny reason or deny science its place, but it puts it in a wider context of social justice, prudence and temperance. Such qualities have tended to be in short supply in the heated public debates over genetic engineering.

Perhaps, with time, the voice of Wisdom will once again be heard. It is a voice that speaks not just on behalf of humanity, but on behalf of the whole natural order in a relationship that spells community and friendship. Yet this is no romantic idealism, rather a searching for right relationships between God, humanity and the natural world that offers a way forward in how to think about the earth. It is an intermediary between the mechanistic model of genetic engineering and idealistic attachment to the earth. It is the contours of such attachment, as expressed in the Gaia hypothesis, to which I will turn in the chapters that follow.

7

An alternative environmental science? Gaia

The method of reductionism that is the basis for much of modern science was mentioned in Chapter 2. While the new physics seems to suggest a more open-ended mythology emerging from the physical processes themselves, the assumption that at the heart of reality we still find physics and mathematics remains intact. Hence, while these models seem to be more 'organic', at one level they still draw methodologically on reductionism. Even chaos theory, which is prepared to consider events in whole systems, seeks to find physical and mathematical explanations of such events. An alternative, more radical approach to science relies on a 'holistic' scientific method, one that is directed deliberately towards understanding the whole system in terms that make sense at the level of the system, rather than simply through individual processes at the chemical or physical level. As discussed earlier in Chapter 2, this has been a general characteristic of the field of ecology for a number of years. However, it took the maverick scientist James Lovelock to popularize this idea and extend it to include other branches of science as well. Now ecological principles are broadened so that the whole earth, not just a single community, is considered to act as a giant ecosystem known collectively as the *Gaia* hypothesis.

Many green theologians and philosophers have warmed to this hypothesis in a way that would have been impossible with more traditional scientific views. Not only does Lovelock's thesis imply a rejection of reductionism, it also implies a rejection of the concept of the world as mechanism. An organic view of the world is presupposed in a way that is suggestive of an alternative model for science. Process philosopher David Griffin, for example, argues against the idea that modern science requires a mechanistic view of nature; instead he suggests that belief in a transcendent God encouraged the 'disenchantment' of science and a mechanistic approach to nature, rather than science as such. The solution now becomes an emphasis on God as immanent in the world, along with a corresponding re-enchantment of science.[1]

It is the purpose of this chapter to examine the different scientific interpretations of Gaia and point to its significance for the philosophy of science, before dealing with the theological and ethical interpretations of Gaia in the following chapter. I will suggest that, as is the case for genetic science, some understanding of the scientific basis for Gaia is necessary in order to come to informed theological and ethical conclusions.

Introduction

James Lovelock freely admits that he is something of an eccentric. He was also prepared to be bold in his ideas later on in life, for only 'the old can happily make fools of themselves. The idea that the earth is alive is at the outer bounds of scientific credibility.'[2] Yet the idea that the earth is alive is precisely what Lovelock goes on to suggest in his Gaia hypothesis. How did he come to such a conclusion?

He describes his scientific journey as a quest in search for evidence for the idea that the earth is alive. His earliest research in this vein involved the invention of an electron captor detector, based on the chemical technique of gas chromatography. Lovelock discovered that this detector was far more sensitive than other methods in finding traces of chemicals, such as pesticides, in living systems, including the gases of the atmosphere. His discovery traced pesticides in 'penguins of Antartica' through to 'nursing mothers in the United States'. Rachel Carson's book *Silent Spring* used these results to argue against widespread use of pesticides. This book, arguably, was the one that launched the green movement of the 1970s.[3] Lovelock's detector proved to be a useful tool in detecting toxic polluting chemicals, such as peroxyacetyl nitrate (PAN) and polychlorobiphenols (PCBs), which are important components of environmental pollution, along with chlorofluoro-carbons and nitrous oxide, which reduce ozone levels in the stratosphere. Moreover, armed with such a detector, he could travel the world and engage with scientists of different disciplines. His background as an inventor was one that lent itself to inter-disciplinarity in a way that would have been much more difficult if he had been an expert in one particular discipline.

Another clue to the puzzle came from Lovelock's invitation by NASA to be part of the search for life on Mars. He describes the thrill of the first invitation in 1961 to be included in NASA's lunar instrument mission as 'as full of promise and excitement as a first love letter'.[4] Back in the 1960s space exploration was culturally the area that most excited the scientific imagination. It seemed full of unlimited promise, and captured a sense of scientific utopia perhaps only paralleled in the 1980s and 1990s by the Human Genome Project. Lovelock was no exception to this mood. He admits that he was disappointed with the degree of interest by biologists in their search for life on Mars. He started asking more fundamental questions about life itself. How do we really know that life on Mars will be the same as that on earth, if it exists? He felt troubled by the specialization of biologists that rendered the more fundamental question – what is life? – unanswered. The automatic, instinctive recognition of life remained undefined and undefinable.

For a physicist, 'life' could best be defined in terms of its neces-sary conditions for existence, that is, in terms of energy flow, so that life is able to decrease entropy and hence increase order at the expense of free energy or substances taken in from the environ-ment. This definition applies not just to biological life but also to physical processes, such as fire, or human products, such as refrigerators. But in spite of its limitations, Lovelock believed that this definition was one that *points us in the right direction* as a way of broadening the meaning of what we commonly understand by the term 'life'. It gave him the important clue that the atmosphere of a planet that supports life would be markedly different from a lifeless one. Since Mars has no oceans, the only external environment with which life could engage would be the gaseous envelope. Furthermore, it would not matter where on the planet the detector landed, since changes to gaseous composition would be detected at a site removed from life itself.

The next stage in the puzzle came from trying to detect evidence of life from sampling the atmosphere of the earth. The results went beyond just detecting life, they suggested that the atmosphere itself was being regulated by the sum total of life processes on the earth. At the time many geochemists simply viewed the gaseous composition of the earth as merely the product of volcanic activity or other gaseous emissions from the earth. This was long before the idea that deforestation might be contributing to a 'greenhouse' effect had become part of common parlance. The idea that the atmosphere was a dynamic extension of the biosphere was hard for scientists of the time to accept. As far as the Martian experiments were concerned, the atmosphere there was known to be mostly carbon dioxide – Mars was therefore almost certainly a lifeless planet. However, Lovelock went on to elaborate the idea of the earth as a living system in a way that would have been impossible without his earlier research into trying to find life on Mars.

When James Lovelock first proposed his hypothesis, he presented Gaia as a single unified model. He recognized that the earth is unique in the solar system in its composition of gases. In particular, it is the presence of a sufficient concentration of oxygen to support higher life forms that marks out the earth as very different from the other planets. Lovelock was able to predict that other planets would be inhospitable for life by analysis of their atmospheres. Mars and Venus, for example, have atmospheres that contain over 90% carbon dioxide and less than 3% nitrogen, while the earth has an atmosphere of 79% nitrogen, 21% oxygen and 0.03% carbon dioxide. He also showed that the temperature of the earth and its gaseous composition have stayed very nearly constant over millions of years. Since the sun is getting progressively hotter, one would have predicted a rise in the earth's temperature and a change in its gaseous composition.

No one disputes these scientific facts. As indicated above, Lovelock proposed a novel explanation to account for the apparently anomalous features found on earth. He suggested that not only does life adapt to environmental conditions, but that life itself serves to regulate those conditions to keep them within the necessary boundaries to support life. Inspired by the poet William Golding, and something of a poet himself, Lovelock gave the name Gaia to his hypothesis, drawn from the idea of the mother goddess of ancient mythology. The idea of the earth as alive is akin to thinking of it like a giant redwood tree. While most of it consists of 'dead' matter, such as cellulose, it is still very much alive.

Lovelock's own description of the Gaia hypothesis in more scientific terms is this, namely

the temperature, oxidation state, acidity and certain aspects of the rocks and waters are at any time kept constant, and that this homeostasis is maintained by active feedback processes operated automatically and unconsciously by the biota. The conditions are only constant in the short term and evolve in synchrony with the changing needs of the biota as it evolves. Life and the environment are so closely coupled that evolution concerns Gaia, not the organisms or the environment taken separately.[5]

The essential elegance of his hypothesis has attracted support from both scientists and the public alike. Moreover, as hinted above, it offered a new way of approaching knowledge of the earth that looked at interactions on a whole planetary level – or *geophysiology*, to use Lovelock's nomenclature. Many scientists, however, were uneasy with Lovelock's ideas. One reason was that it seemed to suggest the idea of a *purpose* for life, namely, to keep the environment constant. Such purpose, or *teleology*, is anathema to traditional science, which aims to provide purely rational explanations.

Lovelock tried to refute the charge of purposefulness by showing that a computer model system called 'Daisyworld' could regulate the temperature of the earth automatically. This model system portrays two populations of daisies, one of which is pale and reflects light and heat, while the other is dark and absorbs heat. The light daisies are presumed to have a higher temperature optimum for growth compared with the dark daisies. As the temperature rises, the numbers of light daisies increase, which leads to a drop in temperature as light is reflected from this variety. By contrast, as the temperature falls, the dark daisies increase in number, which leads to a subsequent increase in surface temperature as more heat is absorbed. This computer model certainly did not 'prove' Lovelock's hypothesis, as some interpreters have suggested, but rather showed that teleology need not be introduced into his model in order for it to work.

There are, in addition, theoretical problems with any proof of Gaia based on computer constructions. If the biota as a living system contains the regulatory device, how can we begin to test such a regulatory feedback system when, since it acts for the biota as a whole, it must involve interspecies communication from microbes to humankind? Merely showing the plausibility of local temperature regulation by a theoretical shift in populations of daisies leaves unanswered both how the detection system 'chooses' the temperature range and how different species act in concert to 'decide' when the negative feedback should begin. Furthermore, it would be quite possible to create destabilizing biological systems that raise the temperature further when the environmental temperature increased.

Let us imagine another theoretical world where lupins were the only species, rather than daisies. Imagine a 'Lupinworld' where there is an association of lupins and microbes. An increase in temperature would increase the activity of microorganisms and so increase respiration rates and carbon dioxide emissions, leading to an increase in temperature. Such an increase in temperature leads to further destabilization of the system, rather than stabilization back to pre-set norms.

The research so far on Gaia begs the question of whether anyone has searched for these biological destabilizing systems, as well as stabilizing ones. Since we know that the earth acts as a stable system, any destabilizing systems would be limited to those that would not, overall, lead to final destabilizing of the systems of the earth. However, there is no reason in principle why some such systems would not exist. The question then is: what is the mechanism whereby stabilizing systems have come to dominate destabilizing ones?

Other scientists are prepared to accept some, but not all of Lovelock's ideas. It is this *range* of possible interpretations of Gaia that can lead to confusion in the debate, especially for non-specialists. Evidence that supports one aspect of Gaia can sometimes be used to support the hypothesis *in toto*. In what follows, I will offer a survey of the different possible scientific explanations of Gaia.

The interconnected model

This interpretation of Gaia requires us to make the least number of assumptions, and is accepted by the majority of scientists. It says, simply, that living organisms on the planet, collectively known as the biota, influence the external environment. In some ways this interpretation of Gaia adds relatively little to scientific knowledge since it has been known for many years that living things alter their external conditions, such as in the production of carbon dioxide in respiration. It does, nonetheless, stress the importance of living things in their *contribution* to changes in the gaseous atmosphere around the earth in a way that was not adequately acknowledged by geochemists in the past. It stops short of suggesting that these atmospheric changes are in some way *regulated* by the living systems. This view does, at least, encourage a more holistic approach to science so that the way different living things influence the atmospheric composition can be examined and tested. According to this understanding of Gaia, it is quite possible that some species, such as certain micro-organisms, will act to shift atmospheric conditions away from equilib-rium required for other higher life forms and so destabil-ize the system. As mentioned earlier, if scientists just look for stabilizing systems they may miss those that act in an opposite way and so distort the evidence in favour of 'regulation' by the biota.

Those biologists who are most attracted to this view are aware of the remarkable ability of microorganisms to adapt to their external conditions. One interesting feature of the history of the earth is not just the relatively constant conditions of temperature and gaseous composition, but also the oscillations of variables such as temperature and gas composition around a mean. Such variations led to successive Ice Ages in our planet's history. Lovelock suggests that the evolution of communities of organisms best suited to regulate the atmospheric conditions around particular norms was favoured in the evolutionary process. Although such a hypothesis is impossible to prove or disprove, the history of microbial adaptation to the earth's earliest conditions gives us some clues.

Prokaryotic organisms are the key elements in any picture of geochemical cycling. Not only do they constitute the bulk of the total biomass of the earth, they are responsible for the geochemical cycles that are central to life's continued existence. To put it bluntly, microbes could survive quite happily without higher organisms, but not the other way round. Many millions of years ago the atmosphere around the earth became aerobic, rather than anaerobic, in what has sometimes been described as a massive 'oxygen' pollution event. Anaerobic is the term used to describe an environment that is free of oxygen, as opposed to aerobic conditions where oxygen is present. Lovelock estimates that the appearance of oxygen as the dominant atmospheric gas was between the Archean and Proterozoic periods. Microbial photosynthesis used sunlight as a source of energy and allowed carbon fixation from carbon dioxide alongside the release of oxygen. Parallel respiratory processes only used some of this oxygen, so the concentration of oxygen gradually rose.

Microbial life has been detected as far back as the oldest sedimentary rocks, at around 4,000 million years ago, when liquid water first appeared on the earth. At this stage Gaia could not have acted as a regulatory system, as the earliest life would have to have simply adapted to the external conditions. The first life forms were likely to be anaerobic fermenters, replaced by free-living photosynthetic microbes. Yet this represents just one aspect of the resourcefulness of microbes. Today we can find bacteria that can use sulphate or carbon dioxide as chemical means for the oxidation of organic compounds needed for life. Even more dramatic is the discovery in volcanic springs, at temperatures of ninety degrees Celsius, of ancient autotrophic species of bacteria that fix carbon dioxide from the energy generated from the reaction of hydrogen with sulphur.

An *autotroph* is defined as any living organism that synthesizes organic substances from inorganic ones using light or chemical energy. All green plants and many planktonic organisms are autotrophs, using sunlight to convert carbon dioxide into sugars by photosynthesis. In the case described here no sunlight is needed, rather the energy is obtained via a chemical reaction. Alongside these bacteria there are heterotrophic bacteria which then oxidize fixed carbon by reducing sulphur or sulphate to hydrogen sulphide, a process known as sulphur respiration.[6] A *heterotroph* is defined as any living organism that obtains its energy from organic substances produced by other organisms. Ultimately all heterotrophs depend on autotrophs. This quite remarkable self-contained ecosystem is independent of oxygen and sunlight as sources of energy.

Bacteria have also been discovered that obtain energy from the oxidation not only of hydrogen, nitrogen or sulphur or iron, but also more unusual elements such as antimony, arsenic, copper, manganese, selenium, uranium or even tin. Furthermore, if we examine even the most extreme environments known to exist on the planet in terms of pressure, salinity, temperature, acidity and so on, we find microbes have exploited these environments.

In addition to this diversity during the history of the planet, microbes have shown a remarkable degree of plasticity. Not only have they responded to a sudden change in oxygen concentration of the atmosphere, by evoking aerobic respiration, they have also responded to the depletion of mineral supply by nitrogen fixation and to the shortage of reducing power by splitting water molecules. The phase of adaptation may merge into a phase of dependence, so the adaptation of some life forms to oxygen, for example, was followed by dependence. The pervasive nature of the dependence of eukaryotes on oxygen obscures the fact that our microbial ancestors actually took advantage and adapted to the presence of oxygen in the atmosphere. By contrast, there is relatively little evidence to suggest that these early microbes adapted by changing or even moderating external conditions.

Furthermore, if the temperature and gases were different then it seems highly probable that microbes would have adapted to these conditions, meaning we would have a very different kind of life from the one that we know today. To postulate that life regulates seems to be a circular argument, as we know of no other life. It is rather like a biological version of the anthropic principle, except in this case all the environmental constants seem to be most suited for life to emerge.

J.W. Kirchner believes that according to the Gaia hypothesis the biota had destablizing effects early in the history of the planet, but now they are supposed to be stabilizing. This leads to a circular argument where:

> I'm left wondering what conceivable events could not be used as evidence for Gaia. If Gaia stabilises and Gaia destabilises, then is there any possible behaviour that is not Gaian? Is Gaia, then, simply a theory so flexible (and by implication free of specific empirical content) that it can be wrapped around any paleoclimatic record?[7]

Of course, if we reject Lovelock's hypothesis and suggest that the microbes failed to moderate the temperature and gaseous composition of earth's atmosphere, then we still need some other explanation to account for the differences in temperature and gases between the planets. The most common explanation offered as an alternative draws on the idea of dissipative structures that represents a type of control systems theory. Control systems can operate in physical, chemical, biochemical and biological spheres. In other words, the existence of a control system does not prove that 'life' is part of the regulation. The theory of dissipative structures was developed by Ilya Prigogine and his co-workers in Brussels, for which he won a Nobel Prize in 1977 – ironically, perhaps, almost coincident with Lovelock's Gaia hypothesis.

Dissipative structures are organized configurations of matter that are held far from equilibrium by a flow of energy. Another common characteristic is that the matter in them goes through cycles or oscillations. Even though Prigogine based his theory around the observation of fluid convection cells in a physical process, dissipative structures of increasing complexity have been discovered, for example, in chemical, biochemical and biological systems. The oscillating cycles of biological systems are good instances of dissipative structures in living organisms, which were recognized not long after Prigogine proposed his theory in 1972.[8] A more intriguing suggestion is whether the earth as a whole functions in some way as a dissipative structure. In this case it can be understood as an organized structure dependent on a flow of energy through the biota.[9] One of the characteristics of dissipative structures held away from equilibrium is that they may swing between two stable states. Such a model could explain the swing in temperatures that we find in the Ice Ages. In this case the ultimate determinant is the flow of solar energy rather than the biota.

Hence, dissipative theory could serve to explain otherwise puzzling features of the earth system, such as the constancy of the atmosphere and temperature held away from equilibrium, the bio-geochemical cycling of biologically important elements and the periodic oscillations of temperature around a pre-set mean. It is ironical, perhaps, that Lovelock himself prefers to define life itself more in terms of a system of energy flow than other possible narrower definitions, such as the ability to reproduce. Hence this model is not all that far from Lovelock's proposal. Indeed, Lovelock cites Prigogine's theory with approval, though he believes that it does not go far enough in any definition of life. Gaia makes a significant step beyond this notion of self-organization.[10] The crucial difference is that dissipative theory makes no special claim to evoke the biota as part of the regulatory process, which, as I show below, is an additional component to Lovelock's argument.

The homeostatic process model

This model of Gaia proposes that the biota regulates the atmospheric conditions of the planet; moreover, it is a view that Lovelock insists is essential for his hypothesis. According to this view, different species act in concert so as to produce conditions necessary for life. More correctly, this could be described as a *rheostat*, as it brings conditions back to pre-set norms. It is quite possible that the regulation system would become 'saturated' and then shift to a new state of equilibrium. This would presumably entail the death of all those species that required the earlier range of conditions. Such a catastrophic event has already taken place in the lifetime of the earth, as mentioned above, with the shift from anaerobic to aerobic conditions in what would have appeared as a massive 'oxygen' pollution event.

This rheostatic model sounds elegant, but it does beg a number of questions. For example, it is impossible to state which process came first, the stable environmental conditions or life adapted to such conditions. It is well known that inorganic systems have feedback mechanisms that keep conditions constant. Biologists have sometimes used control systems theory taken from engineering as models to describe regulation in simple organisms. It becomes far more difficult to envisage a control system with a sensor acting for all living organisms.

There are known biochemical steps in living organisms that regulate the overall flow through the different geochemical cycles, such as the nitrate or sulphur cycle. Nitrate reductase is one good example of an enzyme that is thought to be key in nitrate metabolism. Particular genes code for these enzymes. There are also chemicals that act on such enzymes in order to speed up or reduce their activity.

G. R. Williams has proposed that Gaia can be thought of as having a molecular biology, arguing that the key enzymes that affect overall flux of nitrogen into living organisms are determined by particular genes.[11] While at first sight this seems to be an attractive suggestion, there are a number of difficulties with his proposal that such investigations would be an aid to understanding the Gaia hypothesis itself. The nitrogen regulation system, even in a single species, is far more complicated than Williams assumes.

In the first place particular internal pools of nutrients, which are often very far from the external environmental concentrations, affect the regulatory processes in cells. The internal pools of nitrate in a number of different organisms are controlled by regulation of nitrate uptake in such a way that the internal concentration is kept well above that found in the growing medium.[12] In this case the enzymes necessary for nitrogen assimilation may not be as important in the control of nitrogen flux *from the outside medium*, as Williams assumes. Furthermore, for his model to work the activity of such enzymes would have to be related to *external* nitrogen levels, which is unlikely to be the case if internal pools of nitrogen exist in higher concentrations than the external medium. Moreover, in many systems nitrate uptake processes appear to be just as critical as enzymes such as nitrate reductase in determining overall flux. Of course, the molecular biology of the uptake systems may be identified, but it is unlikely that such genetic information would assist in resolving how *external conditions* are kept within limits.

Secondly, in order to feedback on the process, a sensor would have to act in concert with all other living biota that contribute to the overall external pool. This requires the coordinated genetic activity of myriad different organisms in a way that I find quite frankly far-fetched. This discussion will be resumed in the section below.

While living things could, then, be seen as very much a contributory part of the rheostat system, there seems to be no obvious reason why life itself should persist as such in order for a rheostatic system to exist. In other words, it is entirely possible that the new equilibrium state could be reached which effectively destroys all life, apart from possibly a few extremely resistant bacterial species.

The evidence in support of homeostatic regulation has focused on recently discovered cycles of elements, such as sulphur and nitrogen. The sulphur cycle is well-documented, and I will describe it briefly here by way of illustration. Marine algae are known to reduce sulphate dissolved in seawater to gaseous dimethyl sulphide, or DMS, which is then carried to the land through dissolution in rain droplets. Eventually the sulphate returns to the sea via rivers. Hence the production of DMS is part of the geophysiological recycling of sulphur from the sea to the land. That such recycling takes place is not particularly controversial scientifically. However, Lovelock suggested in addition that DMS produced by the algae is part of a Gaian system of climate regulation.

As the temperature rises the DMS produced by the algae increases. The DMS acts as nucleation sites for cloud droplet formation, which affects the density of cloud above the ocean surface. A higher cloud density reduces the temperature and consequently the DMS flux. This allows an increase in temperature in the absence of cloud formation, which completes the cycle. How far does the evidence suggest such homeostatic regulation of temperature? Experiments show that the regulation of DMS production is not a simple process. For example, as with nitrogen, there appear to be a number of different pools of dimethyl sulphide, which means that the factors that regulate its release into the oceans are highly complex. The production of dimethyl sulphide in marine alga goes through an intermediary dimethyl sulfonio propionate, or DMSP. No clear relationship could be found between the abundance of algal fronds and either DMSP or DMS. Furthermore, there is no evidence of a direct relationship between DMS production and climate changes.

Other experiments suggest that while there is evidence for release of DMS from different species of marine algae, there is no clear relationship between climate and speciation with respect to DMS production.[13] Osmoregulation is defined as the maintenance of cellular salt content, and is particularly critical in saline environments, such as seawater. DMSP acts as an important osmoregulator, and marine biologists have discovered a clear relationship between DMSP and salinity.[14] The use of DMSP as a chemical basis for osmoregulation complicates any possible regulatory function that it may have in temperature control. Other complicating factors include the known influence of carbon dioxide levels on temperature. Polluting compounds are known to have a similar effect to DMS in acting as a nucleation sites for water droplet formation, and serve to complicate any analysis of the effectiveness of the DMS cycle still further.

There is also the added theoretical issue of the effectiveness of DMS production as a temperature regulator in evolutionary terms. In this case the evolution of DMS as a means for climate control is not 'cost-effective' since the main cellular function that needs to be addressed by marine organisms in salty conditions is osmoregulation. Lovelock suggests that the osmoregulatory function may have evolved first, followed by an additional role in temperature regulation.[15] However, this still leaves open the question of how osmoregulation and temperature regulation are co-ordinated, since osmoregulation is acting to keep *internal* cellular conditions constant in a fluctuating environment, while his proposed temperature regulation acts to keep *external* conditions constant. Furthermore, the beneficial effects of temperature regulation would apply to phytoplankton that do not produce DMS, hence these species would have access to more resources and nutrients than the DMS producers. I will return to the possible evolutionary questions around the Gaia hypothesis in the section below.

These apparent inconsistencies in the data are important, since they point to a relationship between sulphur cycling and climate but fall short of providing firm evidence for feedback regulation controlled by the biota. At best it seems to me that there is limited support for local Gaian systems acting in such a way to include biota in geophysiological processes such as the cycling of sulphur between the sea to the land. However, to suggest that Gaia functions in this respect as a way of controlling temperature seems to me to be far more tenuous.

The cooperative evolutionary model

The idea of the earth as a cooperative system draws on Lovelock's belief that Gaia is part of the evolutionary process of the earth. The language used to describe Gaia is that of a single organism, which has evolved so as to allow the persistence of life. The belief among scientists that the earth acts as a single organism is not new. It was held, for example, by the Scottish scientist James Hutton in 1785 and the Russian scientist/philosopher Yergraf Korolenko, who lived in the nineteenth century in the Ukraine. Lovelock acknowledges his debt to Hutton, Korolenko and Korolenko's cousin, Vladimir Vernadsky. An alternative to Lovelock's model is that inorganic material and life evolved *together* through a process described as co-evolution. Lovelock assumes that Gaia evolved independently of life, but emerged as a type of 'awakening' with the evolution of photosynthetic organisms, that is, ones that could use carbon dioxide and sunlight as a form of energy.

The difficulty with all such speculations is that it is not possible to design a scientific test to prove these ideas. While homeostatic regulation could, in theory, be tested, as shown above, the idea of the evolution of Gaia as a single system offers no means for any scientific investigation. It therefore clashes with one of the paradigms of science that requires an idea to be testable if it is to call itself science. Even Darwin's theory of evolution, which remains speculative to the extent that it is never possible to go back to the earliest history of the planet, remains testable through access to evolutionary fossil records and contemporary examples of evolution over shorter periods of history. Any attempt to find fossil record evidence for Gaia has so far proved inconclusive.

The belief that the whole planet cooperates so as to act as a single organism seems to suggest a cooperative model for evolution rather than the competitive model characteristic of Darwin's theory. The idea of co-evolution separates the evolution of life from the response of the inorganic environment, which cannot 'evolve' in the traditional Darwinian sense as it carries no genetic information. Lovelock's model implies that the biota regulates the inorganic environment as well, as part of one genetic complex. All species are acting in concert for the survival of the whole, rather than competing for individual survival.

Although Lovelock speaks in terms of evolution and natural selection, his theory is more closely aligned to E.O. Wilson's sociobiological model as compared to Richard Dawkins's explanation of evolution in terms of genetics. Wilson argued that species evolved in such a way as to encourage cooperation rather than selfish competition. The cooperative behaviour that has evolved in species such as ants and other social animals becomes a model for human behaviour. This impinges on the ethical implications of Gaia, which I will discuss in the next chapter. The opposite alternative is that evolution has favoured the development of behaviour that is based on the preservation of particular genes, the so called 'selfish gene' model of Richard Dawkins mentioned in Chapter 2.

Dawkins strongly rejects any 'organismic' ideas, and argues that individual survival is the prime genetic determinant. He does, nonetheless, admit that genes can interact within populations, but the primary determinant is from within the organism itself rather than from other organisms. He suggests that 'Genes seem likely, other things being equal, to exert more power over nearby phenotypic characters than over distant ones.'[16] Williams tries to get round this difficulty by agreeing that the level of genetic interaction between organisms is not as important as the genetic interaction at the level of individual organisms. However, he then makes the assertion that Gaia represents the regulation of such metabolic steps writ large at a global scale, so that the coordination of cellular metabolism at the level of an organism affects both local and global ecology.[17]

Such a suggestion seems to me to be naïve in its resistance to the complexity of global interactions. In the first place, there is a lack of correlation between activities of particular metabolic pathways and environmental concentrations, even at a relatively local level. Secondly, Williams has ignored the specific membrane transport steps that are just as important in influencing concentrations of metabolites in cells, which are then held far from external concentrations. Finally, his attempt to fit Gaia into a molecular explanation is counter to the overall philosophy of Gaia, which seeks physiological interpretations of results rather than their reduction to molecular processes.

Ford Doolittle is similarly sceptical of the Gaia hypothesis in evolutionary terms, suggesting that the feedback loops that Lovelock cites as evidence for his theory are accidental rather than created by natural selection. Doolittle believes that creating Gaia as a kind of 'protective device', which has its own evolutionary history in addition to the evolutionary history of different species, is not really necessary. He prefers the idea that natural selection at the level of species is responsible for the evolution of life.[18] Of course, not all protagonists of Gaia believe that it has evolved in the way Lovelock implies. Furthermore, Doolittle argues that just as life has not manipulated the physical constants that go to make up what physicists call the anthropic principle, so equally life need not be invoked to account for stable environmental conditions necessary for life. The difference between an evolved Gaian system and one that is dependent simply on chance physical constants relates to the ability of Gaia to withstand threats to its survival. If Gaia as a unitary living system with its own evolutionary history does not exist, then the earth is far more fragile than Lovelock's theory would suggest. This has implications for human behaviour, as will be discussed in the next chapter.

Dawkins's model of the 'selfish gene' has attracted more hostility, perhaps, than the cooperative model of E.O. Wilson. Both seek to extend biology into the realm of ideology through evolutionary ideas. Many biologists have rejected any extension of animal behaviour to human behaviour as an oversimplification of the much more complex construct of human culture. Dawkins's use of the concept of 'memes' was discussed in Chapter 2.

Stephen Clark seems surprised at the 'hasty scorn' of Gaia by some biologists. However, his suggestion that it 'conflicts with no known evolutionary principle' does not reflect the controversial claims of the evolutionary emergence of Gaia. Conventional geneticists find the notion of Gaia feeding back on hereditary material of the biota 'mythical' because it is untestable.[19] It is for this reason that the eminent biologist John Postgate insists that Gaia should remain a 'metaphor', not a mechanism.[20]

The ideological/teleological model

The above cooperative evolutionary model slides into an ideological/teleological model for Gaia where she becomes part of a philosophical 'quest'. While Lovelock has specifically denied that

Gaia is teleological, some of the language he uses opens up the possibility of a teleological interpretation. He admits that over two-thirds of those who wrote to him after the publication of his Gaia books were concerned about the meaning of Gaia in the context of religious faith. The way that Lovelock describes Gaia implies a consciousness, though that is not necessarily his intention. For example, in describing the ability of the earth to withstand violent interruptions from outer space, he muses: 'It is a tribute to the strength of Gaia that our planetary home was restored so promptly and effectively after these events.' In his reflections on God and Gaia Lovelock remarks:

> Belief in God is an act of faith and will remain so. In the same way it is otiose to try and prove that Gaia is alive. Instead, Gaia should be a way to view the Earth, ourselves and our relationships with living things.[21]

The directedness of Gaia is, then, towards the persistence of life, rather than any particular form of life, such as humans. The resonance of Gaia as science with the ancient religious understanding of the earth goddess has been taken up by the eco-feminist Anne Primavesi.[22]

Bound up with the concept of Gaia as ideology is the belief that human beings need to move away from understanding themselves as 'technologist toolmakers' reconstructing the earth to one where they consider themselves as cooperating with the earth in a balanced relationship. Kit Pedler rejects the idea of human beings acting as 'toolmakers', which presupposes the earth is a machine, in favour of human beings identifying with the planet as a living organism. He uses Gaia as a basis for the idea of a 'sustainable' future, that is, one where human beings and their environment are in harmony and are part of the Gaian organism. Pedler claims that 'the blueprint for a sustainable future can only reappear if we look outside our own lives to Gaia and make that the primary, and not the secondary centre of our attention'.[23] The idea that Gaia is both ideological and teleological has clear theological and ethical implications, and I intend to develop this further in the chapter that follows.

Conclusions

It is clear from the above that Gaia as a grand theory can neither be disproved nor proved, and its varied interpretation by scientists reflects their own particular philosophical presuppositions. Those who are still influenced by reductionist methodology in science and logical positivism would be inclined to dismiss Gaia altogether as mythology, tainted further by a creeping form of teleology that seems to imply that Gaia has a purpose in sustaining life. Yet, even for those who are prepared to consider the possibility of Gaia as science, different levels of interpretation come to mind.

The interconnected model acknowledges the core philosophy behind Gaia, namely, that we need to look at interrelationships between organisms and their environment and consider them together. In this model it is still possible to distinguish the influence of different factors affecting the global biosphere. Extending this model a little further, the theory of dissipative structures is invoked in order to explain the constancy in temperature and oscillations that we discover at the level of the whole earth. This automatic system depends on energy flow through the biota, but does not involve the biota in any feedback mechanism. Gaia is important as it resists reductionism in science, while being at the boundary between a model of the world as organic and mechanism. On one level Gaia is organic in that the biota are integral to the process, but on another it is mechanistic in that the system of feedback does not depend directly on sensors in the biota. Clearly, if we define life as the ability of a system to sustain itself away from equilibrium, then even in this model the earth is in some sense alive.

However, Lovelock would like to take us further than this, and offer an organic model of the earth where the biota does play an active role in regulating the environmental conditions. The biota and environment are necessarily joined together in such a way that to separate them is artificial and creates a false impression of autonomy. He rejects the idea that his theory is teleological, that is, purposeful, by proposing an ideal world that can theoretically regulate temperature just by changing populations of white daisies. Of course, this begs the question of how the daisies or any other creature might have evolved so as to keep conditions within a given range needed for growth. If higher temperatures or other conditions had been the norm, maybe other species would have evolved. Nonetheless, the idea that the biota is part of a giant feedback system in a living earth has a certain aesthetic appeal, given the strangeness of the earth compared with other planets.

Whether we explain such cooperation through a selfish gene idea, as does Dawkins, or some other sociobiological process, depends on our own particular presuppositions. If the ultimate level of explanation is the gene, then the selfish gene idea is the only one that is really plausible. However, if we are prepared to consider other levels of complexity, then the dynamics of social cooperation will have evolved through a range of interacting factors of which the gene is just one component. Dawkins and Lovelock represent the two poles of the spectrum, one advocating mechanism and one organicism. Both models have a long history in the story of science, and both have a long-standing relationship with both philosophy and religion. In as far as Gaia becomes a scientific myth, it becomes a form of scientism, an ideology, in much the same way as aspects of Dawkins's ideas.

How far as Christian theologians we are prepared to travel down the path paved by Lovelock is an important question. For the way we see the science will influence the degree to which we chose to incorporate Gaia into theology. What different possibilities might we envisage? How far are we justified in using Gaia terminology in detachment from the science? What are the implications for ethics, in particular for the relationship between humanity and the earth? What does it suggest for anthropology and our own self-understanding of who we are? In particular, what are the implications for environmental ethics? I will begin to explore possible answers to these questions in the chapter that follows.

8

Gaia: debates in theology and ethics

The most striking image of Gaia is that the earth is a single living organism, rather than a mechanism. Nonetheless, the variety of scientific approaches to Gaia reflects Gaia's own ambiguous position as science. Perhaps, hardly surprisingly, we find a number of theologians adopting Gaia in different ways in order to support their particular theological views. These range from the most conservative through to the most radical eco-feminist positions. While Gaia's rehabilitation in theological discourse might seem relatively harmless, the difficulties become greater when she becomes the basis for philosophy and environmental ethics. In this chapter I will explore the different mythologies associated with Gaia, and suggest that the way forward in the debate may come through a greater appreciation of the ambiguities in science. For, once the concrete reality of Gaia is called into question, then any claim for the earth-centred basis for her existence becomes highly problematic.

Gaia in theology

Lovelock always denied that Gaia had religious connotations, though, as mentioned earlier, he is quite ready to admit that most of the correspondence he has received comes from those writers who have a particular religious interest in Gaia. While he insists that his own starting point is atheistic, at times he shows an attraction to more mystical and even pagan forms of religion. He describes his childhood as 'amazingly superstitious', comparing the kind of Christmases he experienced with a pagan solstice feast. He is also attracted to the idea of linking Gaia with the Virgin Mary, speculating:

Those millions of Christians who make a special place in their
hearts for the Virgin Mary possibly respond as I do. The concept of Jahweh as remote, all-powerful, all-seeing is either
frightening or unapproachable . . . Mary is close and can be
talked to. She is believable and manageable. It could be that the
importance of the Virgin Mary in faith is something of this
kind, but there may be more to it. What if Mary is another name
for Gaia? Then her capacity for virgin birth is no miracle or
parthenogenetic aberration, it is a role of Gaia since life began
. . . She is of this Universe and, conceivably, a part of God. On
Earth she is the source of life everlasting and is alive now; she
gave birth to humankind and we are a part of her . . . That is
why, for me, Gaia is a religious as well as a scientific concept,
and in both spheres it is manageable.[1]

Such ideas would send shivers down the spine of those scientists
wishing to keep the language of science away from that of theology. For some scientists, even an idea such as 'Gaia is alive' carries
too much of a connotation of a vital life force, with its mystical
overtones, to be helpful scientifically. For these scientists Gaia
becomes reduced to a complex regulatory system that includes the
biota, but is neither 'alive' nor has any degree of singularity. Such
a view would still fall within the homeostatic interpretation of
Gaia, but without taking the next step of claiming that the earth is
alive. However, there are still scientific problems with this interpretation since it is difficult to test for regulatory devices at this
level of complexity. It does, however, show that it is possible for
Gaia to be interpreted as a homeostatic process, but without
invoking any grander mythological or quasi-spiritual process.

From a theological point of view linking the Virgin Mary with
Gaia in the form of a quasi earth mother would be contradictory to
traditional Roman Catholicism. There may be occasions when the
adoration of Mary has superseded that of Christ in forms of folk
religion loosely connected to the Roman Catholic Church. Lovelock is, perhaps, correct in his suggestion that Mary seems far
more approachable for many ordinary believers than traditional
images of God as remote and all-powerful. However, linking the

Virgin Mary explicitly with the divinity in the way he suggests, from the perspective of the Roman Catholic tradition, distorts the role of Mary, understood for centuries as one who pointed to Jesus, who is the Christ. It is her example of obedience to God that the tradition of the church suggests is one that needs to be emulated, rather than any association with the mother earth. Furthermore, prayer to Mary is on the basis of her humanity rather than her divinity. Of course, Lovelock would probably have no qualms about straying into folk religious ideas, since for him these would more likely to be the source of true spirituality compared with established forms of faith. The fact that his suggestions cannot be supported theologically from the tradition of the church is irrelevant as far as he is concerned, even though he is keen for his ideas to find a hearing in the mainstream scientific community that has largely rejected him.

Once we move into an understanding of Gaia as evolved, it becomes much more difficult to avoid the idea of Gaia having a particular identity or even a consciousness. Although Lovelock insists that the biota operates according to an unconscious process that is free of teleology, the apparent purpose of Gaia remains the persistence of life. It seems to me that this goal-directedness of Gaia fills something of the gap left by the collapse in the idea of divine providence. However, in this case Gaia is not necessarily working for the good of humanity, as in traditional theism. Rather, the aim of Gaia is for life to persist, even if this means the elimination of humankind. Those who develop an ideological vision of Gaia seem quite ready to admit that humanity is more like a pathogenic parasite on the whole planetary system.[2]

Given this rather sinister face of Gaia, it is perhaps surprising that some theologians have taken up and used the language of Gaia in Christian theology. Hugh Montefiore, for example, has managed to incorporate Gaia into a more traditional theological framework, apparently equating the work of Gaia with the Holy Spirit. For him 'Gaia is a kind of sacrament through which the power and Wisdom of God shines . . . the outward and visible earth shows us something of the inner workings of the Holy Spirit within it'.[3] Jürgen Moltmann also cites the Gaia hypothesis with approval, though in rather less explicit ways. He seems to take Gaia for granted as that which describes the earth system, and once more loosely associates Gaia with the activity of the Holy Spirit, for:

> Through the Spirit human societies as part systems are bound up with the ecosystem 'earth' (*Gaia*); for human societies live in and from the recurring cycles of earth, sun, air and water, day and night, summer and winter. So human beings are participants and subsystems of the cosmic life system, and of the divine Spirit that lives in it.[4]

Given the ambiguities in the science of Gaia and its interpretation discussed in the last chapter, it seems to me to be highly problematic to identify Gaia with the work of the Holy Spirit in the way that Montefiore and to some extent Moltmann suggest. Such identification would lead to confusion in the role of God as Holy Spirit in natural processes rather than its clarification. Furthermore, Lovelock's association of Gaia with the idea of Mary, understood as divine mother earth, would resist any translation of Gaia into one of the persons of the Trinity. Finally, linking Gaia as female with the Holy Spirit implies that it is only in this person that the feminine nature of God becomes displayed.[5]

It is, nonetheless, more usual for Gaia to be taken up by those who advocate a more monistic understanding of the relationship between God and the world. In this Gaia seems to cohere with New Age spirituality. While New Age writers have not developed the Gaia hypothesis as science in any significant way, some neo-pagans have proposed a mystical version of Gaia.[6] Lovelock's Gaia and New Age writing in general seem to bear some resemblance to the romantic works of Goethe or Oken. Such romantic views of science and organic visions of nature are certainly not new and have recurred throughout the history of the relationship between science and religion. D. Abram comments that the church in the sixteenth and seventeenth centuries was threatened by the idea of the earth as a 'living matrix of spiritual powers and receptivities'.[7] He argues that the idea of the earth as mechanism fitted in with the church teaching of the time, which fostered a deification of the human. The concept that the earth is *more* like an organism than a mechanical watch seems close to the idea that Gaia is a *metaphor*. However, the language of Gaia resists being contained simply in metaphorical categories. The extension of Gaia into more mystical forms of spirituality leads ultimately to patterns of thought that look back not just to the organic, but also to the goddess.

When we turn to the appropriation of Gaia by eco-feminist theologians, it is easy to find examples of authors who use Gaia terminology. However, more often than not this is a deliberate attempt to rehabilitate the idea of Gaia as goddess rather than any claim to identify with Lovelock's Gaia hypothesis. The Greek term for Mother Earth was *Gaia* or *Ge*. According to Hesiod, writing in about 700 BC, Gaia is the mother or grandmother of Zeus, his rule dependent on her approval. This affirms the importance of the female in the Greek pantheon. While some eco-feminist writers find inspiration from other goddess figures such as Isis, Gaia does find a place in their writing.

Charlene Spretnak is a good example of a writer who, while claiming to be post-Christian, still draws on traditional theological concepts, such as divine grace. However, she believes that traditional images of God need to be rejected in favour of goddess images that stress divine immanence. In her book, *States of Grace*, she argues that it is only through an earth-centred spirituality that we can recover a sense of meaning following the radical deconstruction that stems from postmodernity. She advocates Buddhist meditation as a way of entering into a deeper union with the cosmos. The model for ethical ecological practice for her is that of Native American spirituality. However, she takes deliberate inspiration from Lovelock's Gaia hypothesis, citing his ideas without calling them into question.[8] Gaia leads to a new form of spirituality, holding together different strands from different spiritual traditions. Spretnak considers Gaia to have an integrity, a 'dynamic unfolding that was established long before our emergence'. Hence our 'ethics should include the fulfilling of our vital needs with minimal damage to our cosmic relations'.[9] She joins this view of Gaia with a goddess spirituality that welcomes the body, with its embeddedness in nature. While she seems to recognize that there are some difficulties in close identification between the earth and femaleness as such, she insists that the most important idea to retain is an understanding of the planet as a body, an organism. This bears little resemblance to Lovelock's Gaia hypothesis, which is used in an indiscriminate way for her own theological purposes.

Rosemary Radford Ruether is another eco-feminist theologian who has used Gaia terminology, in particular in her book *God and Gaia*.[10] Her notion of Gaia seems to be related to a recovery of the sacramental tradition, especially a reworking of the early cosmological images of the presence of the divine. Ruether draws on an eclectic mixture of Matthew Fox, Teilhard de Chardin and process theology, and for her *Gaia* becomes the feminine voice in the heart of matter itself. By contrast, *God* is seen as the voice that speaks on behalf of the weak, one that comes from power and law. She admits that a simplistic return to the goddess is not really adequate, and what we need is a 'coincidence of opposites' of God and Gaia in the manner that she suggests we find in subatomic physics.

Ruether only mentions Lovelock's thesis briefly, but she uses Gaia in a mythological sense in order to describe the world as a living organism. How far is her proposed union of God and Gaia really tenable in the manner she suggests? A union of God and Gaia is one that Lovelock would endorse as a proper way to understand Gaia from a religious point of view. He is attracted to the idea of linking God and Gaia in order to present a unified perspective, so that theology and science, biology and physics are not separated but presented as a single way of thinking.[11] However, I suggest that such a union of God and Gaia is hard to sustain in any really meaningful way, especially where more traditional transcendent images of God are rejected. As a basis for linking theology and science it becomes highly problematic, for Gaia almost always takes precedence. Certainly, in Ruether's later writing, the uneasy tension between Gaia and God is lost and replaced with a single unified understanding, so that we are left with a single image of Gaia / God fully immanent in the world. In particular, Ruether suggests that humanity has to see itself as part of an organic community, one that accepts that following death it will rise up again in new forms. Hence our bodily matter

> lives on in plants, animals and soil, even as our own living bodies are composed of substances that once were part of rocks, plants and animals, stretching back to prehistoric ferns and reptiles, before that to ancient biota that floated on the first seas of earth, and before that to the stardust of exploding galaxies.[12]

While Ruether makes no mention here of Gaia as such, her implication that human beings are part of the overall evolution of biota considered as an organic whole with the earth and all its processes draws on Gaian imagery.

The different theological interpretations of Gaia discussed here range from an assimilation into a pantheistic idea of an pagan earth deity or an earth goddess, through to more traditional interpretations of God acting through the Holy Spirit to bring about the process of Gaia. All such theological interpretations seem to be problematic.

In the first place, the identification of Gaia with the Deity seems to weaken Gaia's status as science, since it can no longer avoid the charge of mythology.

Secondly, identification of Gaia with the earth in a form of neo-mysticism fosters the suspicion of more traditional theologians that any theological concern for the earth slides into a form of pantheism that is incompatible with an understanding of God as Trinity. The retreat of much theology into history and biblical studies at the expense of creation and wider issues in science is entirely understandable if creation theology takes these forms.

Thirdly, identification of Gaia with a goddess figure seems to encourage identification of the earth with women in a way that could serve to reinforce rather than counter the patriarchal modes of thought. Feminists have consistently argued against any separation of, for example, women from men, nature from spirit,

emotion from reason. If Gaia becomes a goddess, then this reinforces such identification of women and earth. While Ruether has
tried to avoid this problem by suggesting a combination of God
and Gaia, the identity of God seems lost from view once she
considers the meaning of redemption. In this case the future of
humanity is one that is entirely consistent with Gaia as science.
The death of humanity leads to life in different forms, including
both inorganic and organic life as part of a single unified system.

Finally, while many feminist writers draw on the imagery of
Gaia, I wonder how far they have really considered the way it
counters the value that many place on diversity. While Lovelock
suggests that biodiversity does lead to the most stable system,
clearly some species can be eliminated with no ill effects. Gaia as a
whole system seems to weaken not just the value of individuals but
also the value of marginal communities. I will return to this issue
again in my consideration of postmodern philosophy.

Gaia in philosophy

The idea that the earth might be an organic unity of living beings
and the environment that displays intelligence and purposefulness, with a 'world soul' or *anima mundi*, resonates with the
philosophy linked with Lovelock's interpretation of Gaia. An
alternative philosophy associated with the weakest scientific
version of Gaia is that the world as a whole is more like a mechanism, where such feedback processes are automatic mechanical
processes, with no participation of intelligent life.

The organic model has very ancient roots, reaching far back
into the early philosophy of Pythagoras, where rocks and minerals
were understood to be elemental forms of life that grow from
metallic seeds. According to this scenario, mining would not
destroy the metals, which would grow back after excavation. However, Pythagoras also believed that the real world could be known
through mathematical reasoning. For him, such a reasonable and
perfect world was hidden behind our illusion of disorder. Hence,
overall his philosophy supported a mechanical model of the earth.
On the other hand, the Stoic philosophy of both the ancient

Greeks and the Romans was much more explicitly organic; in this case the earth was seen as both living and intelligent, hence mining was discouraged for fear of damage to mother earth.

Giving value to the earth, or naturalism, was revived in the twelfth century. Here the earth was perceived as delicately tuned, and any injury would have serious consequences. However, for much of the Middle Ages the harmony of the earth was perceived to be the result of the action of a Creator God.[13] The Renaissance period saw the revival of the idea that the earth is organic, though it took a Neo-Platonic form that included the idea of a separate world soul. In this case an intelligent force or world soul directed passive matter. This is rather different from the idea of the world as a super-organism, where the life force is inseparable from matter. Once the soul was considered separate from matter, it was relatively easy to replace the idea of soul with that of mechanism.

The rise of early modern science effectively dismissed any ideas of an intelligent earth, so that by the eighteenth century the earth came to be viewed predominantly as a grand harmonious machine. Of course, there were some scientists and writers who retained a more romantic view of the earth even in this period, but the main institutions of power adopted the mechanistic model. Nonetheless, even in the mechanical model, belief in harmony persisted, though now it was through natural laws.

Elizabeth Sahtouris is one philosopher who wonders what would have happened if those ancient philosophers who argued against Pythagoras for a living earth had eventually won the day.[14] What if organic biology rather than mechanical physics had become the basis for modern science, and physics had developed in the shadow of biology rather than the other way round? The question is an intriguing one, though she believes that it is in our time that a recovery of an organic view has become possible.

Sahtouris insists that the most important thing about Gaia is not the recovery of an earth goddess but the idea that the earth is alive, rather than just inert matter with living things on it. The kind of questions that scientists want to ask about whether individual physical processes or biota contribute most to the stability of the gaseous envelope around the earth become less significant if the earth is alive, since such investigations still tend to treat the earth as if it were a mechanism. Hence, once we see the earth as a living whole, the parts are related to the earth in an analogous manner to the different organs of the body. She suggests that to reject the idea of a living earth as impossible is as premature as the rejection of the paradox that we find in quantum physics, where light is both a particle and wave at the same time. It is the refusal of our imaginations to make such a leap that is problematic. However, it seems to me that to liken Gaia as 'living' with quantum physics ignores the fact that the experiments in physics actually pointed in this direction, while the idea of a living earth is pure speculation.

Of course, saying that the earth is alive depends in part on how we define such life. I have already alluded to this in the previous chapter. Sahtouris favours the idea of *autopoiesis*, which means that which is self-producing, as a definition of life. An autopoietic system defines its own boundaries and is capable of replacing components of the system. This is very different from earlier biological definitions of life as that which is capable of growth, reproduction and genetic inheritance. The autopoietic definition of life allows for alternative life forms on other planets. While the biologists who defend the definition of life as autopoietic do so on the basis of molecular events, Sahtouris applies this model to the earth as a whole. She is, nonetheless, hopeful that this model of the earth will eventually come to be accepted by the scientific community.

I am less convinced that the earth can be viewed in autopoietic categories, especially as communication between different components is very hard to conceive. The earth may have some autopoietic-like qualities, but a simpler model of dissipative theory could equally explain these qualities. One of the classic rules of science is that the simpler model is favoured over the more complex, unless there is good reason to reject the simpler model. It seems to me that, however intriguing, the idea of the earth as autopoietic is one that is read into the functions of the earth through a basic belief in an organic philosophy, rather than anything more substantial scientifically.

For Sahtouris humanity as part of Gaia is simply an experiment in free choice, in which we are the first to become conscious of ourselves as the 'eye' of the cosmos. She suggests that in our contemporary culture such consciousness has turned in on itself and become a form of egotism. She believes we need to learn the lesson of cooperation, rather than competition, that she perceives to be the underlying principle of Gaia. But is Gaia really as benign as she seems to suggest? Sahtouris is not alone in finding Gaia suggestive for environmental philosophy. However, there are some problems in giving humans the role of 'mind' of the earth or 'consciousness' of the planet. For if humans are responsible for earth's mind, then it becomes difficult to give equal value to non-humans, which is the opposite of Sahtouris' intention.[15]

Mary Midgley is another philosopher of science who is perhaps surprisingly positive about Lovelock's Gaia. Of course, his stance against the specialization and fragmentation of science would concur with her interpretation of many of the problems with modern science. Midgley is particularly critical of the way the machine metaphor in science has come to dominate scientific activity, leading to all kinds of fantasies, especially in popular scientific writing.[16] In particular, the idea of a machine without a designer does not really make sense, so we invent one to replace the idea of a purposeful designer, either a benign one, such as evolution, or a more sinister one, such as the selfish gene or ruthless necessity. The dream of artificial intelligence is just one more example of this kind of progression. Even though Richard Dawkins would no doubt object to his theories being parodied in this way, the language that he uses is ripe for such appropriation.

Given this context, Midgley suggests that in Lovelock's Gaia 'the imagination is being rightly used to guide and supplement scientific thinking'.[17] She believes that the most important philosophical point of Gaia is that life is not a mechanism but is continuous with the surrounding world, and that it naturally and gradually arises out of the system. She suggests that Gaia gives us an important image of belonging to the earth that is badly needed in our fragmented world. She also suggests that the combination of science with religion should neither be surprising nor shocking. For, once we see ourselves as intricately part of a whole, then we will treat the earth with reverence and respect. However, like Sahtouris, she rejects any sense that the earth takes the form of a deity; rather, the respect due is one that resonates with religious belief. This is analogous to the way in the past that Isaac Newton and other early scientists have given due respect for the earth without making the earth itself an object of Deity.

It is, perhaps, the maverick nature of Lovelock's work that offers a certain appeal for Midgley, for it is surprising that she does not seem to recognize that Gaia can be aligned with more dangerous forms of scientism, just as can any other kind of science. She is quick to point to the scientism characteristic of popular science writing based on more mechanical models, such as that of the selfish gene. She points to the 'last chapters' of books written by scientists that move into all kind of speculative theories. However, the final chapter of Lovelock's book *The Ages of Gaia* also contains fantastically speculative religious material already alluded to earlier. The difference may be that while Lovelock is ready to admit that he is speculating, the scientists that she describes write as if their views are emergent from the science.

The philosopher Stephen Clark is surprised at the rejection of Lovelock's Gaia by scientists. He suggests that the main reasons for this rejection may lie in Lovelock's lack of affiliation with mainstream science and his identification with organic views, long since rendered obsolete by the modern Western scientific enterprise. The main moral Clark gleans from Gaia is that humans are effectively parasites on the planet, and that we must struggle to become symbiotic with the earth or die.[18] Clark is, nonetheless, highly critical of the recovery of the idea of the earth as a mother goddess, in the way it tends to become attached to Lovelock's Gaia.[19] He does agree with the basic concept of Lovelock's Gaia that the earth is a single unity, suggesting that the thesis is 'a simple and profoundly plausible one'.[20] However, Clark seems to accept a form of Gaia theory that rejects any sense of the earth as a single organism or a single organizing principle. In this he does seem to depart from Lovelock's own version of the hypothesis and render it in a weaker form, especially compared with Sahtouris.

Process philosophy is, in general, more critical of the Gaia hypothesis. Process philosophy is interesting, as it seems to bear some resemblance to Gaia in that it considers the whole world as part of a single process, including inorganic and organic life forms together. Furthermore, some Christian theologians have quite readily adopted process philosophy as a basis for their theology. One criticism of Gaia by process theologians is that it is limited in its consideration of the earth rather than the whole universe. A second criticism is that it lacks adequate consideration of the individual.[21] While both Gaia and process philosophies acknowledge 'processes' in the material world, Gaia takes a holistic stance that is lacking in process thought. Furthermore, the purpose or teleology that emerges in Gaian thought is very different from the teleology in process ideas, which are always directed towards individual maximum 'enrichment'. For Gaian thought the directedness, if it exists, is more general and towards the maintenance of life.

Process philosophy pinpoints a trend in Gaian philosophy that has become much more difficult to sustain in the more recent context of postmodern culture. Postmodernism in general rejects any grand narrative as an adequate explanation of reality. Postmodernity has become the principal challenge to modernity to such an extent that grander holistic ideas become difficult to accept from a cultural perspective. While it could be argued that a grand narrative is *also* characteristic of traditional forms of Christianity, Lovelock's hypothesis is not normally aligned with such forms, but presents itself as a radical alternative that is identified with more liberal theological alternatives. Hence Lovelock's Gaia is not only facing attack from within science, it is also a possible subject of criticism from cultural forces within society as well.

While the philosophy emerging from Gaia seems to swim against the tide of modernity, with its presupposed reductionist method in science, it reclaims an ancient myth that becomes equally hard to accept in the present postmodern culture. Those who object to any form of grand narrative believe they are disguised attempts at a will to power over others. Such a critique would counter any claims for a humbler, more reverent attitude towards the earth that Gaian philosophy is supposed to instill. Postmodernity welcomes the local, the novel, the particular context in which ideas are shaped and developed. A postmodern science is much more hesitant about any metanarrative. It is perhaps one reason why there has been a shift in modern ecology from an exploration of systems to one that looks at the dynamic interplay between different organisms in fluid boundaries. Biological science today is much more resistant to the idea of natural harmonies. Ecological systems seldom display tendencies towards balance in the way early ecologists envisaged. There is also a scepticism about the long-term direction of natural systems. Such shifts make Gaian theory even harder to sustain than when it was first proposed.

Gaia in ethics

There is a wide spectrum of possible approaches to environmental ethics, from those who give priority to individuals to those who consider collectives such as species, ecosystems and the biosphere. In recent years there has been a move towards an affirmation of collective value. The Gaia hypothesis, even in its weakest form, reinforces this shift towards collective value and uses a similar language of 'community' and 'organism'. Gaia challenges the ethical stance that opts for more individualistic or anthropocentric, that is, human-centred positions. John Passmore, for example, suggests that the only valid basis for defining moral worth comes from consideration of humanity. Others are prepared to extend the idea of worth to all individual organisms, including humanity. Such a view is known as biocentric, rather than anthropocentric. One such position is that of Paul Taylor, where all individual organisms have their own particular purpose, or *telos*. It is this *telos* that gives individual organisms worth.[22] According to Taylor's biocentric view, all living beings have equal moral status, whereas according to *Gaia* the value lies in the collective activity of the biota.

An ethic of resource management

An understanding of Gaia that includes homeostatic processes can, ironically perhaps, lead to two completely different ethical positions. The first stance is adopted by those concerned with the idea of the earth providing resources for human use. This view seems to counter the stress on collective value suggested by the notion of Gaia as an interdependent community of organisms outlined above.

A resource management approach is not novel, and is the most common attitude adopted by political organizations concerned with the environment. The focus is human-centred, and action is judged according to the possible benefit or otherwise for human beings. Hence it might seem anomalous that any Gaian view could be used to support an anthropocentric stance. The argument would run something like as follows. The most extreme view, which barely deserves to be described as an 'ethic', is that since the science of Gaia shows that the earth will correct itself after change, human pollution is relatively incidental.[23] It is for this reason that not all conservationists welcome Gaian theory, as it seems to encourage a robust view of the earth as one that can withstand many more millennia of abuse by humans.

A more sophisticated view is that human responsibility is to conserve those parts of the planet that act like the 'vital organs'; that is, the tropical rainforests, the deep-sea algae and the prokaryotic bacteria. Those species that are not essential to Gaian function would be dispensable. If Gaia was forced to a new equilibrium state, this would lead to the destruction of many species, including humans. The survival of human beings, then, depends on avoiding any action that would force Gaia into a new equilibrium state.

Lovelock seems to object to any 'resource management' ideas, as if human beings could 'manage' the affairs of the earth when we have failed to manage our own human relationships. He believes that ideas such as 'stewardship' still encourage a short-term focus and one that is too anthropocentric. This fails to consider the over-all health of the planet. He draws a graphic parallel between the idea of 'stewardship' and 'management' of artificial kidneys in a disabled body. He implies by this image that any attempt at stewardship is misplaced as we are setting ourselves up as care-takers, instead of simply recognizing our place as simply 'part of Gaia'.

Yet he does seem to allow some unique function for humanity. In this case he argues that we should consider ourselves as part-ners to the planet, acting as 'shopstewards' and 'representatives' of 'bacteria, fungi, slime moulds and fish, birds and animals'.[24] The difference between humanity and the other creatures of the earth is that humanity is aware of Gaia. Furthermore, the human ability to be self-conscious becomes in effect the consciousness of Gaia. Lovelock seems to be moving away from a purely anthro-pocentric stance, though the threat of human extinction is still part of his call for humans to live in partnership. If we fail to adopt this approach, 'the rest of creation, will, as part of *Gaia* uncons-ciously move the earth itself to a new state, one where humans may no longer be welcome'. Lovelock objects to the idea that Gaia 'gives industry the green light to pollute at will'. Rather, he insists that 'her unconscious goal is a planet fit for life', and if humans stand in the way 'we shall be eliminated with as little pity as would be shown by the micro-brain of an intercontinental ballistic nuclear missile in full flight to its target'.[25]

An ethic of environmental care

Lovelock's earlier research on detection of pesticides in remote regions of the planet brought him into the limelight as far as environmentalists were concerned. He seemed to welcome this role, seeing the rising tide of pollution as something that had to be stemmed at our own peril. It is therefore not surprising that his vision of Gaia is one that fosters human responsibility, rather than the opposite, as indicated above. Although Lovelock has not worked out his ethical position in any rigorous way, his focus on partnership and consideration of the overall process of Gaia bears some resemblance to the land ethic of Aldo Leopold and the envi-ronmental ethic of the American philosopher Holmes Rolston III.

Aldo Leopold's work, *A Sand County Almanac*, written in 1949, was highly influential in the more recent shift towards collective value.[26] He argued that the land, that is, soils, waters, plants and animals, deserves moral consideration as part of the community of life. Conservationists admire his pioneering work in recognition of the value of all organisms on the planet. Leopold's insistence, in particular, that the land has value as well as the creatures on it, bespeaks of an ethic that coheres with the system approach in Gaia.

Holmes Rolston III possibly comes closer to a Gaian approach in that he gives value to the ecosystem and biosphere as that which is 'life creating'. Holmes Rolston describes systemic value as a process that leads to 'intrinsic values woven into instrumental relationships'.[27] His valuation of the system, while at the same time giving value to individual components of that system, avoids the implicit danger of eco-fascism. However, in certain respects the biological basis of his ideas is naïve. His views tend to reinforce the concepts of 'integrity' and 'stability' in ecosystems in a way that does not exist in practice. As discussed in Chapter 2, ecology today has not only moved beyond a consideration of ecology as systems that are stable, it also views ecosystems as far more fragile and fluid in their boundaries compared with previous understandings.

An ethic grounded in Gaia as philosophy

Elizabeth Sahtouris is more explicit in her use of Gaia as a paradigm for both philosophy and ethics. She finds in Gaia clues for human behaviour.[28] She assumes that we are like immature adolescents who can only make progress by becoming more in tune with the inner workings of the planet. In this she echoes the eco-theology of Sallie McFague, who regards sin as a failure to recognize our place in our planetary home.[29]

There are various possible objections to this idea. The first, most obvious one is that Gaia herself is not as benevolent as in Sahtouris' portrayal. Even Lovelock admits that Gaia is

no doting mother tolerant of misdemeanors, nor is she some fragile and delicate damsel in danger from brutal mankind. She is stern and tough, always keeping the world warm and comfortable for those who obey the rules, but is ruthless in her destruction of those who transgress. Her unconscious goal is a planet fit for life.[30]

A second objection to using Gaia as a basis for ethics is that it identifies something that exists, in this case Gaia, with something that is of value. At the turn of the twentieth century G.E. Moore developed a stinging critique of John Stuart Mill's work in what has come to be known as the naturalistic fallacy. Briefly, this stated that it was philosophically illegitimate to base a value on something that exists in the natural world. In other words, we cannot move from an 'is' to an 'ought'. Moore developed the earlier work of David Hume, who suggested that no value statements could be validly derived from facts.

Moreover, as hinted at earlier, arguing the case for an ethic from Gaia develops just one strand of Gaia. More ignoble qualities of the 'system', including the ability of Gaia to 'hit back' at humans, are toned down as models for human behaviour. Furthermore, as indicated earlier, those parts of the planet that are most valuable for sustaining the earth system are the tropical forests, prokaryotic bacteria and algae.

Gaia as a basis for ethics also shares many of the problems of the so-called 'deep ecology' of Arne Naess, Warwick Fox and others. Pedler, for example, speaks of a new lifestyle that is 'Gaian' where the 'human race is an integral part of a single life force, sometimes called the earth organism, the earth spirit of Gaia', which in practice is an 'alternative to the ready made solutions offered by the industrial machine'.[31] It is a new consciousness that pervades every aspect of life, which is similar to deep ecology's focus as a 'consciousness movement', rather than an ethic per se.

The new consciousness, which calls for an extension of the self into an all-inclusive idea, where there are no distinctions between self and non-self, is highly problematic. Identification with everything leads to a form of eco-fascism. Ironically, perhaps, an extension of the self tends to project self into the world in an 'anthropocentric' way, which is the opposite of the supposed holistic 'dream' of deep ecology. While the Gaia hypothesis does not, in itself, imply this form of mergence of self with the earth, those who have taken up the 'quest' for Gaia in a rigorous way seem to share the same 'consciousness'. It is as if the biological fact that we share the same molecules as non-living matter gives us a rationale for a new metaphysics where all distinctions are ignored.

Conclusions

I suggest that the range of possible interpretations of Gaia from a scientific perspective means that there is an equally wide range of theological and ethical outcomes. This diversity leads to confusion in the debate since it is not always clear which particular version of Gaia is being used in support of a particular view. This especially highlights the problems of any attempt to find in the natural world a basis for ethics. A return to nature in Gaia is not likely to lead to clear ways forward, and shares some of the problems of moral pluralism in general. There is an obvious danger of using Gaia as a way of supporting predetermined ethical outcomes.

There are, nonetheless, important lessons to learn from Gaia. First of all, to attempt to formulate a mythology from science is both problematic and fraught with difficulties. Secondly, Gaia as science does show the determination of the human spirit, the risk of staking claims against a background of scientific dogma in a way that leads to fruitful discussions. Thirdly, few would wish to return to a sterile view of the earth as simply existing in isolated compartments. An organic view of the earth is a more helpful image compared to the purely mechanistic one, as long as it does not stray into the more scientifically dubious notion of the earth as a living organism. But would more organic, relational concepts of science have been possible if women, rather than men, had dominated the scientific enterprise? Do the philosophical and theological issues raised by Gaia amount to a reaction against a male-centred view of reality? It is to an exploration of these questions that I turn in the next chapter.

Feminist horizons in science and religion

In general the contemporary science and religion debate has largely ignored the feminist critique of either science or, for that matter, theology, apart from nodding approval in places to some eco-feminist ideas, such as Sallie McFague's metaphor for the world as God's body. The challenge posed by feminists, that science is itself gendered knowledge, is left out of the discussion. What is not debated is that the participation of women in science has been both frustrated and largely devalued. In what Eileen Byrne calls the 'Snark Sydrome', women are declared to be deficient in scientific abilities, especially the 'hard sciences', such as physics.[1] She suggests that the situation is more complex than a simple exclusion of all women in all science – for example, some sciences, notably biology, are androgynous in their ability to attract women to undergraduate programmes. Sciences such as chemistry or statistics are 'non-traditional' for women, while women in engineering are perceived as 'abnormal'. At the research level the situation is more complex, with women progressively diminishing in numbers further up the academic ladder.

What are we to make of such results? Does the difference in status of men and women in science reflect difference in biology, gender or exclusion through territorial boundaries imposed by men? I will explore different feminist responses to science, ranging from outright rejection to transformation. I will also suggest that debates in biology and religion need to be informed by such discussions. For they point to ways in which the future of science might be envisaged, which will be the subject of the following chapter.

The place of women in historical perspective

Some historians of science have even gone as far as suggesting that religious belief actually contributed to oppressive attitudes towards women in the history of science. Margaret Wertheim argues that a major psychological force behind the evolution of physics was the theological assumption that the structure of the natural world was determined by a set of transcendent mathematical relations.[2] The religious impetus for the idea of transcendence was prior to Platonic idealism and served to reinforce the mindset of those in early modern science. Once we view God as a mathematician, then this reinforced even further the cultural framework for the exclusion of women, barred as they had been throughout history from the religious priesthood of the church. As physics became more secularized, the role of priest was given to science, along with parallel exclusion of women. Like other historians, she recognizes that much early science from the thirteenth century through to the eighteenth century was inspired by religious belief. The novelty in her presentation is her suggestion that this alliance served to reinforce women's exclusion in a way that cannot be attributed simply to the prevailing sexism of the period.

Compatibility theories

Given the observation that women have been marginalized from science, what other factors might have been significant? Linda Schiebinger argues strongly that there is nothing specifically masculine about science.[3] Rather, the social and cultural forces in Europe at the time of the rise of modern science dismissed women from the public realm and thereby excluded them from science. In particular, she suggests that the compatibility theories, which became popular towards the end of the eighteenth century, were especially significant. Such theories of compatibility stemmed originally from the philosophy of Aristotle, and divided the world into the dualistic realms of male / female; active / passive; form / matter; perfection / imperfection; actual / potential. Hence it was not just women excluded from science, but a set of values around the ideal of 'femininity'. Such exclusion was not as prominent in the early stages of amateur science. However, once science became a profession, its link to the public sphere was strengthened, along with an association with masculinity. In this period, while femininity was virtue to be admired in the private world of the home, masculinity prevailed as dominant in the public, abstract, political sphere. Once the compatibility idea had taken hold, women could no longer compete in the public realm as they were thought to be unsuitable candidates for such a venture.

Influential writers, such as Rousseau, believed that the more abstract creative work of the sciences, especially the physical sciences, was simply impossible for women to achieve. Furthermore, women who did try to engage in science would 'blemish' their femininity and not be acting in a way that was true to their nature as women. Some women, such as the mathematician Sophie Germain, achieved results by writing under a male pseudonym, in her case Antoine August Le Blanc. Yet women were admitted to the study of botany, as long as they remained amateurs, allied as it was to herbal healing and gardening. Men believed that such studies would bring women closer to God and thus strengthen their role as moral guardians in the home. Such affiliation of women with botany remained and persisted even after 1735 when Linnaeus' classification of science depended on sexual characterization of plants. Such connotations of polyandry and polygamy could be deemed unsuitable subjects of study for 'delicate females'. Linnaeus adjusted descriptions of plant sexuality so that they were compatible with European mores of the time. Hence, 'through rich metaphors Linnaeus suggested that plants joined in lawful marriages whereas stamens and pistils met as bride and grooms on verdant nuptial beds'.[4]

In spite of these cultural obstacles, women did manage to become scientists as assistants to husbands or brothers, and often came from the more educated aristocratic classes. As assistants women could be kept hidden in the domestic sanctuary, often prevented from using the most sophisticated equipment. Hedwig Dohm dared to criticize science in the nineteenth century. However, her work was rejected by scientists on the basis that it was too polemical. Today there exists a similar hostility by some scientists towards the works of contemporary feminists, which are branded in an amorphous way as 'political'. Some nineteenth-century writers such as J. S. Mill attempted to defend the place of women in philosophy by suggesting that abstract thought could be complemented by the more practical experience of women. In this he still held to the complementarity thesis, but he turned it on its head and used it for women's advantage. Nonetheless, at the time his call was largely ignored.

There were two possible reactions by women to the idea of complementarity. One was to reject it altogether and declare that the mind has no sex, so that women and men are basically similar in their ability to think and reason in science. Any difference is superficial rather than actual. The other response was to accept difference and use it as a basis for a new framework for thought. As I will show later, both approaches become evident in the contemporary feminist approach to science and the philosophy of science. In theological reflection we find similar responses by women. One is to reject the idea that women are inferior in their theological reasoning and argue that, like men, they need to be heard for the contribution they can make to theological discourse in a way that is largely independent of their sexuality. Another response is to declare that the methods of women and feminism in general are different from those of men, so that they have something distinct to contribute to theology from the side of practical experience.

Righting the record

Another possible approach to the history of science it to search for those women who have made significant contributions. This has parallels with the approach of feminist theologians, such as Rosemary Radford Ruether and Elisabeth Schüssler Fiorenza, who have rewritten the biblical record in terms of a narrative of women, rather than men. There are striking examples of women biologists who have made highly significant contributions to the advancement of science.[5] However, the sexism is still evident in the way their achievements seem to be forgotten far earlier than those of men. Furthermore, even in biology women in the nineteenth century could only function as assistants to men. The few more recent exceptional cases, such as Barbara McClintock, whose work was discussed in Chapter 3, may have been able to achieve notoriety eventually, although McClintock was considered eccentric and largely rejected for most of her life. Among other women medical researchers, Ruth Sager, who pioneered the idea of cytoplasmic inheritance, remained a research fellow for most of her life and published more than fifty articles before she was appointed as a lecturer.[6] I have already mentioned that Rosalind Franklin's contribution to the structure of DNA was marginalized. The Nobel Prize was awarded to the theoreticians James Watson and Francis Crick and was also shared with Maurice Wilkins, even though they relied on Franklin's experimental X-ray diffraction work. Furthermore, the main achievements of women in medical science have been in women's health areas, such as gynaecology, which men have traditionally sidelined.

While women do seem to have been excluded in various ways in the history of science, they have been far more successful in establishing themselves as writers in popular science. Many of the popular writers of the nineteenth century were women, often motivated by a commitment to natural theology.[7] Taking inspiration from the *Natural Theology* (1802) of William Paley, women writers at the turn of the nineteenth century, such as Priscilla Wakefield, linked the wonders of nature with the wonders of creation and the Creator. This may, however, not have been a particularly positive move as far as the entry of women into mainstream science was concerned, for it widened the gap between women and 'proper' science.

Women popularizers of science have continued to achieve prominence right up to the present day, though usually now without any reference to natural theology. Moreover, in many cases twentieth-century women have had specific scientific training as well as a desire to communicate to a wider audience. Rachel

Carson, for example, used nature writing to challenge the individualism of much of Western society. In her work the natural world became the basis for human joy and celebration, such as her books *The Sea Around Us* or *A Sense of Wonder*.[8] Her well-known exception to this approach, *Silent Spring*, considered the devastating consequences of the use of insecticides, such as DDT. Carson was concerned particularly with the social aspects of the way science was done. For example, 98% of the funding of entomologists in the USA then was directed towards the development of insecticides. Hence any protest that DDT was safe was highly suspicious. Yet her complaint was not just against environmental damage, it was directed towards the men who had designed scientific method to function in a certain way and who demanded concrete proof before any action could be justified. Carson was bold in her suggestion that:

> The 'control of nature' is a phrase conceived in arrogance, born of the Neanderthal age of biology and philosophy, when it was supposed that nature exists for the convenience of man. The concepts and practices of applied entomology for the most part date from that Stone Age of science. It is our alarming misfortune that so primitive a science has armed itself with the most modern and terrible weapons, and that in turning against the insects it has also turned them against the earth.[9]

In a sense Rachel Carson was a pioneer not just of the ecological movement, that caught the imagination of men and women alike, but also the contemporary feminist critique of science that I will discuss in more detail below.

Feminist critiques of science

Feminist critiques of science are broadly similar in some respects to the more general critiques of feminism in that they follow patterns of liberal, cultural or romantic feminist approaches. I will give an overview of these different patterns first before suggesting ways in which feminist thinkers have tried to develop new philosophies of science.

Science and liberal feminism

The feminist critique that is possibly the most familiar is that arising from the liberal tradition, namely, a fight for equality in education, opportunities, employment and status for women in science.
Such a tradition has existed since the seventeenth century. A
similar movement exists in relation to theology, though now it
takes the form of a campaign for equal opportunities of women in
the theological hierarchy and access to the priesthood. Those who
have campaigned long and hard for access of women to science
believe that any claim by science to be objective or value-neutral is
false as long as women are excluded from its institutions. In addition, the exclusion of women has given science in a patriarchal
society an even greater social power and authority. The claim that
science was neutral obscured the invisibility of women's presence.

Liberal feminists challenged the complementarity thesis that
stated that men and women had different, but complementary
roles in the public and private realm. They strongly rejected the
idea that there was a biological difference between men and
women that rendered women inapt or incompetent in science.
The view that the biological difference between men and women
is such that their mind works in a completely different way is
known as *essentialism*. Such a view also draws on the early historical belief that the biological difference between men and women
reflects the incomplete growth of female bodies. Even up to the
middle of the eighteenth century women's reproductive organs
were thought to be simply imperfect male sex organs. As late as
1860, the French brain surgeon Paul Broca, in a study that
involved 292 male and 140 female cadavers, claimed that the
brains of women were 14% lighter than those of men.[10] Stephen J.
Gould challenged Broca's results in recent times, charging that
Broca had not taken into account that both age and height affect
brain size. The fact that his views were accepted without question
for over 120 years reflects their coherence with both the essentialist views of the time and the particular social bias against women.

Many liberal feminists believe that more contemporary sociobiological theories about women are just contemporary versions
of essentialism. Sociobiology seeks to explain our behaviour in

terms of genetics, hence it amounts to a modern form of biological determinism. Ruth Bleier is especially critical of the way socio-biology has tried to narrow human development to genetic categories. She suggests, in particular, that environmental influences must be taken into account in defining the way humans develop:

> There is no way to tease apart genetic and environmental factors in human development, or to know where genetic effects end and environmental ones begin; in fact this is a meaningless way to view the problem.[11]

We find here a resurfacing of the debate between how far we are the products of nature or nurture, our biology or our environment. Bleier refuses to accept that we can find an instinct or biological 'nature' beneath or outside culture and learning in the way that sociobiology suggests. She believes that the claim by socio-biologists that certain characteristics of men and women are universal is itself faulty in its logic, in that it tries to explain in biological categories stereotypical views of women. These stereotypical views include ideas such as that women are attached to the home, faithful, selective and nurturing while men are attached to business and professions, fickle, promiscuous and aggressive. These assumptions about the universality of such characteristics are problematic, reaching a zenith in the final proclamation of the 'naturalness' of rape.[12] The extent to which sociobiologists try to extrapolate from animal behaviour to humans is also faulty in that animals too have their own culture that is distinct from pure biological determinism.

Yet biological explanations of differences between men and women continue to remain popular, especially through studies exploring the effect of sex hormones on human behaviour. Doreen Kimura, for example, has investigated the role of sex hormones on cognitive differences between men and women.[13] She found that exposure to sex hormones affected both men and women, but both responded along a particular range associated with male and female patterns of cognitive ability. In general women outperform men on perceptual speed, verbal fluency, fine motor coordination and mathematical calculation. However, men outperform women on spatial tasks, target-directed motor skills and mathematical reasoning. Nonetheless, even these results show that there was a continuum in the cognitive ability of men and women, so that female sex hormones are not determinative in any absolute sense. The study did not attempt to investigate the effects of cultural influences on cognitive ability. Hence, it is quite possible that given certain learning environments women could outperform men in the characteristics identified as male-dominant.

Another issue associated with all sociobiological explanations of behaviour is that the threat of eugenics looms large. However, it seems to me that it is important to distinguish between the kind of sociobiology that extrapolates from studies of animal behaviour from that which draws inferences from the physiological studies of scientists, such as that of Kimura. Feminist critiques of science have tended to bracket all such studies together in an unhelpful way. It is clearly unacceptable to describe 'rape' or any other violent behaviour as 'natural'. However, a study of the effect of hormones on particular cognitive patterns does suggest that there is a biological component to human thinking and behaving. Yet finding such a biological component should not then lead to the next step that this is the only or necessarily the most important explanation.

The liberal feminist critique of the lack of women's participation in science has become more widely accepted, and is reflected in governmental moves to encourage girls and women to take up science. On a practical level it is often difficult to gain access to information about the presence of women in science in industry. Much of the data in the United Kingdom comes from the 1991 Census. Part of the problem seems to be that if employers do not see an economic advantage in giving positions to women, then they will not implement policies to promote women.[14] The 1994 government report on women in science, engineering and technology, *The Rising Tide*, showed some increase in women in science, but still a very low percentage in senior positions in universities or industry, even in those science subjects, such as biology, where the majority of undergraduates are women.

Science and cultural feminism

For cultural feminists of the nineteenth century and beyond the attempts by liberals to instate women in science do not go far enough. Rather, they insist that we take far more account of gender differences. The basis of the liberal argument so far might imply that women are the same as men and so should be accepted into male science. In other words, this approach suggests that women can only be successful in science by aping men. Much the same sort of critique exists in theology, where cultural feminists argue that any theological language needs to draw on the experience of women, rather than simply through imitation of male-dominated categories.

While the liberals reject any account of biological difference as a basis for exclusion, cultural feminists look to the particular social and cultural factors that shape gender differences. In particular, they accept that men and women are different, but this is on account of cultural differences, such as education, rather than biology as such. In this case the traditional traits of women are not rejected but become the spearhead of social reform. Cultural feminists take up the suggestion of J. S. Mill in that they bring to bear the particular experience of women in asking how to shape the institutions, goals and research priorities of science. Of course, by identifying such traits as defined by gender, rather than biology, the possibility that men could be included exists. Cultural feminists argue for a reformation of science, so that any pursuit of power is rejected in favour of greater equality and freedom. Such feminine qualities are not those of women alone, but rather the eternal feminine also animates men who adhere to the same values.

If women perceive science in a different way, then it follows that the choice of problems so far identified by science has been influenced by gender differences. Evelyn Keller suggests that, from the very earliest psychological stages in childhood development, science is associated with boys and non-science with girls.[15] Hence social, psychological, political and cultural factors influence science in particular ways. One example of how such differences come to be expressed is that of the choice of research priorities. There is some evidence, for example, that until recently the lack of research on contraception and women's health issues, such as menstruation, reflects the lack of participation of women in science.

A more radical example of gender difference in science is that it influences research design. In this case the choice of male rats predominantly over female rats for experiments on animal learning could be an example of how gender choice affects design.[16] While in this case the scientific justification for exclusion of females was that the females had four-day cycles that complicated the results, the exclusion of female rats does not seem justified. Keller suggests the implication is that it is the *male* that represents the species.

Another possible area where bias seems to apply is in the interpretation of observations, especially in the more socially orientated sciences. Over the last forty years or so years women working in primatology have challenged the traditional male-dominated interpretation of primate behaviour. However, more recent critical analysis of the way their work has been perceived in the popular mind shows an interesting twist to the story. Jane Goodall was popularized in the 1960s and 1970s as one who represented a unification of culture with nature in a way that avoided issues of colonization, race or gender. She seemed to offer a means of redeeming the world of Western science by her example of maternal compassion.[17] The idea of the primitive then was romantic, seen as gentle, in touch with nature and almost paradisiacal.

Dian Fossey and Birute Galdikas, on the other hand, worked in the late 1970s and 1980s when the feminist challenge to science was becoming more vocal and a negative view of the primitive was heightened in popular culture. Fossey, in particular, came to represent an 'infernal primitive', while Galdikas typified a naïve white explorer. Fossey's accounts of the way gorillas had been hacked to death helped to shift the image of the primitive from that of paradise to nightmare, showing once more that the old colonial ideas that Africa was the seat of ignorance and suspicion were just beneath the surface. Yet the photographer's expectation that Fossey would show a 'feminine' nature was disappointed. In reaction to this she became the highly unflattering opposite, a 'white woman going to seed by failing to live up to Western standards of beauty'.[18] She was portrayed as one who came close to madness in her attempts to stamp out poaching. In one *National Geographic* issue a poacher was shown tied to a stake. She was also portrayed as socially outcast, sexually unstable, hinting that she even resembled a witch. Her example shows that in this case the popular representation of women's work in science has still suffered from gender bias. More often than not aberrant behaviour of male scientists has been tolerated under the cover of eccentricity.

It does, however, become far more difficult to argue that women would significantly affect the way 'harder' sciences are done, such as physics. However, Wertheim does just that in claiming that the way physicists have spent resources for some of their projects is irresponsible.[19] In particular, the 'dream of finding a unified theory of the particles and forces of nature' becomes an obsession that leads to more and more expenditure on particle accelerators. The pressing forward of this theory to resemblance with God becomes a further justification of the work and signals a 'decadent priesthood' that has lost touch with ordinary human needs and responsibilities. For her, women's rejection of this kind of work is not surprising, as it functions in a way that is totally alienating to women.

Science and romantic eco-feminism

Once we move into this type of feminism, the critique of both science and theology comes together in an interesting way. While there are some elements in common with cultural feminism, the basis for more romantic forms of feminism is that women's difference in both biology and gender needs to be affirmed. Romantic feminists argue that liberals are mistaken in identifying access to science as the key problematic. However, they also accept that biological differences in the way men and women function do exist. But they believe that men have, in the past, defined such differences. Instead, the task of women is now to redefine their own sense of self in the light of their own experiences of body and gender. Furthermore, this leads on to a different view of the way science is done.

Romantic feminists seem to suggest that feminine values are superior to male values. In this they run the risk of replacing one kind of hierarchy with another. The close association of gender with biology reinforces this tendency. For, once the locus of gender difference becomes identified with women, then this leads back to the problems associated with essentialism. However, in this case essentialism is used to justify the dominance of women rather than men.

Eco-feminism is the term used to describe the link between women's concern for the earth and gender issues. More romantic forms of eco-feminism are associated with romantic feminism's rejection of science as totally capitulated to male values. Of course, such versions of eco-feminism exist alongside liberal and cultural eco-feminism, all of which have had a significant role in the shift towards greater concern for the needs of both women and ecology. Like those liberal campaigners for women in science, liberal eco-feminists sought to challenge governments to change laws so that they were more environmentally friendly. On the other hand, those known as cultural eco-feminists situated an exploration of the relationship between women and nature within an overall critique of patriarchy.

Eco-feminism suggests that it is possible to understand all aspects of human experience as marking an association between women and nature. For example, emotional ties in relationships are thought to be more characteristic of the psychology of women as compared to men, and such ties are deemed to be closer to 'nature', as compared to the detached reasoning of the intellect. Secondly, the social roles historically assigned to women are the practical, domestic chores, considered to be more rooted in contact with the 'earth', compared with the roles assigned to men. Finally, the biological basis of women's physiology, including in particular menstruation and childbirth, roots the experience of women in the natural cycles of the earth.

There are various ways to respond to this association of women and nature. One might be to call for direct political action in order to liberate both women and the natural world, the cry of the oppressed becoming a joint chorus of women and nature. This would be the response of social and political forms of feminism. Another response associated with more romantic forms of feminism is to celebrate the association between women and nature as a means of reclaiming women's power. In this case the power of women may be recast by looking back to ancient time when there was religious worship of a goddess. Their popularity stems, perhaps, from the interconnectedness portrayed in romantic versions of eco-feminism, a holism that even cultural eco-feminists fail to develop.

One of the landmark contributions in the development of an earth-based spirituality and a romantic portrayal of the relationship between women and nature is the book by Susan Griffin, *Woman and Nature: The Roaring Inside Her*.[20] This is no standard text in theology, but a poetic interpretation of the intense closeness between humanity and nature. In this book Griffin traces the interrelated dualisms between soul/flesh, mind/feelings and culture/nature to the terror of patriarchal man faced with mortality. Men choose to oppress women when faced with this terrifying reality. For Griffin the solution is total identification with the earth. Further, the joint voice of women and nature is an impassioned, embodied voice, unashamed in its rejection of the so-called objectivity of patriarchal modes of thought. Even though Griffin does not use the language of spirituality, she seems to hint at this by association.

Carol Christ is more insistent that the crisis that threatens the earth is spiritual as well as economic and social.[21] Both Susan Griffin and Carol Christ believe that reconstruction of an adequate relationship with the natural world must follow deconstruction of existing patterns of thinking. For Carol Christ ideas such as the goddess, earth and life are all symbolic of the whole of which we are part, so that 'the divinity that shapes our ends is life, death and change, understood both literally and as metaphor for our daily lives'.[22] Yet there seems to be little notion of any salvific role of the divine, since for her there is no ultimate justice or injustice, and the promise of life remains what it is now. Hence the only religious insight is that we are just part of the whole process of life and death.

Romantic eco-feminism seems to have arrived at an impractical solution, one that advocates the unity of all in a goddess figure, but one that suffers from the possible difficulties associated with a close identification of women and nature through essentialism. Such essentialism is problematic as it forms the basis and rationale of the very structures of oppression against women, for example, the compatibility theories discussed earlier. I would agree with those who reject essentialist forms of feminism that the association of essentialism with oppressive structures cannot be shaken off in the way that romantic eco-feminism suggests. Charlene Spretnak writes in a similar vein, drawing on the Gaia hypothesis. I discussed the problems associated with this particular understanding of the transformation of science in the last chapter. The romantic versions of eco-feminism of Carol Christ or Susan Griffin are also problematic in that while they are perhaps comforting to some feminists, they are even less likely to have any influence at all on the practice of mainstream science.

Carolyn Merchant's response to the unsatisfactory nature of spiritual/romantic eco-feminism is to present the case for a socialist form of eco-feminism, one that explores the means of production advocated by capitalist economies and asks what is at stake for women and nature.[23] Furthermore, she suggests that particular forms of production have particular consequences on biological reproduction, for example, the effects on the unborn of chemical or nuclear pollutants in the environment, the interventionist technologies practised, such as chemical methods of birth control, amniocentesis and so on. While Merchant's analysis comes from a different starting-point than traditional cultural feminism, her solution unfortunately still seems to be based more on a romantic ideology rather than on politics. She suggests that new forms of socialist ecology could bring human production and reproduction into balance with nature's production and reproduction, leading to a sustainable global environment. But what are the philosophies behind different feminist ideas about science? Are there ways of redescribing science from a feminist philosophical perspective? It is to these questions that I now turn.

Feminist philosophies of science

Feminist empiricism

A feminist empiricist approach to science asserts that we do not need to reject science as such, but says the distortions of science come from gender and other cultural biases. Any distortion of the results owing to gender influences needs to be challenged. The assumption is that the quest for pure objectivity is a fair one, and that eventually such cultural influences will be recognized by the scientists themselves. Stephen Jay Gould is one influential scientist who believes that feminist science at its best is quite simply good science. Even for practising ecologists, who view the world in more holistic categories than some scientists, empiricism is still the pillar on which their science is built.[24] Pickett and his colleagues suggest that as long as we recognize that science works as a *community* exercise, then it is capable of correcting cultural and gender influences.

This form of contextual empiricism is a step away from the logical positivism of the nineteenth century, but is it really realistic about the way science works in practice? In particular, this suggestion fails to consider the way that feminist thinkers from outside the scientific community have exposed the particular gendered framework of science. Nonetheless, a version of empiricism is, in practice, the view taken by many women scientists, as will be discussed later.

but are they necessarily feminists?

The turn to romanticism

A philosophical approach to science that perhaps has a wide appeal to many feminists is the notion of the organic, as opposed to the mechanistic, way of viewing the earth. In this it largely rejects the assumption of scientific reductionism. This idea was mentioned in the previous chapter and several times earlier in this book.

In particular, Carolyn Merchant, in her book *The Death of Nature*, suggests that it was only with the rise of modern experimental science that nature was considered inert and dead.[25] She suggests that up until this time the belief that the earth was in some sense alive prevailed, along with a strong sense of the supernatural at work in the created world. She is particularly critical of Francis Bacon, who she believes portrayed nature as a female to be tortured by men of science, hinting by his use of language of the torment of witches. Such language, she suggests, paved the way for the acceptance of the exploitation of nature. However, she does not reject the association of the female with the earth that Bacon presupposed. Rather, Merchant insists that the twin ideas of the earth as mother and organism served to constrain the activity of humans.

There seems to be a paradox here. On the one hand, Merchant suggests that the portrayal of the earth in the form of a female figure encouraged Bacon to exploit and 'rape' nature for the benefit of humankind. Yet, on the other hand, the idea of the earth as female organism served to constrain human exploitation in earlier generations. Her argument does seem somewhat inconsistent, reflecting perhaps the dilemma that is always associated with the identification of women with the earth.

There are further historical issues worth noting that Merchant seems to have overlooked. She draws on the seventeenth-century writer Gottfried Wilhelm Leibniz for her understanding that the world is alive in a version of his cosmic vitalism. However, she incorporates, in addition, a notion of mutual intersubjectivity that is completely lacking from Liebniz's position.[26] Furthermore, Leibniz's organic views did not, as Merchant implies, automatically lead to a rejection of hierarchy. Rather, he seemed quite content with the status quo, accepting all that comes as the will of God. To view the world through the stark lens of either that of death in mechanistic science or life in organicism seems too crude an interpretation. Both aspects offer some insight into reality, and it is easy to adopt either metaphor in a whole-hearted way that Janet Biehl describes as simply 'childish'. Moreover, it is hard to see how science might be transformed back to an organicism in the way Merchant suggests. Even 'evidence' for the Gaia hypothesis, in as far as it exists, relies to some extent on experimental methods based on traditional science. The most that we might hope for is a shift towards a more organic and less wholly mechanistic approach to the natural world.

Feminist science and standpoint theory

The possibility that a feminist approach to science is capable of generating a different form of science is associated with standpoint theory. It rejects empiricism as the model for science as it seems to accept that women would not change the way knowledge is gained. Above all, standpoint theory insists that all knowledge is gendered. Moreover, it also rejects the postmodern alternative that seems to make no value judgment on any form of science, becoming just preferred belief. Standpoint theory accepts, with empiricism, that realism is possible, but argues that it must be approached from a feminist perspective. It is, therefore, the feminist philosophy that seems to me to be the one that offers the greatest challenge to science, since postmodern philosophy in its extreme form is likely to be dismissed by scientists as nonsense. Hilary Rose believes that one way this revisioning may be possible is through the theme of caring. In particular, she suggests that once we think from a perspective of caring our rationality becomes more responsible to others.[27]

Sandra Harding has also argued strongly for feminist standpoint theory as the basis for a new philosophy of science.[28] The fluid categories of both science and feminist make it hard to envisage what a feminist science might be like. She rejects the idea of a 'feminine' science, even if the qualities of femininity have been undervalued in the history of science. Harding suggests that feminist science needs to take into account the fact that it has in the past ignored the perspective of women or any less dominant groups. In this she does argue for a greater 'objectivity', but one that is not simply modelled on the claim for objectivity of the past.

The turn to the experience of women as a basis for a new philosophy of science is significant as it is an attempt to avoid the issue of essentialism that is inevitable once women are defined in terms of their nature or biology. Once gender is evoked to replace biological body boundaries, this leads to a further difficulty in that it seems to imply a split between the social construct of gender and the biological sexual body. The difficulty for many feminists with social reconstruction in terms of gender is that it is theoretical and abstract, thereby avoiding the material, mechanistic images of the body, which most feminists are keen to challenge.

One fascinating way out of this dilemma for feminists is to draw on more recent quantum images of the body that refuse to accept Cartesian dualism between mind and body.[29] In this case intelligence is thought to pervade the entire body. More recent endocrinology studies have shown that neuropeptides and thoughts are interrelated with each other. There is no 'causal link' between neuropeptides and thoughts, rather they are different aspects of the same reality.[30] Consciousness acts more like a quantum field that finds expression both materially and mentally, even though it is outside our own conscious awareness. In this case holistic science is coming to the service of feminism in order to reject previous mechanistic images of science.

Feminist science and postmodern alternatives

Feminist cultural studies and debates in the humanities are replete with references to postmodernity. In fact, a postmodern culture is assumed to be the case in a way that contrasts sharply with the scientific acceptance of critical realism. Postmodernity in general stresses the way models of culture are social constructs. Even science is met with the razor-sharp gaze of social deconstruction, so that any idea is as good as any other and comes from a particular understanding of reality. However, in areas such as the new physics and ecology a more open approach to existence is possible and could in some sense be thought of as postmodern.[31] In this sense scientists would reject any absolute truth claims, even though the search for truth remains. Yet it seems to me that in the humanities postmodernity is capable of going much further than this in that it rejects any claim for reality in the discoveries of science.

Those feminists who have drawn on postmodernity use it as a basis for the deconstruction of science. All views are taken as contextual and are accepted, apart from those that make universal metaphysical claims or construct a 'grand narrative', which are dismissed. There is a clear difficulty here for feminists in that it becomes much harder to respond in a way that offers a challenge to science other than simple deconstruction. While the openness that this approach suggests leaves behind rigid, constricting views of reality, its free-floating nature seems diffuse and undefined. Furthermore, even those scientists who do move into areas of chaos theory still search for the reality that is at the heart of the discoveries. A postmodern philosophy taken to its limit amounts to a total rejection of the scientific project in a way that leads not so much to its transformation as mutual hostility and marginalization.

Practical implications of feminist science

What might be the practical implications of the feminist critique of science and associated alternative philosophies? Liberal feminism is often associated with an empiricist philosophy. In this case the reformation of science is such that it takes into account justice issues, such as access of women to scientific employment. In practice this is likely to be easier in universities than in industry, where any attempt to change the system has to be justified primarily by reference to market forces. Of course, if the company image is one that supports women this may improve its status, but a groundswell of public opinion in favour of women in science is necessary first. Empiricists accept that other aspects of the design of science and the research priorities may need to be scrutinized in order to eliminate cultural biases against women.

Those who argue for a shift to a more holistic or organic view of science would promote those sciences that look at systems rather than scientific reductionism. It is important to note that sciences, such as ecology, can reject both organicism and reductionism in favour of the idea of a philosophy based on scientific community and consensus. It is surprising that feminists do not so far seem to have taken up this idea to any great extent and used it in their critiques of science. This contrasts with feminist theology, where the idea of community is much more important, especially the community around women. There is, however, an acceptance that the wider experience of women is important, as will be discussed in more detail below.

Standpoint theory is one that leads to a different overall framework for science. A particular theme, such as caring, holism or maternal thinking, becomes the basis for a new approach to scientific priorities and issues. How far the scientific community at large will respond to these challenges is hard to say. Postmodernity, on the other hand, is more radical in its deconstruction of all universal claims. While it gives an important corrective to over-enthusiastic or even utopian claims for feminist science, I suggest that science in order to be science cannot reject its search for reality, even though it can respond by becoming more modest about making universal truth claims.

From my own practical experience of working as a woman in plant physiology research, the idea that scientific knowledge was gendered was not obvious to me at the time. Nonetheless, I was aware of the lack of representation of women in senior positions in science, and the tendency of some of those men in power to have sexist attitudes. I was also aware of the lack of interest by the majority of scientists in the wider issues of philosophy and ethics raised by applied biology. However, it did not occur to me at this time that the lack of concern could be gender-related. It seemed to me that the specialization of science gave it great strength, but also arrogance towards other ways of knowing. By contrast, once I moved into theological studies the gender issue was far more obvious. Now the subject became all-important in interpretation. Furthermore, the hostility of a significant percentage of my fellow male students towards women in theology was no longer veiled, coinciding as it did with the struggle towards the ordination of women in the late 1980s and early 1990s.

Another question that is worth asking here is whether there are particular reasons for women not wishing to become included in mainstream science. Certainly, recent work in the USA suggests that women are attracted to the margins of established scientific communities. In addition, a recent study has shown how the early increase of women in mainstream science in the 1970s and 1980s has tailed off in recent years.[32] The authors, Eisenhart and Finkel, believe that factors such as sexism in the workplace or unequal opportunities are not the only ones involved in the lack of women's participation in science. Their research showed that the kind of scientific work to which women were attracted was something that had practical consequences, such as conservation groups or work with political or social relevance. This 'lower-status' science offered a science that was more socially aware, but was also unstable in financial terms. The common view of the women who worked in these areas that they were 'better places' for women to be, disguised the fact that their employment was often unstable, and they often did not have the necessary institutional supports in areas such as child care.

Finally, given that the experience of women in science is from the margins, might this have any further implications for science? One argument is that more support needs to be given to women engaged in more practical research. However, this fails to challenge the philosophy of elite science. A more radical suggestion is that the framework of science itself must change by taking into account the views of ordinary women.[33] While this applies more specifically to the way science is taught, taking particular account of its social context, it also serves to redefine what science is. For example, knowledge brought to science from non-conventional sources such as African experiences of healing needs to be valued rather than dismissed as 'quackery'.[34] However, while the authors suggest that this is still 'subject to empirical check, like any other scientific knowledge', it is not clear how such checking could apply in these experiences. Nonetheless, the demand to make science more accessible, more related to everyday experiences and emotions and more 'human' in its orientation is a valid enterprise. Yet it is also fair to say that many practising scientists claim that it *does* involve the whole person and it is *not* as coldly objective as it might appear. The transformation that is asked for is one that is more inclusive, but it also highlights the way science does happen in practice, as suggested in Chapter 2.

Conclusions

I have argued in this chapter that feminist critiques of both science and theology need to be taken into account in mapping the debates between science and religion. Biological science, in particular, raises issues for feminists in that it has helped to define women and men in terms of their bodies. There are three possible feminist reactions to the largely male exclusivity of science, especially the hard sciences like physics. One is the liberal campaign for greater equality of access by women. In this model the essentialism associated with the exclusion of women from science in the past and through current models of sociobiology becomes deeply suspect. However, this leaves untouched empiricism as the basis for the philosophy of science, except in so far as the presence of women will make a difference to scientific culture.

A second reaction is to highlight issues of gender exclusion, so that those educational and cultural factors that tend to exclude women from science are explored. Science becomes transformed through a new gendered perspective. Yet such a reaction might suggest that there are no real differences between men and women other than those associated with gender. Once more biological issues seem to be separated from theoretical ones in a way that is counter to the feminist desire to collapse Cartesian dualisms of mind/body, men/women, soul/matter and so on.

A third reaction is to retrieve something of the ideas of essentialism, but now use them as a way of celebrating women's difference from men. A romantic feminist approach denies any value to androcentric visions of reality. In more extreme versions women draw on religious motifs, such as the female goddess, as a counter to the claim by men to have discovered God in the theory of everything. Other eco-feminists claim to have found in the natural world new forms of cosmic vitalism. Yet any association of women with nature has a highly chequered history. I suggest that in this case the association works less in favour of women and more to reinforce the very patriarchy that feminism rejects.

The possible alternatives in terms of philosophy are either to argue from a particular view, or standpoint theory, or to dismiss all claims to universality in the acceptance of a radical postmodern analysis of culture. A more intermediate position is one that insists on taking account the experience of women, especially those of ordinary women in their everyday lives. Such experiences include an acceptance of emotion, intuition and common sense as valid ways of knowing. Perhaps the feminist contribution to the transformation of science is to help scientists to be bolder in their acknowledgment of this human dimension. Once this happens, then the space opens up for a genuine dialogue with feminist issues, such as a shift in orientation of science so that it becomes a more fully humane enterprise, taking more account of wider social and cultural issues. Yet how might biological science be transformed in the future? What are the particular theological issues that are raised by any revisioning of science? I begin to address these questions in the final chapter.

10

Shaping a future science

Working at the interface of biological science and theology is no
easy task, not least because those who are committed to either one
or the other disciplines are enthralled by the image of the natural
world from their particular perspective. A slow thaw in relations of
science with theology has begun to take place in the new physics,
with a new openness to forms of religion and mysticism. I have
suggested in this book that such openness is a double-edged
sword. On the one hand, it may lead to less scepticism about
religious ways of knowing, yet on the other it may relegate theology to 'wishy-washy' forms of spirituality that have very little real
theological content. I still come across biologists who may have
heard of eminent physicists, such as Paul Davies, but think that
the theological task must be somehow to prove that God exists or
even emerges from the sciences. Such a truncated view of theology actually makes the dialogue with biology harder, rather than
easier. Or again, while biologists may recognize that ethical issues
in the new genetics are very important, any connection with
religion or theology has not even entered their consciousness.

From a theological perspective suspicion is also likely to be
present; all engagement with biological sciences may be viewed as
detracting from the main theoretical task of contemporary theology, namely, to develop an adequate systematic approach within a
theological framework. Like many other theologians who have also
been scientists, it seems to me that theology cannot afford to
ignore science if it is to have something to say that is relevant in the
twenty-first century. This is not the same as suggesting that all
theology must be applied in some way to particular issues. Rather,

the particular way that theology emerges needs to take account of the scientific context, just as it takes into account other cultural contexts such as feminism, poverty, race and so on. The temptation now is that theology may begin to lose its identity and not challenge, where appropriate, aspects of the scientific philosophy in which it is situated.

The intention throughout this book has been to show how theology not only can learn from science, but also science needs to listen to insights from theology as well. I intend in this chapter to offer an overview of the book as a way of pointing to the future of science, especially the biological sciences, given that the examples I have used are illustrative, rather than exhaustive. Yet such a future is one that also serves to challenge theology even further to engage more fully with scientific issues. Hence this is not just about a future for science, but a future for the theological task as well.

As we enter a new millennium, some consciousness of how our attitudes to nature have shifted and developed historically helps to put in perspective our current anxieties about genetic engineering and environmental issues. Nonetheless, many of our images of nature have tended to coexist alongside each other and find their roots as far back as the ancient Greek civilizations. The belief that in the ancient world nature was organic and that this was then replaced with a mechanical view through the philosophy of Descartes is popular, but rather an oversimplification. Instead, both romantic and more mechanistic understandings of the world have coexisted for a long time, even if at certain periods of history one or other has tended to take cultural prominence.

I suggested that a more interesting shift for us to consider concerns the move away from an understanding of nature as symbolic. There was a belief in the early church Fathers, right up to the Protestant Reformation, that the natural world acted as a symbol of something in the spiritual or transcendent realm. Hence any reference to nature in the biblical texts pointed to this spiritual dimension. According to this scenario, the physical and biological reality of the natural world was far less important than its spiritual dimension. Indeed, an investigation of the empirical

basis for the spiritual insights might even be considered blasphe-
mous. Once the symbolic role of nature faded through changing
methods of exegesis and biblical interpretation, this opened the
way for more detailed empirical work. Such observations of nature
had, of course, already begun in the Middle Ages, especially once
Aquinas adopted an Aristotelian framework for his theology. Yet it
was the demise of the symbolic understanding of nature that
permitted empirical investigations of the natural world in a way
that had been much more difficult in an age gripped by the notion
of nature as symbol.

The belief that nature might become a mirror for the divine
mind became popular among the experimental scientist–theologians of the seventeenth century, such as John Ray, and was taken
up later by other writers, such as William Paley. Much of this
physico-theology sounds rather odd from a contemporary perspective, but it was a way of trying to show that all discoveries in the
natural world could point to the divine mind. Unlike the symbolic
view of nature, the idea of nature as mirror actually encouraged
scientific investigation and became a way of 'thinking God's
thoughts after him'. This was not a full-blown natural theology in
the sense understood by the Roman Catholic Church, for the
natural world only hinted at who God is, rather than expressed a
true revelation of God. As Protestant writers, these scientists still
insisted on the primacy of the revelation of God in the Word,
rather than the world. Nonetheless, it did at least show a positive
attitude towards the natural world that eventually became lost in
subsequent neo-Calvinistic works.

The stinging critique of all natural theologies by David Hume,
alongside the momentous evolutionary thesis of Charles Darwin,
effectively dampened the quest for a physico-theology. Instead,
the belief that nature is autonomous, governed by its own internal
laws, gradually took hold. It is this belief that is still the most
popular among biologists today. It renders a deep resistance to any
discussion of the significance of theology. Nonetheless, in physics
the idea that the natural world might in some sense act as a mirror
for God is beginning to come back in vogue, even among those
who do not think of themselves as being particularly religious.

Contemporary biological writers, such as Richard Dawkins or Matt Ridley, have effectively quelled most attempts to retrieve a religious dimension in the biological world.

Yet the challenge remains for biological scientists who are also Christian believers and in some cases theologians, namely, how to interpret divine action in a world that is shaped by evolution. Certainly, it is not impossible for excellent work in biology to include a more spiritual dimension, as the writings of Barbara McClintock show. Yet, even here, such spirituality never entered her writing in the way that mysticism has entered the writing of modern physicists. It is as if the resistance in biology is part of the legacy of Darwin. For all his brilliance, the post-Darwinian scientism that has emerged from Darwin's theory casts a shadow over any contemporary attempts at reconciliation. Suggestions that really Darwin is a 'disguised friend' to theology, while perhaps comforting to those who are Christians, do not sound convincing to those who have adopted an atheistic or agnostic framework for their biology. I suggest that it is important for theologians to acknowledge the strength of the claim that nature is autonomous, rather than arriving at too facile an accommodation. For if we simply locate the work of God in all the molecular changes in evolution, such as mutations, the problem of theodicy appears in a new form. If we locate the action of God only in those mutations that lead to the emergence of new species, the choice again seems arbitrary, and set by our own preconceptions of what it means to declare the creation as good.

Nonetheless, once we engage a little further in the dialogue between science and religion, we can find examples where science could be said to have a religious dimension. Certainly, the early-seventeenth-century chemists and physicists were as committed to their faith as they were to their science. The temptation, of course, is for the religious insights to be assimilated to a scientific world view and become simply a product of science. Yet there is another problem with this particular form of dialogue as well, in that through the assimilation a new mythology emerges, one that takes its bearing from science, while claiming to be supportive of religious belief. In this case the theological content emerging from the assimilation process is so changed as to render any claim for dialogue somewhat superfluous. While, on the one hand, it is important not to dismiss as irrelevant those scientists who claim to have religious insights, however heterodox they seem to us, it is the task of any responsible theology to critique the religious content of such claims. The hostility between science and religion in the past has tended to encourage those engaged at the interface to welcome with open arms any attempt at reconciliation, however spurious from a theological point of view. Nicholas Lash has done more than anyone to force us to consider the superficial nature of some attempts at dialogue between theology and the sciences.[1]

Of course, the dialogue may also become distorted in other ways as well, in those situations where claims are made for science that go far beyond its own capacity as science. In these cases science takes the place of religion and actually becomes the means of salvation, even though theological language as such is probably not used. Certainly, we can find examples of biologists, such as Richard Dawkins, who make claims for the role of the imagination in science and its capacity to induce wonder to the extent that any other means to arrive at a similar experience is dismissed as based on fantasy rather than fact. The spurious nature of such claims becomes more obvious once we start to tease out the values in science, the *fact* that science can never become totally value-free, even if its goal is to become totally objective and removed from the subject. While there are some scientists who acknowledge the culture of all science and realize that this culture will help solve the questions it sets itself, many ordinary practising scientists still see science as somehow being a superior form of knowledge, beyond culture.

Yet there are aspects of scientific knowing that theologians may welcome in the face of the deeper uncertainties presented by other cultural changes, such as those posed by postmodernism. The search for truth in science is one that theologians can recognize, even if they resist any claim by scientists that this truth is sufficient in and of itself to provide meaning. Traditional approaches to scientific method consider whether the data are primary, known as induction, or secondary, known as deduction. While deductive methods are said to supersede inductive ones, the biological sciences still tend to rely largely on inductive approaches. Furthermore, frameworks for scientific method, such as the falsification hypothesis, sit uneasily with the approaches used in the biological sciences. Hence any attempt to somehow fit theology into a model of falsification is ignoring the fact that this philosophy of science is inappropriate for the study of the natural world in the biological sciences.

I suggested, instead, that a narrative approach to scientific method not only brings the characters alive from a literary perspective, but also allows the cultural dimension of science to come into view in a way that is difficult for the more sterile methodological approaches such as deduction and induction. The narrative of the way the new ecology has emerged in our more recent history puts a new slant on philosophical and theological reflection in this area. The new ecology now speaks not just in terms of ecosystems, but also in terms of unstable and fluid 'patches', changing in a dynamic way as a result of particular disturbances. Gone is the fixed belief in stability in ecosystems. Yet such a change has a profound influence on theology as well. The politics of ecology and the philosophy of environmental ethics have tended to rely on an image of ecology as a system of stable, interconnected relationships. Even if there is an acknowledgment that the ecosystems are in dynamic relationships, this is within an understanding that the system is a stable whole. Theologians such as Jürgen Moltmann, too, have taken ecological metaphors and applied them to God, considered to be a social, ecological Trinity. Yet once the biological basis for ecology shifts, how might this affect any proposal for an ecological Trinity?

Barbara McClintock is a very significant biologist in the context of this discussion of method. I suggest that her biography is another way of demonstrating how science proceeds in a way that would be impossible if we just examined her scientific papers alone. Indeed, once her biographer opens up the particular religious aspects to McClintock's approach to her subject, it becomes obvious that without her religious belief she could not have

continued in the way she did against considerable forces of oppo-
sition. Her work is interesting in that although she resisted the
scientific dogma of the time, she did so on the basis that her own
observations of the natural world forced her to declare herself
different. It was this sensitivity to her material, this 'feeling for
the organism', that kept her going in those times when she must
have felt that she had 'fallen from grace' as far as the scientific
establishment was concerned. Fortunately, her story has a happy
ending, in that she eventually won a Nobel Prize for Medicine, but
one wonders if science has really taken this lesson to heart. The
new molecular biology continues to hold its grip on the scientific
imagination of many of the most able scientists. While all
scientists are necessarily committed to their work, as Michael
Polanyi has demonstrated, when it excludes all other voices it
becomes particularly problematic.

The science of genetic engineering has grown enormously
since McClintock first made those early discoveries of transposable elements in the chromosomes of maize plants. Some might
argue that genetic engineering is a way of artificially transposing
different gene combinations. However, while the movements that
McClintock discovered were within a single species, genetic
engineering allows genetic transfer between species that are very
different from one another. The methods used in the transfer of
genetic material are fairly crude in practice and lead to a fairly low
'success rate'. Yet, in spite of these problems, genetic engineering
has been applied in a number of different ways for particular
purposes. Examples include the treatment of genetic disease in
humans, the cloning of animals to produce pharmaceuticals for
medical purposes, the applications to crops so that yield is
enhanced or new products made and so on. Nonetheless, many
ecologists and some medical practitioners resist genetic engineering because of the risks to human health and the environment.
While there is little direct evidence to support the claim for deleterious effects of genetic engineering, the possibility is still very
real and cannot be dismissed. The use of patents in genetic engineering raises other issues of both animal 'rights' and justice in the
human community. The possible use of genetic engineering in

biological warfare is very real, and a subject that few biologists are prepared to discuss.

Genetic engineering offers an ambivalent promise, one that is reflected in the mixed reaction of the churches, especially evident in the reports of the World Council of Churches. Yet it is notable that the official response of the Anglican Church towards genetic engineering seems to have become more positive, at least at the time of writing of this book, even if considerable doubts are raised at the grass roots. Almost all the churches resist genetic manipulation of the human germ-line, while welcoming somatic therapy where it is used to treat human diseases. The concern of the official Roman Catholic Church is related to its stance on abortion, namely, any manipulations that seem to encourage the destruction of life are vigorously resisted. For example, the Vatican is particularly hostile towards genetic diagnostic testing where it is used to promote termination of pregnancy. Yet, on the other hand, it does seem to take a very different attitude to manipulations of animal and vegetable matter where the outcome is one that seems to benefit humanity. The Church of Scotland has taken the lead in exploring ethical issues associated with the genetic engineering of non-humans through the Society, Religion and Technology Project. It is particularly hesitant to endorse the patenting of life. The mixed response of the churches shows some cooperation at the level of the World Council, but in general a lack of any theological framework for the discussion of the issues. I suggested that one way that the ecumenical debate may move forward is through the rediscovery of the Wisdom motif, common to the biblical, Thomistic and Orthodox traditions.

This rediscovery of Wisdom offers a way into approaching the theology of the new genetics. Taking the case studies of genetically modified food and animal/human cloning, I argued that theological positions can be made both in favour and against. Yet it seemed to me that in these more difficult cases Wisdom tended to point to a greater need for caution on the part of scientists. Food, in particular, has religious significance that goes beyond just simple consumption of organic materials for energy. I suggested that the issues raised by the possibility of human cloning are highly significant for theological reflection, for it impinges on our understanding of what it means to be made in the image of God, *imago Dei*.

These theological questions cannot be separated from ethical debate, as became clear in the response of the different churches discussed earlier. I argued next that the secular ethical approach has looked at narrow questions of risk and benefit, taking a consequentialist approach to ethics. This approach inevitably leads to deadlock and mistrust between those who are in favour and those who are against, since clear evidence of either the long-term benefits or the risks is not yet forthcoming. Moreover, it tends to reduce ethics to an empirical discussion of measured and quantifiable risks and benefits. I suggest that this imposes a straitjacket on the ethical discussion in that it is imposing a scientific model on ethics in an area where science has failed to find the answers.

Deontological approaches do not fare much better either. However, by looking at the intrinsic arguments for and against genetic intervention, a greater honesty may be brought into the discussion. It seems to me that the language of consequentialism betrays a much deeper commitment either for or against the new technologies. An alternative approach that may lead to greater possibilities for dialogue is a recovery of the virtue tradition in ethics, in particular the virtue of Wisdom. I have already outlined the way Wisdom can become incorporated into a more ecumenical approach to the issues and a framework for theological reflection. In this scenario Wisdom does not present those who search for her with rigid answers, but remains open in its approach to new possibilities in science as well as being aware of its dangers. Yet in every given case some sort of appraisal is possible and constructive. The ambiguity remains prior to reflection, but becomes clearer through dialogue and discussion. Of course, there may be some situations that are necessarily ambiguous, especially as even in a Wisdom ethic the consequences will be taken into account. But, in addition to consequences, the motive and intention of the players are significant as well. I have argued that by building up a Wisdom ethic, an ethic that leads to character formation, the ability to make decisions even in these difficult circumstances is facilitated.

Wisdom opens up wider issues for discussion of the new genetics, and looks at social and environmental consequences rather
than just the narrow scientific issues. Yet we could ask if there
might be other models for science that are more organic and less
mechanistic in their philosophy. The Gaia hypothesis is a good
example of a very different approach to science. However, even
within Gaia theory we find scientists taking markedly different
approaches, viewing Gaia as a simple way of explaining the interconnections between living things and their environment on a
planetary level, through to teleological models of the earth as
a giant organism. Such different approaches to the science of
Gaia are mirrored in a wide diversity of theological and ethical
responses, though often in ignorance of the scientific alternatives.
I suggested that on this basis Gaia proves to be an unhelpful model
for theological reflection, stirring up as it does a latent religious
memory of the earth goddess.

This discussion dovetails into considerations about the place of
women in science, especially the biological sciences. I suggested
that an appreciation of the way feminists have responded to questions about women in science is significant, not just for feminist
theology, but also for current debates in science and religion. This
is an area that has been sorely neglected by those working at the
interface, possibly because there is a distinct lack of women's voices.
Yet if the institutional church and theology in general has tended
to exclude women, so too has science, even if the biological
sciences proved to be rather more accommodating. The relationship between women, science and nature is a particularly complex
but interesting area for discussion. The early scientists attempted
to exclude women on the basis of compatibility theories, that by
nature women were incapable of rational science.

The responses of women to such exclusion from science follow
a pattern that is similar in some respects to that in theology. One
is to dredge through the history of science and find forgotten
examples of women who have contributed to science but who have
become written out of the record. The issue for these liberal feminists is simply one of reclaiming the rights of women to equality of
treatment. Another approach of cultural feminism is to claim that

the way women have been excluded is a reality that reflects gender differences in the way boys and girls are socialized into different roles, rather than biological differences. In both scenarios all notions of biological compatibility are rigorously rejected. A third, more romantic response is to acknowledge that differences exist, but now to interpret them very differently so that women serve to shape a new way of doing science, one that accepts that nature and women are in some sense intricately connected. Of course, the charge of essentialism hovers close to this position.

A way out of this dilemma, while still refusing to let go of the possibility of a different sort of science, is through the development of feminist standpoint theories. Such theories emphasize the experience of women as paramount for the development of a new science. This kind of approach is perhaps the one most feared by traditionalist scientists, for it seems to suggest that it is possible to find alternatives in scientific policy-making. Another option, which is one that is also favoured by many feminist theologians, is to stress the postmodern culture in which science is now situated. Yet, taken to its extreme, dialogue with science no longer becomes possible, since all scientific theories are seen as simply cultural constructs. Such a view is not likely to impinge on the scientific enterprise, other than triggering a laugh of dismissal.

Where does all this lead in terms of a future for science? I suggest that, paradoxically perhaps, the postmodern context in which we find ourselves does open up more room for dialogue between disciplines. In particular, postmodernity gives us the tools to challenge reductionist science as the only way of knowing. Yet there are clearly limits to the deconstruction approach to science. Postmodernity on its own leaves an empty space in which all kinds of spurious forms of mysticism can flourish. Instead, a future for science can best be imagined from a theological perspective through the lens of Wisdom.[2]

One of the problems of the new biology is that in its very newness it has not yet had time to be tested. From a psychological perspective Wisdom is a quality that often grows with age and experience. It is the employment of decision strategies that are effective, as they have been learned over time. It involves solving a complex set of questions simultaneously, looking in particular to the future in order to consider long-term effects as well as short-term ones. The ability to see things in ways that take account of many different factors arises from the gendered experience of women. It is therefore women who are the most likely candidates in taking the lead in this respect, though Wisdom is certainly not related to biological nature. Rather than being one character trait, Wisdom is a blend of qualities that come together in a certain way. Hence, even in terms of biological science, Wisdom is a good that needs to be fostered.

From a theological perspective Wisdom is an alignment not just with any value or any outcome, but with the purposes and intentions of God. Wisdom or Sophia is the feminine face of God, reflected not just in the biblical tradition of Lady Wisdom but even in traditions that have excluded a prominent institutional place for women, as in Eastern Orthodoxy. Wisdom gives theology a distinct voice that prevents it from merely assimilating to the needs of science alone.[3]

The way this would work out in practice to develop science in the future relies on dialogue and greater communication between scientists, policy-makers, members of the public, ethicists and theologians. Fortunately, there are some signs of a greater appreciation of the importance of such dialogue though the development of committees that are more inclusive, rather than less inclusive. The shift in 1999 of the composition of those elected to be members of the Advisory Commission on Releases into the Environment is a good example of such a change. The suggestion of Pope John Paul II is relevant, that scientists need to

> continue their efforts without ever abandoning the *sapiential* horizon within which scientific and technological achievements are wedded to the philosophical and ethical values which are the distinctive and indelible mark of the human person.[4]

Yet John Paul II does not answer how such a sapiential horizon may be recovered within science. I suggest that it is through dialogue, through exploring the boundaries of science and theology, that such a sapiential horizon comes into view. Yet such Wisdom is not just for the benefit of science, but also for theology as well. A theology that is informed by science and the possibilities of science is a theology that is unfolding, one that is open to the future, while still true to its task to reflect an understanding of God that is appropriate for the culture in which we find ourselves.

The new biology presents us with very novel and challenging perceptions of how we view the natural world. Yet it also challenges our anthropology, how we think about who we are in relation to God, humanity and the earth. Wisdom, as an anthropological term as well as a theological term, reminds humanity of its frailty before God. For the Wisdom of theology is also the Wisdom of the cross. Such stark contrast with secular Wisdom will no doubt be unpalatable to the positivistic attitudes that still pervade the new biology. Yet it seems to me that if science is to have any future at all, it *must* be prepared to take a sacrificial stance for the greater common good. It is no longer possible to suggest that just because something is achievable that it is automatically good. Wisdom affirms the good in science where it is in alignment with moral values of prudence, justice and temperance, but rejects those developments that work against human dignity and respect for animals and the natural environment.

The future of science, especially biological evolution, is undoubtedly in our hands. How far we use this power for the good of the environment and the wider good of the human race depends on decisions that we are making now. It would be foolish to put the full responsibility for this new science into the hands of scientists alone. We are all indirectly responsible for the way science comes to be shaped in our society. I will finish this book with a plea for greater cooperation between all parties, including policy-makers and lay persons, not just specialist theologians and scientists. Above all, we need to recover a sense of realistic hope, that anything we can contribute, however small, really makes a difference. This small step becomes the sign of true faith, one that acknowledges that our limited search for Wisdom will never be complete, yet it is still giving honour and glory to God, who is the author of all our Wisdom.

Notes

Preface

1. See, especially, R. J. Russell et al., (eds), *Evolutionary and Molecular Biology*, Vatican City and CTNS, Berkeley 1999.
2. For example, A. Peacocke, *Theology for a Scientific Age*, enlarged edition, London: SCM Press 1993; C. Southgate et al., (eds), *God, Humanity and the Cosmos*, Edinburgh: T. & T. Clark 1999.

Acknowledgments

1. C. Deane-Drummond, 'Theology and the Culture of the Sciences', *New Blackfriars* 81, 2000, pp. 36–46.
2. C. Deane-Drummond, 'Come to the Banquet: Seeking Wisdom in a Genetically Engineered Earth', *Ecotheology* 9, July 2000 pp. 27–37; 'Wisdom: A Voice for Theology at the Boundary with Science', *Ecotheology*, January 2001, *in press*.
3. C. Deane-Drummond, *Genetic Engineering for a New Earth?*, Cambridge: Grove Ethical Series E114 1999; *Creation Through Wisdom*, Edinburgh: T. & T. Clark 2000.

Chapter 1

1. P. Hooper with M. Palmer, 'St Francis and Ecology' in E. Breuilly and M. Palmer (eds), *Christianity and Ecology*, pp. 82–3.
2. See, in particular, J. Brooke and G. Cantor, *Reconstructing Nature*; for a contrasting view, see C. Merchant, *The Death of Nature*.
3. I am indebted to Peter Harrison for many of the historical details of the following discussion. See P. Harrison, *The Bible, Protestantism and the Rise of Modern Science*.

4. This book is still in print: J. Ray, *The Wisdom of God Manifested in the Works of Creation.*

5. Preface to *The Great Instauration,* Francis Bacon (1620) in J. Devey (ed.), *The Physical and Metaphysical Works of Lord Bacon.*

6. C. Raven, 'Synthetic Philosophy in the Seventeenth Century: A Study of Early Science', Herbert Spencer Lecture.

7. C. Raven, *John Ray, Naturalist.*

8. F. W. Dillistone, *Charles Raven.*

9. C. Raven, *Natural Religion and Christian Theology.* It is interesting to note that Raven vigorously defended Teilhard's work, even to the point of suggesting that he *had* paid sufficient attention to the problem of evil. See C. Raven, *Teilhard de Chardin,* pp. 174–84.

10. C. Raven, *Science, Religion and the Future,* p. 29.

11. Ibid., p. 17.

12. Ibid., p. 66.

13. J. R. Jacob, 'The Ideological Origins of Robert Boyle's Natural Philosophy', *Journal of European Studies* 2, 1972, p. 16. I am indebted to John Brooke for providing the source of references to Boyle, Kepler and Chambers. See J. H. Brooke, 'Religious Belief and the Content of the Sciences', *Osiris* 16, 2001, *in press*; and J. H. Brooke, *Science and Religion: Some Historical Perspectives,* pp. 52–116.

14. M. Caspar, *Kepler,* p. 267.

15. R. Chambers, *Vestiges of the Natural History of Creation and Other Evolutionary Writings.*

16. P. Teilhard de Chardin, 'The Spirit of the Earth' in *Human Energy,* pp. 32–4. See also P. Teilhard de Chardin, *The Human Phenomenon.*

17. J. Moltmann, *The Way of Jesus Christ,* p. 294.

18. B. Bruteau, *God's Ecstasy.*

19. See, for example, U. King, *Christ in All Things.*

Chapter 2

1. See, for example, J. Polkinghorne, *One World,* pp. 17–19; M. Fuller, *Atoms and Icons,* pp. 17–20; I. Barbour, *Religion and Science,* pp. 106–8; A. E. McGrath, *Science and Religion,* pp. 76–80; C. Southgate (ed.), *God, Humanity and the Cosmos,* pp. 65–73.

2. S. Hughes, 'The Naked Postmodernists', *The Times Higher Educational Supplement,* 10 October 1997, p. 22.

3. L. Gilkey, *Religion and the Scientific Future,* p. 4.

4. R. Dawkins, 'The Values of Science and the Science of Values' in W. Williams (ed.), *The Values of Science*, pp. 13–14.
5. M. Polanyi, *Personal Knowledge*.
6. H. Brown, *The Wisdom of Science*, p. 123.
7. A. Peacocke, *Theology for a Scientific Age*, pp. 11–14, 50–4.
8. D. Deutsch, *The Fabric of Reality*.
9. Pope John Paul II, *Faith and Reason*, pp. 41–5.
10. R. Dawkins, *The Selfish Gene*, p. 21.
11. R. Dawkins, 'A Reply to Poole', *Science and Christian Belief* 71, April 1995, p. 46.
12. R. Dawkins, *Unweaving the Rainbow*, p. x.
13. M. Ridley, *The Origins of Virtue*.
14. Dawkins, 'The Values of Science and the Science of Values', p. 36.
15. R. Dawkins, 'Is Science a Religion?', p. 2.
16. M. Midgley, *Science as Salvation*.
17. S. Hawking, *A Brief History of Time*, p. 175.
18. For further discussion, see C. Deane-Drummond, 'Theology and the Culture of the Sciences', *New Blackfriars* 81, January 2000, pp. 36–46.
19. For a more detailed discussion of scientific reductionism as a method used in biology, see, in particular, Peacocke, *Theology for a Scientific Age*, pp. 39–41.
20. E. Fox Keller, *A Feeling for the Organism*, pp. xiv, 198–9.
21. Ibid., p. 202.
22. D. Scott, *Michael Polanyi*, p. 46.
23. See D. Worster, *Nature's Economy*.
24. J. A. Bissonette (ed.), *Wildlife and Landscape Ecology*.
25. I. Lakatos and A. Musgrave (eds), *Criticism and the Growth of Knowledge*.
26. For further discussion on this issue, see J.W. van Huyssteen, *Duet or Duel?*
27. K. Popper, *Conjectures and Refutations*.
28. S. T. A. Pickett et al., *Ecological Understanding*.
29. R. V. O'Neill et al., *A Hierarchical Concept of Ecosystems*.

Chapter 3

1. For further details of DNA replication and genetic engineering methods, see M. Reiss and R. Straughan, *Improving Nature*, pp. 11–41.

2. M. Wilson, 'Vaccination Made Easy' in D. Bruce and A. Bruce (eds), *Engineering Genesis*, pp. 41–5.

3. I. Wilmut et al., 'Viable Offspring Derived from Fetal and Adult Mammalian Cells', *Nature* 385, 1997, pp. 810–13.

4. A report entitled *Cloning Issues in Reproduction, Science and Medicine* was produced by the Human Genetics Advisory Commission and the Human Fertilisation and Embryology Authority in December 1998. As this book goes to press, a report chaired by Professor Liam Donaldson from the 'Chief Medical Officer's expert group reviewing the developments in stem cell research and cell nuclear replacement to benefit human health', entitled *Stem Cell Research: Medical Progress with Responsibility*, was published (Department of Health, 2000). As might be expected, the report was very positive about the possible medical benefits of therapeutic cloning, using a consequentialist framework to endorse the use of human embryos for stem cell research. A Government White Paper was produced in August 2000 broadly endorsing these recommendations. By the time this book is published, it can be expected that legislation will be in place in the UK.

5. Crops that have been altered by inserting genes in order to express a desired characteristic are known as *transgenic*. I prefer to use the term to refer to cases where genes are inserted from unrelated species, though it can also be adopted to describe genetic engineered crops in more general sense.

6. B. Halweil, 'Transgenic Crops Proliferate' in L. Starke (ed.), *Vital Signs 1999/2000*, pp. 122–3.

7. D. Atkinson, 'A Thousand and One Uses of Oil-seed Rape' in D. Bruce and A. Bruce (eds), *Engineering Genesis*, p. 38.

8. British Medical Association report, *The Impact of Genetic Modification on Agriculture, Food and Health*.

9. For more details of these examples, see ENDS, 'The Spiralling Agenda of Agricultural Biotechnology', *ENDS Report* 283, pp. 21–2, 24.

10. The Royal Society, 'GMOs and Pusztai – The Royal Society Reviews the Evidence', http://www.royalsoc.ac.uk.press/pr-15–99. htm (May 1999).

11. ENDS, 'Applying a BioDiversity Break to Genetically Modified Crops', *ENDS Report* 289, p. 24. For more discussion, see C. Deane-Drummond, *Genetic Engineering for a New Earth?*

12. See ENDS, 'The Spiralling Agenda of Agricultural Biotechnology', *ENDS Report* 283, p. 22.

13. Reported in April 1997, Editorial, 'The Final Doomsday Scenario', in the publication *Jane's Land-Based Air Defence*, cited in W. Barnaby, *The Plague Makers*, p. 143. The source of information was from Western intelligence activities and defectors.
14. See Barnaby, *The Plague Makers*, pp. 125–43.
15. British Medical Association, *Biotechnology, Weapons and Humanity*.
16. T. Horimonto and Y. Kawaoka, 'Reverse Genetics Provides Direct Evidence for a Correlation of Hemagglutinin Cleavability and Virulence of an Avian Influenza A Virus', *Journal of Virology* 68, 1994, pp. 3120–8.

Chapter 4

1. J. Williams, *Christian Perspectives on BioEthics*, pp. 56ff.
2. P. Abrecht (ed.), *Faith and Science in an Unjust World*, p. 49.
3. Ibid.; also, A. Dyson, 'Genetic Engineering in Theology and Theological Ethics' in A. Dyson and J. Harris (eds), *Ethics and Biotechnology*, pp. 263–4.
4. J. Polkinghorne, 'The Unity of Truth in Science and Theology' in D. Gosling and F. Rajotte (eds), *Science and the Theology of Creation*, p. 31.
5. Ibid., p. 31.
6. G. Altner, 'Theology and Natural Science: The Debate Today' in Gosling and Rajotte (eds), *Science and the Theology of Creation*, p. 13.
7. Ibid., p. 20. Italics mine.
8. Church of England Board for Social Responsibility, Bishop D. Sheppard (chair), *Submission to the House of Commons Science and Technology Committee's Inquiry into Human Genetics*, p. 1.
9. Ibid., p. 10.
10. Pope John Paul II, *Origins* 13 (23), 17 November 1983, pp. 388–9.
11. Also published in English: J. de D. V. Correa and E. Sgreccia (eds), *Human Genome, Human Person and the Society of the Future*.
12. For further discussion, see T. A. Shannon, *Made in Whose Image?*
13. Only published in Italian: G. Ancora et al., *Biotechnologie: Animali e Vegetali*.
14. Society, Religion and Technology (SRT) Project leaflet, *Genetic Engineering: How Far Should We Go?*, p. 1.
15. SRT Project leaflet, *Cloning Animals and Humans*, p. 2.
16. SRT Project leaflet, *Patenting Life*, p. 2. The Church of Scotland General Assembly was unsuccessful in its attempt to modify the

European legislation, which agreed to patenting whole life forms in May 1998.

17. D. Hardy, Beckly Lecture, *Human Genetic Engineering*, p. 29.
18. Ibid., p. 43.
19. Methodist Church, *Making Our Genes Fit*.
20. M. Midgley, *Wisdom, Information and Wonder*, pp. 3–22.
21. J. D. G. Dunn, 'The Body in Colossians' in T. E. Schmidt and M. Silva (eds), *To Tell the Mystery*, pp. 163–81.
22. J. Mahoney, *Seeking the Spirit*, p. 71.
23. S. Bulgakov, 'The Unfading Light' in R. Williams, *Sergii Bulgakov*, p. 136.
24. Ibid., p. 140.

Chapter 5

1. Church of England Board for Social Responsibility, J. Polkinghorne (chair), *Response to the Nuffield Council on Bioethics Consultation Document on Genetically Modified Foods*.
2. P. Hefner, *The Human Factor*.
3. T. Peters, *Playing God*, pp. 15, 83–4.
4. R. Cole-Turner, *The New Genesis*, p. 102.
5. J. Brooke and G. Cantor, *Reconstructing Nature*, p. 16.
6. Cole-Turner, *The New Genesis*, pp. 103–4.
7. Ibid., p. 104.
8. Ibid., p. 108.
9. See also C. Deane-Drummond, *Creation Through Wisdom*.
10. B. Ashley and K. O'Rourke, *Health Care Ethics*.
11. Ibid., pp. 307–27.
12. Peters, *Playing God*, pp. 157–78.
13. Nuffield Council on Bioethics, *Genetically Modified Crops*.
14. Church of England Board for Social Responsibility, *Response to the Nuffield Council on Bioethics Consultation Document*.
15. MAFF, J. Polkinghorne (chair), *Report of the Committee on the Ethics of Genetic Modification and Food Use*.
16. 'Transgenic Food' in D. Bruce and A. Bruce (eds), *Engineering Genesis*, pp. 180–4.
17. Press release, *Christian Ecology Link*, 25 November 1999.
18. The recent Nuffield Council on Bioethics report on *Genetically Modified Crops* has argued for greater access to the benefits of the technology in the poorer communities.

19. C. Deane-Drummond, *Theology and Biotechnology*, pp. 105–32.
20. S. McDonagh, 'Creation Groans: Living in the World in the Light of the Kingdom'.
21. C. Deane-Drummond, 'Biotechnology: A New Challenge for Theology and Ethics' in C. Southgate (ed.), *God, Humanity and the Cosmos*, pp. 355–87.
22. M. Douglas, *Purity and Danger*, pp. 42–58.
23. M.P. Carroll, 'One More Time: Leviticus Revisited', *Archives Européennes de Sociologie* 19, 1978, pp. 339–46.
24. L.L. Grabbe, *Leviticus: Old Testament Guides*, pp. 58–9.
25. J.E. McKinlay, *Gendering Wisdom the Host*, pp. 48–56.
26. Food Ethics Council, *Novel Foods*.
27. See Deane-Drummond, 'Biotechnology: A New Challenge for Theology and Ethics', pp. 355–87.
28. P. Hefner, 'Biocultural Evolution and the Created Co-creator' in T. Peters (ed.), *Science and Theology*, p. 174.
29. Ibid., p. 181.
30. P. Chapman, 'Calf Cloned From World's Only Seaweed Eating Cow', International News, www. *Electronic Telegraph*, Issue 1177, Saturday, 15 August 1998.
31. J. Moltmann, *The Way of Jesus Christ*, p. 307.
32. See C. Deane-Drummond, *Creation Through Wisdom*.
33. For a discussion of different dimensions of image bearing, see C. Deane-Drummond, *Ecology in Jürgen Moltmann's Theology*, pp. 146–56.
34. T. Peters, 'Cloning Shock: A Theological Reaction' in R. Cole-Turner (ed.), *Human Cloning*, p. 18.
35. J. de D.V. Correa and E. Sgreccia, 'Reflections on Cloning'. See also 'Declaration on the Production and the Scientific and Therapeutic use of Human Embryonic Stem Cells', http://www.vatican.va/roman_curia/pontifical_academies/acdlife/documents/rc_pa_a staminali_en.html
36. For a critique from a feminist perspective, see A. Adam, *Artificial Knowing*.
37. J. Polkinghorne, 'Cloning and the Moral Imperative' in Cole-Turner (ed.), *Human Cloning*, pp. 35–42.

Chapter 6

1. For a useful discussion of ethical issues in the genetic engineering of

the non-human world, see D. Bruce and A. Bruce (eds), *Engineering Genesis*, especially pp. 77–109.

2. I have listed these in C. Deane-Drummond, *Genetic Engineering for a New Earth?*

3. J. de D. V. Correa and E. Sgreccia, 'Reflections on Cloning'. http://www.vatican.va/roman_curia/pontifical_academies/acdlife/documents/rc_pa_acdlife_doc_30091997_c. See also G. Ancora et al., *Biotecnologie: Animali e Vegetali.*

4. For a further discussion, see M. Junker-Jenny and L. Sowle Cahill (eds), *The Ethics of Genetic Engineering.*

5. See A. Holland and A. Johnson (eds), *Animal Biotechnology and Ethics.*

6. For a philosophical approach in support of cloning, see J. Harris, *Clones, Genes and Immortality.*

7. For an excellent discussion of the implications of genetic engineering of humans, see M. Junker-Jenny (ed.), *Designing Life?*

8. For a discussion of issues of social justice connected with the Human Genome Project, see T. Peters (ed.), *Genetics.*

9. A. Ochert, 'A Germ of an Idea Leads to GM People', *The Times Higher Educational Supplement*, 28 January 2000, p. 22.

10. For a discussion of these aspects, see C. Deane-Drummond, 'Theology and the Culture of the Sciences', *New Blackfriars* 81, January 2000, pp. 36–46.

11. P. Taylor, *Respect for Nature*, pp. 72–90.

12. R. Attfield, *The Ethics of Environmental Concern*, p. 158.

13. A. Linzey, *Animal Theology.*

14. A full discussion of animal rights is outside the scope of this chapter on genetic engineering. For further reading, see P. Singer, *Animal Liberation*; S. R. L. Clark, *The Political Animal.*

15. J. Harris, 'Is Cloning an Attack on Human Dignity?', *Nature* 387, 1997, p. 754.

16. See R. Stone, 'Religious Leaders Oppose Patenting Genes and Animals', *Science* 268, 1995, p. 1126.

17. T. Peters, *Playing God*, pp. 116–30.

18. Appendix to the Society, Religion and Technology Project report to the General Assembly of the Church of Scotland, pp. 62–4.

19. For further references to sources, see C. Deane-Drummond, *Creation Through Wisdom.*

20. M. Banner, 'Ethics, Society and Policy: A Way Forward' in A. Holland and A. Johnson (eds), *Animal Biotechnology and Ethics*,

pp. 325–39.

21. D. Cooper, 'Intervention, Humility and Animal Integrity' in Holland and Johnson (eds), *Animal Biotechnology and Ethics*, pp. 145–55.

22. Peters, *Playing God*.

23. A. McIntyre, *After Virtue*.

24. S. Hauerwas, *Character and the Christian Life*.

25. S. Wells, *Transforming Fate into Destiny*.

26. J. Milbank, *Theology and Social Theory*, pp. 12–13.

27. See, for example, T. Peters (ed.), *Genetics*.

28. See, for example, A. Carlberg, *The Moral Rubicon*.

Chapter 7

1. D. R. Griffin (ed.), *The Re-Enchantment of Science*, pp. 1–46.

2. J. Lovelock, *The Ages of Gaia*, p. 3. See also J. Lovelock, *Gaia: A New Look at Life on Earth*.

3. R. Carson, *Silent Spring*.

4. Lovelock, *The Ages of Gaia*, p. 4.

5. Ibid., p. 19. Note that *biota* is the term used to describe the sum total of living things on the planet.

6. T. D. Brock and M. T. Madigan, *Biology of Microorganisms*.

7. J. W. Kirchner, 'The *Gaia* Hypotheses: Are they Testable? Are they Useful?' in S. H. Schneider and P. J. Boston (eds), *Scientists on Gaia*, p. 41.

8. G. Nicolis, 'Dissipative Structures and Biological Order', *Advances in Biological and Medical Physics* 16, 1977, pp. 99–113.

9. Craik's proposal that the earth as a whole is a dissipative structure is supported by his analysis of both the history and current knowledge of the adaptability of microorganisms. See J. C. A. Craik, 'The Gaia Hypothesis: Fact or Fantasy?', *Journal of the Marine Biological Association (UK)* 69, 1989, pp. 759–68.

10. Lovelock, *The Ages of Gaia*, p. 26.

11. G.R. Williams, *The Molecular Biology of Gaia*, pp. 176–82.

12. C. Deane-Drummond, 'Nitrate Uptake into *Pisum sativum* L.cv. Feltham First Seedlings: Commonality with Nitrate Uptake into *Chara carollina* and *Hordeum vulgare* through a Substrate Cycling Model', *Plant, Cell and Environment* 9, 1986, pp. 41–8.

13. See, for example, M.O. Andreae, 'Geophysiological Interactions in the Global Sulphur Cycle' in Schneider and Boston (eds), *Scientists on Gaia*, pp. 131–8.

14. K. Caldeira, 'Evolutionary Pressures on Planktonic Dimethyl-sulphide Production', in Schneider and Boston (eds), *Scientists on Gaia*, pp. 153–8.

15. Lovelock, *The Ages of Gaia*, pp. 144–51.

16. R. Dawkins, *The Extended Phenotype*, p. 248. The phenotype is a biological term that represents the expression of the gene in an organism, that is, genotype plus environment.

17. Williams, *The Molecular Biology of Gaia*, p. 179.

18. W. Ford Doolittle, 'Is Nature Really Motherly?', *Coevolution Quarterly* 29, Spring 1981, pp. 58–63; extract also reproduced in C. Barlow (ed.), *From Gaia to Selfish Genes*, pp. 32–3.

19. See S. Clark, *How to Think About the Earth*, p. 29; Kirchner, 'The *Gaia* Hypotheses: Are they Testable? Are they Useful?', pp. 38–46.

20. J. Postgate, '*Gaia* Gets Too Big For Her Boots', *New Scientist* 118, 1988, p. 60.

21. Lovelock, *The Ages of Gaia*, p. 207.

22. A. Primavesi, *From Apocalypse to Genesis*, pp. 14, 34. Anne Primavesi's *Sacred Gaia* was published as this book goes to press.

23. K. Pedler *The Quest for Gaia*, p. 17.

Chapter 8

1. J. Lovelock, *The Ages of Gaia*, p. 206.

2. J. Ravetz, 'Gaia and the Philosophy of Science' in P. Bunyard and E. Goldsmith (eds), *Gaia*, p. 135.

3. H. Montefiore, *Credible Christianity*, p. 31.

4. J. Moltmann, *God in Creation*, p. 18.

5. Such an exclusive link has been heavily criticized by Sarah Coakley. See, for example, S. Coakley, 'Femininity and the Holy Spirit?' in M. Furlong (ed.), *Mirror to the Church*, pp. 124–35.

6. Tim Zell, the founder of the Church of All Worlds, is a good example. See M. Alder, *Drawing Down the Moon*, p. 303.

7. D. Abram, 'The Mechanical and the Organic: Epistemological Consequences of the Gaia Hypothesis' in P. Bunyard (ed.), *Gaia in Action*, pp. 234–47.

8. C. Spretnak, *States of Grace*, pp. 80, 272 note 1.

9. Ibid., p. 110.

10. R. R. Ruether, *God and Gaia*.

11. Lovelock, *The Ages of Gaia*, pp. 208–12.

12. R. R. Ruether, *Introducing Redemption into Christian Theology*, p. 119.

13. For further discussion, see J. Visvader, 'Gaia and Myths of Harmony: An Exploration of Ethical and Practical Implications', in S. H. Schneider and P. J. Boston (eds), *Scientists on Gaia*, pp. 33–8.

14. E. Sahourtis, *Gaia*, pp. 20ff. See also E. Sahourtis, 'The Gaia Controversy: A Case for the Earth as an Evolving Organism' in Bunyard (ed.), *Gaia in Action*, pp. 324–38.

15. See A. Weston, 'Forms of Gaian Ethics', *Environmental Ethics* 9 (3), 1987, pp. 217–30.

16. M. Midgley, *Utopias, Dolphins and Computers*, pp. 136–49.

17. Ibid., p. 148.

18. S. Clark, 'The Parasites' Future', *Times Literary Supplement*, 26 October 1989, pp. 1143–4.

19. S. Clark, *How to Think About the Earth*, pp. 23–4.

20. Ibid., p. 27.

21. D.R. Griffin, *The Re-Enchantment of Science*, p. 21.

22. P. Taylor, *Respect for Nature*, p. 986.

23. For examples, see Bunyard and Goldsmith (eds), *Gaia*.

24. J. Lovelock, 'Planetary Medicine: Stewards or Partners on Earth?', *The Times Literary Supplement*, 13 September 1991, pp. 7–8.

25. Lovelock, *The Ages of Gaia*, p. 212.

26. A. Leopold, *A Sand County Almanac*.

27. Holmes Rolston III, *Environmental Ethics*, p. 188.

28. Sahtouris, *Gaia*, p. 19.

29. S. McFague *The Body of God*, pp. 112–29.

30. Lovelock, *The Ages of Gaia*, p. 212.

31. K. Pedler, *The Quest for Gaia*, p. 174.

Chapter 9

1. E. Byrne, *Women and Science*, pp. 1–12.

2. M. Wertheim, *Pythagoras' Trousers*, pp. 7–12.

3. L. Schiebinger, *The Mind Has No Sex*.

4. Ibid., p. 242.

5. For examples, see G. Kass-Simon and P. Farnes, *Women of Science*.

6. Cytoplasmic inheritance is based on the fact that non-nuclear organelles in cells, known as mitochondria, also contain genetic information in the form of DNA. See ibid., pp. 232–6.

7. B. T. Gates and A. B. Shteir, *Natural Eloquence*, pp. 11ff.

8. R. Carson, *The Sea Around Us*; R. Carson, *A Sense of Wonder*.

9. R. Carson, *Silent Spring*, p. 297.

10. Byrne, *Women and Science*, p.15.

11. R. Bleier, *Science and Gender*, p. 43.

12. Ibid., p. 6.

13. See M. Morse, *Women Changing Science*, pp. 22–3.

14. N. J. Lane, 'Women in Science, Engineering and Technology: The Rising Tide Report and Beyond' in M. Maynard (ed.), *Science and the Construction of Women*, pp. 37–54.

15. E. Fox Keller, 'Feminism and Science' in E. Fox Keller and H. E. Longino (eds), *Feminism and Science*, pp. 28–40.

16. Ibid., especially pp. 29–30.

17. J. Krasner, 'Ape Ladies and Cultural Politics' in Gates and Shteir, *Natural Eloquence*, pp. 237–51.

18. Ibid., p. 243.

19. Wertheim, *Pythagoras' Trousers*, pp. 13–15.

20. S. Griffin, *Woman and Nature*.

21. C. Christ, 'Rethinking Theology and Nature' in J. Plaskow and C. Christ (eds), *Weaving the Visions*, pp. 314–25.

22. Ibid., p. 321.

23. C. Merchant, *Radical Ecology*, pp. 196–201.

24. S. T. A. Pickett et al., *Ecological Understanding*, p. 30.

25. C. Merchant, *The Death of Nature*.

26. J. Biehl, *Rethinking Ecofeminist Politics*, pp. 74–7.

27. H. Rose, *Love Power and Knowledge*, pp. 71–96.

28. S. Harding, *Whose Science?: Whose Knowledge?*

29. A. Scott, 'The Knowledge in our Bones: Standpoint Theory, Alternative Health and the Quantum Model of the Body' in Maynard (ed.), *Science and the Construction of Women*, pp. 106–25.

30. D. Chopra, *Quantum Healing*.

31. See J. W. van Huyssteen, *Duet or Duel?*

32. M. A. Eisenhart and E. Finkel, *Women's Science*.

33. J. Barr and L. Birke, *Common Science*.

34. Ibid., p. 133.

Chapter 10

1. N. Lash, *The Beginning and the End of Religion*, pp. 92–102. For further discussion, see Deane-Drummond, *Creation Through Wisdom*, in press.

2. C. Deane-Drummond, 'FutureNatural? A Future for Science

Through the Lens of Wisdom', *The Heythrop Journal* 40, 1999, pp. 41–59.

3. C. Deane-Drummond, 'Wisdom: A Voice for Theology at the Boundary with Science', *Ecotheology*, January 2001, *in press*.

4. Pope John Paul II, *Faith and Reason*, p. 152.

Bibliography

Abrecht, P. (ed.), *Faith and Science in an Unjust World*, vol. 2, Geneva: WCC 1980.

Adam, A., *Artificial Knowing: Gender and the Thinking Machine*, London: Routledge 1998.

Alder, M., *Drawing Down the Moon: Witches, Druids, Goddess Worshippers and Other Pagans in America Today*, Boston: Beacon Press 1983.

Ancora, G., E. Benevenuto, G. Bertoni, V. Buonomo, B. Hoinings, A. Lauria, F. Lucchini, P. A. Marsan, V. Mele, A. Pessina and E. Sgeccia, *Biotechnologie: Animali e Vegetale: Nuove frontiere e muove responsabilita*, Vatican City: Libreria Editrice Vaticana 1999.

Ashley, B. and K. O'Rourke, *Health Care Ethics: A Theological Analysis*, second edition, St Louis: Catholic Health Association of the United States 1982.

Attfield, R., *The Ethics of Environmental Concern*, Oxford: Blackwell 1983.

Barbour, I., *Religion and Science: Historical and Contemporary Issues*, London: SCM Press 1998.

Barlow, C. (ed.), *From Gaia to Selfish Genes: Selected Writings in the Life Sciences*, Cambridge, Mass.: MIT Press 1991.

Barnaby, W., *The Plague Makers: The Secret World of Biological Warfare*, London: Vision 1999.

Barr, J. and L. Birke, *Common Science: Women, Science and Knowledge*, Bloomington: Indiana University Press 1998.

Biehl, J., *Rethinking Ecofeminist Politics*, Boston: Southend Press 1991.

Bissonette, J. A. (ed.), *Wildlife and Landscape Ecology: Effects of Pattern and Scale*, New York: Springer 1997.

Bleier, R., *Science and Gender: A Critique of Biology and its Theories on Women*, Oxford: Pergamon Press 1984.

Breuilly, E. and M. Palmer (eds), *Christianity and Ecology*, London: Cassell 1992, pp. 82–3.

British Medical Association, *Biotechnology, Weapons and Humanity*, London: BMA, January 1999.

British Medical Association, *The Impact of Genetic Modification on Agriculture, Food and Health*, London: BMA, May 1999.

Brock, T. D. and M. T. Madigan, *Biology of Microorganisms*, fifth edition, Englewood Cliffs, N.J.: Prentice Hall 1988.

Brooke, J., *Science and Religion: Some Historical Perspectives*, Cambridge: Cambridge University Press 1991.

Brooke, J., 'Religious Belief and the Content of the Sciences', *Osiris* 16, 2001, *in press*.

Brooke, J. and G. Cantor, *Reconstructing Nature: The Engagement of Science and Religion*, Edinburgh: T. & T. Clark 1998.

Brown, H., *The Wisdom of Science: Its Relevance to Culture and Religion*, Cambridge: Cambridge University Press 1986.

Bruce, D. and A. Bruce (eds), *Engineering Genesis: The Ethics of Genetic Engineering in Non-Human Species*, Society, Religion and Technology Project, London: Earthscan 1998.

Bruteau, B., *God's Ecstasy: The Creation of a Self-Creating World*, New York: Crossroad 1997.

Bunyard, P. (ed.), *Gaia in Action: Science of the Living Earth*, Edinburgh: Floris Books 1996.

Bunyard, P. and E. Goldsmith (eds), *Gaia: The Thesis, The Mechanism and the Implications*, Wadebridge Ecological Centre 1989.

Byrne, E., *Women and Science: The Snark Syndrome*, London: The Falmer Press 1993.

Carlberg, A., *The Moral Rubicon: A Study of the Principles of Sanctity of Life and Quality of Life in Bioethics*, Lund: Lund University Press 1998.

Carroll, M. P., 'One More Time: Leviticus Revisited', *Archives Européennes de Sociologie* 19, 1978, pp. 339–46.

Carson, R., *The Sea Around Us*, Cambridge/New York: Cambridge University Press 1951.

Carson, R., *Silent Spring*, Boston: Houghton Mifflin 1961

Carson, R., *A Sense of Wonder*, New York: Harper & Row 1965.

Caspar, M., *Kepler*, London: Abelard Schuman 1959.

Chambers, R., *Vestiges of the Natural History of Creation and Other Evolutionary Writings*, Chicago: Chicago University Press 1994.

Chapman, P., 'Calf Cloned From World's Only Seaweed Eating Cow', International News, www. *Electronic Telegraph*, issue 1177, Saturday, 15 August 1998.

Chopra, D., *Quantum Healing: Exploring the Frontiers of Mind/Body Medicine*, New York: Bantam Books 1989.

Church of England Board for Social Responsibility, Bishop D. Sheppard (chair), *Submission to the House of Commons Science and Technology Committee's Inquiry into Human Genetics*, Church of England, January 1995.

Church of England Board for Social Responsibility, J. Polkinghorne (chair), *Response to the Nuffield Council on Bioethics Consultation Document on Genetically Modified Foods*, Church of England, August 1998.

Clark, S., 'The Parasites' Future', *The Times Literary Supplement*, 26 October 1989, pp. 1143–4.

Clark, S., *How to Think About the Earth*, London and New York: Mowbray 1993.

Clark, S. R. L., *The Political Animal: Biology, Ethics and Politics*, London and New York: Routledge 1999.

Cole-Turner, R., *The New Genesis: Theology and the Genetic Revolution*, Westminster: John Knox Press 1993.

Cole-Turner, R. (ed.), *Human Cloning: Religious Responses*, Westminster: John Knox Press 1997.

Craik, J. C. A., 'The Gaia Hypothesis: Fact or Fantasy?', *Journal of the Marine Biological Association (UK)* 69, 1989, pp. 759–68.

Dawkins, R., *The Selfish Gene*, London: Paladin 1978.

Dawkins, R., *The Extended Phenotype*, Oxford: Oxford University Press 1982.

Dawkins, R., 'A Reply to Poole', *Science and Christian Belief* 71, April 1995, p. 46.

Dawkins, R., 'Is Science a Religion?', 1996 Address to the American Humanist Association, also published in *The Humanist* 57 (1), 1997.

Dawkins, R., *Unweaving the Rainbow: Science. Delusion and the Appetite for Wonder*, London: The Penguin Press 1998.

de D. V. Correa, J. and E. Sgreccia, Pontifica Academia Pro Vita, 'Reflections on Cloning', Vatican City: Libreria Editrice Vaticana 1997.

de D. V. Correa, J. and E. Sgreccia (eds), *Human Genome, Human Person and the Society of the Future*, Vatican City: Libreria Editrice Vaticana 1999.

Deane-Drummond, C., 'Nitrate Uptake into *Pisum sativum* L.cv. Feltham First Seedlings: Commonality with Nitrate Uptake into *Chara carollina* and *Hordeum vulgare* through a Substrate Cycling Model', *Plant, Cell and Environment* 9, 1986, pp. 41–8.

Deane-Drummond, C., *Ecology in Jürgen Moltmann's Theology*, Lampeter: The Edwin Mellen Press 1997.

Deane-Drummond, C., *Theology and Biotechnology: Implications for a New Science*, London: Geoffrey Chapman 1997.

Deane-Drummond, C., 'FutureNatural? A Future for Science Through the Lens of Wisdom', *The Heythrop Journal* 40, 1999, pp. 41–59.

Deane-Drummond, C., *Genetic Engineering for a New Earth?: Theology and Ethics of the New Biology*, Cambridge: Grove Ethical Series E114 1999.

Deane-Drummond, C., 'Come to the Banquet: Seeking Wisdom in a Genetically Engineered Earth', *Ecotheology* 9, 2000, pp. 27–37.

Deane-Drummond, C., *Creation Through Wisdom: Theology and the New Biology*, Edinburgh: T. & T. Clark 2000.

Deane-Drummond, C., 'Theology and the Culture of the Sciences', *New Blackfriars* 81, January 2000, pp. 36–46.

Deane-Drummond, C., 'Wisdom: A Voice for Theology at the Boundary with Science', *Ecotheology*, January 2001, *in press*.

Department of Health, *Stem Cell Research: Medical Progress with Responsibility*, London 2000.

Deutsch, D., *The Fabric of Reality*, Harmondsworth: Penguin 1997.

Devey, J. (ed.), *The Physical and Metaphysical Works of Lord Bacon*, London: George Bell 1901.

Dillistone, F. W., *Charles Raven: Naturalist, Historian, Theologian*, London: Hodder & Stoughton 1975.

Doolittle, W. Ford, 'Is Nature Really Motherly?', *Coevolution Quarterly* 29, Spring 1981, pp. 58–63.

Douglas, M., *Purity and Danger: An Analysis of the Concepts of Pollution and Taboo*, second edition, London: Routledge 1984.

Dyson, A. and J. Harris (eds), *Ethics and Biotechnology*, London: Routledge 1994.

Eisenhart, M. A. and E. Finkel, *Women's Science: Learning and Succeeding From the Margins*, Chicago/London: Chicago University Press 1998.

ENDS, 'The Spiralling Agenda of Agricultural Biotechnology', *ENDS Report* 283, August 1998, pp. 18–30.

ENDS, Applying a BioDiversity Break to Genetically Modified Crops', *ENDS Report* 289, February 1999, pp. 21–7.

Food Ethics Council, *Novel Foods: Beyond Nuffield*, Southwell: Food Ethics Council 1999.

Fox, A, *Whose Life is it Anyway? God, Genes and Us*, 1998 Heodway Methodist Conference Lectures, Ilkeston: Moorley's 1998.

Fuller, M., *Atoms and Icons: A Discussion of the Relationship Between Science and Theology*, London: Mowbray 1995.

Furlong, M. (ed.), *Mirror to the Church: Reflections on Sexism*, London: SPCK 1988, pp. 124–35.

Gates, B. T. and A. B. Shteir, *Natural Eloquence: Women Reinscribe Science*, Madison: University of Wisconsin Press 1997.

Gilkey, L., *Religion and the Scientific Future*, London: SCM Press 1970.

Gosling, D. and F. Rajotte (eds), *Science and the Theology of Creation: Report of a Seminar Held at the Ecumenical Institute, Bossey*, Church and Society Documents, no. 4, Geneva: WCC 1998.

Grabbe, L. L., *Leviticus: Old Testament Guides*, Sheffield: Sheffield Academic Press 1993.

Griffin, D. R. (ed.), *The Re-Enchantment of Science*, New York: State University of New York Press 1988.

Griffin, S., *Woman and Nature: The Roaring Inside Her*, London: The Women's Press 1984.

Harding, S., *Whose Science?: Whose Knowledge?; Thinking from Women's Lives*, Ithaca: Cornell University Press 1991.

Hardy, D., *Human Genetic Engineering: Good or Evil?*, Beckly Lecture, Division of Social Responsibility of the Methodist Church, June 1993.

Harris, J., 'Is Cloning an Attack on Human Dignity?', *Nature* 387, 1997, p. 754.

Harris, J., *Clones, Genes and Immortality: Ethics and Genetics*, Oxford: Oxford University Press 1998.

Harrison, P., *The Bible, Protestantism and the Rise of Modern Science*, Cambridge: Cambridge University Press 1998.

Hauerwas, S., *Character and the Christian Life: A Study in Theological Ethics*, San Antonio: Trinity University Press 1975.

Hawking, S., *A Brief History of Time*, New York: Bantam Press 1988.

Hefner, P., *The Human Factor: Evolution, Culture and Religion*, Minneapolis: Fortress Press 1993.

Holland, A. and A. Johnson (eds), *Animal Biotechnology and Ethics*, London: Chapman & Hall 1998.

Horimonto, T. and Y. Kawaoka, 'Reverse Genetics Provides Direct Evidence for a Correlation of Hemagglutinin Cleavability and Virulence of an Avian Influenza A Virus', *Journal of Virology* 68, 1994, pp. 3120–8.

http://www.vatican

Hughes, S., 'The Naked Postmodernists', *The Times Higher Educational Supplement*, 10 October 1997, p. 22.

Human Genetics Advisory Commission and Human Fertilisation and Embryology Authority, *Cloning Issues in Reproduction, Science and Medicine*, HGAC and HFEA, December 1998.

Jacob, J. R., 'The Ideological Origins of Robert Boyle's Natural Philosophy', *Journal of European Studies* 2, 1972.

John Paul II, *Origins* 13 (23), 17 November 1983, pp. 388–9.

John Paul II, *Faith and Reason, Encyclical Letter 'Fides et Ratio'*, London: Catholic Truth Society 1998.

Junker-Jenny, M. (ed.), *Designing Life? Genetics, Procreation and Ethics*, Aldershot: Ashgate 1999.

Junker-Jenny, M. and L. Sowle Cahill (eds), *The Ethics of Genetic Engineering*, Concilium, London: SCM Press 1998.

Kass-Simon, G. and P. Farnes, *Women of Science: Righting the Record*, Bloomington: Indiana University Press 1993.

Keller, E. Fox, *A Feeling for the Organism: The Life and Work of Barbara McClintock*, New York: Freeman 1983.

Keller, E. Fox and H. E. Longino (eds), *Feminism and Science*, Oxford: Oxford University Press 1996.

King, U., *Christ in All Things: Exploring Spirituality with Teilhard de Chardin*, London: SCM Press 1997.

Lakatos, I. and A. Musgrave (eds), *Criticism and the Growth of Knowledge: Proceedings of the International Colloquium in the Philosophy of Science*, Cambridge: Cambridge University Press 1970.

Lash, N., *The Beginning and the End of Religion*, Cambridge: Cambridge University Press 1996, pp. 92–102.

Leopold, A., *A Sand County Almanac*, Oxford: Oxford University Press 1949.

Linzey, A., *Animal Theology*, London: SCM Press 1994.

Lovelock, J., *Gaia: A New Look at Life on Earth*, Oxford: Oxford University Press 1979; second edition, 1987.

Lovelock, J., *The Ages of Gaia*, Oxford: Oxford University Press 1988.

Lovelock, J., *Gaia: The Practical Science of Planetary Medicine*, London: Gaia Books 1991.

Lovelock, J., 'Planetary Medicine: Stewards or Partners on Earth?', *The Times Literary Supplement*, 13 September 1991, pp. 7–8.

MAFF, J. Polkinghorne (chair), *Report of the Committee on the Ethics of Genetic Modification and Food Use*, Ministry of Agriculture, Fisheries and Food, HMSO 1994.

Mahoney, J., *Seeking the Spirit: Essays in Moral and Pastoral Theology*, London: Sheed & Ward 1981.

Margulis, L. and D. Sagan, *Slanted Truths: Essays on Gaia, Symbiosis and Evolution*, New York: Springer-Verlag 1997.

Maynard, M. (ed.), *Science and the Construction of Women*, London: University College London Press 1997.

McDonagh, C., 'Creation Groans: Living in the World in the Light of the Kingdom', paper presented at Newman College (Birmingham) Study Day, *Creation and the Environment in Christian Perspective*, 19 February 2000.

McFague, S., *The Body of God*, London: SCM Press 1993.

McGrath, A. E., *Science and Religion: An Introduction*, Oxford: Blackwell 1998.

McIntyre, A., *After Virtue: A Study in Moral Theory*, second edition, London: Duckworth 1985.

McKinlay, J. E., *Gendering Wisdom the Host: Biblical Invitations to Eat and Drink*, JSOT, Sheffield: Sheffield Academic Press 1999.

Merchant, C., *The Death of Nature: Women, Ecology and the Scientific Revolution*, London: Wildwood House 1982.

Merchant, C., *Radical Ecology: The Search for a Liveable World*, New York/ London: Routledge 1992.

Methodist Church, *Making Our Genes Fit: Christian Perspectives on the New Genetics*, London: The Methodist Church, 1999.

Midgley, M., *Wisdom, Information and Wonder: What is Knowledge For?*, London: Routledge 1989.

Midgley, M., *Science as Salvation*, London: Routledge 1992.

Midgley, M., *Utopias, Dolphins and Computers: Problems of Philosophical Plumbing*, London: Routledge 1996.

Milbank, J., *Theology and Social Theory*, Oxford: Blackwell 1990.

Moltmann, J., *God in Creation: An Ecological Doctrine of Creation*, London: SCM Press 1985.

Moltmann, J., *The Way of Jesus Christ*, London: SCM Press 1990.

Montefiore, H., *Credible Christianity: The Gospel in Contemporary Culture*: Mowbray London and New York 1993.

Morse, M., *Women Changing Science: Voices from a Field in Transition*, New York: Plenum Press 1995.

Nicolis, G., 'Dissipative Structures and Biological Order', *Advances in Biological and Medical Physics* 16, 1977, pp. 99–113.

Nuffield Council on Bioethics, *Genetically Modified Crops: The Ethical and Social Issues*, London: Nuffield Council on Bioethics 1999.

O'Neill, R. V., D. L. De Angelis, J. B. Waide and T. E. Allen, *A Hierarchical Concept of Ecosystems*, Princeton: Princeton University Press 1986.

Ochert, A., 'A Germ of an Idea Leads to GM People', *The Times Higher Educational Supplement*, 28 January 2000, p. 22.

Peacocke, A., *Theology for a Scientific Age*, enlarged edition, London: SCM Press 1993.

Pedler, K., *The Quest for Gaia*, London: HarperCollins 1991.

Peters, T., *Playing God: Genetic Determinism and Human Freedom*, London: Routledge 1997.

Peters, T. (ed.), *Genetics: Issues of Social Justice*, Cleveland: The Pilgrim Press 1998.

Peters, T. (ed.), *Science and Theology: The New Consonance*, Boulder and Oxford: Westview Press 1998.

Pickett, S. T. A., J. Kolasa and C. G. Jones, *Ecological Understanding: The Nature of Theory and the Theory of Nature*, London/Boston: Academic Press 1994.

Plaskow, J. and C. Christ (eds), *Weaving the Visions: New Patterns in Feminist Spirituality*, San Francisco: Harper & Row 1989.

Polanyi, M., *Personal Knowledge*, London: Routledge & Kegan Paul 1958.

Polkinghorne, J., *One World: The Interaction of Science and Religion*, London: SPCK 1986.

Popper, K., *Conjectures and Refutations: The Growth of Scientific Knowledge*, London: Routledge & Kegan Paul 1963.

Postgate, J., '*Gaia* Gets Too Big For Her Boots' *New Scientist* 118, 1988, p. 60.

Primavesi, A., *From Apocalypse to Genesis*, Tunbridge Wells: Burns & Oates 1991.

Primavesi, A., *Sacred Gaia*, London and New York: Routledge 2000.

Raven, C., *John Ray, Naturalist: His Life and Works*, Cambridge: Cambridge University Press 1942.

Raven, C., *Science, Religion and the Future*, first edition, 1943; London: Mowbray Morehouse 1994.

Raven, C., 'Synthetic Philosophy in the Seventeenth Century: A Study of Early Science', Herbert Spencer Lecture, Oxford: Blackwell 1945.

Raven, C., *Natural Religion and Christian Theology: The Gifford Lectures, 1952*, Cambridge: Cambridge University Press 1953.

Raven, C. E., *Teilhard de Chardin: Scientist and Seer*, London: Collins 1962.

Ray, J. *The Wisdom of God Manifested in the Works of Creation* (1695), New York: Arno Press edition 1977.

Reiss, M. and R. Straughan, *Improving Nature: The Science and Ethics of Genetic Engineering*, Cambridge: Cambridge University Press 1996.

Ridley, M., *The Origins of Virtue*, Harmondsworth: Penguin 1997.

Rolston III, H., *Environmental Ethics: Duties to and Values in the Natural World*, Philadelphia: Temple University Press 1988.

Rose, H., *Love, Power and Knowledge: Towards a Feminist Transformation of the Sciences*, Cambridge: Polity Press 1994.

Royal Society, The, 'GMOs and Puszati – The Royal Society Reviews the Evidence', http://www.royalsoc.ac.uk.press/pr-15-99.htm (May 1999).

Ruether, R. R., *God and Gaia: An Ecofeminist Theology of Earth Healing*, London: SCM Press 1993.

Ruether, R. R., *Introducing Redemption into Christian Theology*, Sheffield: Sheffield Academic Press 1998.

Russell, R. J., W. R. Stoeger and F. J. Ayala (eds), *Evolutionery and Molecular Biology: Scientific Perspectives on Divine Action*, Vatican City and Berkeley: Foundation and Center for Theology and the Natural Sciences (CTNS) 1999.

Sahourtis, E., *Gaia: The Human Journey from Chaos to Cosmos*, New York: Pocket Books 1989.

Schiebinger, L., *The Mind Has No Sex: Women in the Origin of Modern Science*, Cambridge, Mass.: Harvard University Press 1989.

Schmidt, T.E. and M. Silva (eds), *To Tell the Mystery: Essays in Honour of Robert H. Gundry*, Sheffield: Sheffield Academic Press 1994.

Schneider, S.H. and P.J. Boston (eds), *Scientists on Gaia*, Cambridge, Mass.: MIT Press 1991.

Scott, D., *Michael Polanyi*, London: SPCK 1996.

Shannon, T.A., *Made in Whose Image? Genetic Engineering and Christian Ethics*, New York: Humanity Books 2000.

Singer, P., *Animal Liberation*, London: Pimlico 1995.

Society, Religion and Technology Project, *Report to the General Assembly of the Church of Scotland*, Edinburgh: Church of Scotland, May 1997.

Society, Religion and Technology Project, *Patenting Life*, Church of Scotland, 16 April 1998.

Society, Religion and Technology Project, *Genetic Engineering: How Far Should We Go?*, Church of Scotland, June 1998.

Society, Religion and Technology Project, *Cloning Animals and Humans*, Church of Scotland, revised version, 26 July 1998.

Southgate, C. (ed.), *God, Humanity and the Cosmos: A Textbook in Science and Religion*, Edinburgh: T. & T. Clark 1999.

Spretnak, C., *States of Grace: The Recovery of Meaning in a Postmodern Age*, San Francisco: HarperCollins 1993.

Starke, L. (ed.), *Vital Signs 1999/2000: The Environmental Trends that are Shaping our Future*, London: Earthscan 1999.

Stone, R., 'Religious Leaders Oppose Patenting Genes and Animals', *Science* 268, 1995, p. 1126.

Taylor, P., *Respect for Nature: A Theory of Environmental Ethics*, Princeton: Princeton University Press 1986.

Teilhard de Chardin, P., *Human Energy*, London: Collins 1969.

Teilhard de Chardin, P., *The Human Phenomenon*, first edition trans. as *The Phenomenon of Man*, 1959; new edition, Brighton: Sussex Academic Press 1999.

van Huyssteen, J. W., *Duet or Duel? Theology and Science in a Postmodern World*, London: SCM Press 1998.

Volk, T., *Towards a Physiology of Earth*, New York: Springer-Verlag 1997.

Wells, S., *Transforming Fate into Destiny: The Theological Ethics of Stanley Hauerwas*, Carlisle: Paternoster Press 1998.

Wertheim, M., *Pythagoras' Trousers: God, Physics and the Gender Wars*, London: Fourth Estate 1996.

Weston, A., 'Forms of Gaian Ethics', *Environmental Ethics* 9 (3), 1987, pp. 217–30.

Williams, G. R., *The Molecular Biology of Gaia*, New York: Columbia University Press 1996.

Williams, J., *Christian Perspectives on BioEthics*, Ottawa: Novalis 1997.

Williams, R., *Sergii Bulgakov*, Edinburgh: T. & T. Clark 1999.

Williams, W. (ed.), *The Values of Science*, Boulder and Oxford: Westview Press 1999.

Wilmut, I., A. E. Schnieke, J. McWhir, A. J. Kind and K. H. S. Campbell, 'Viable Offspring Derived from Fetal and Adult Mammalian Cells', *Nature* 385, 1997, pp. 810–13.

Worster, D., *Nature's Economy: A History of Ecological Ideas*, New York: Cambridge University Press 1977.

Index of Names and Subjects

Index of Terms